Springer Series on Asian Criminology and Criminal Justice Research

Series editor

Jianhong Liu, University of Macau, Macao, China

The series publishes both theoretical and empirical work along several themes in Asian Criminology, with a focus on research-level monographs and edited volumes. It aims to cover 4 main themes: the elaborations and adaptations of research models and established theories (established mainly by Western scholarship) to Asian contexts; an introduction of innovative concepts, theories and policies originating in Asian societies to Western audiences; and in-depth studies of particular Asian countries, as they reflect local traditions and cultures one hand, and a general understanding of criminal behavior or criminal justice, on the other. It will feature authors from any country of origin doing research about or pertaining to Asian countries.

The series encourages submissions of both quantitative and qualitative research approaches, as well as mixed methods and comparative approaches, with a focus on studies using rigorous methods and presenting new research results. It will be of interest to researchers in criminology and criminal justice, as well as related fields such as sociology, demography and international studies.

More information about this series at http://www.springer.com/series/15738

R. Thilagaraj · Jianhong Liu
Editors

Restorative Justice in India

Traditional Practice and Contemporary Applications

Springer

Editors
R. Thilagaraj
Department of Criminology
University of Madras
Chennai, Tamil Nadu
India

Jianhong Liu
University of Macau
Macao
China

Springer Series on Asian Criminology and Criminal Justice Research
ISBN 978-3-319-47658-2 ISBN 978-3-319-47659-9 (eBook)
DOI 10.1007/978-3-319-47659-9

Library of Congress Control Number: 2016963778

Printed on acid-free paper

This Springer imprint is published by Springer Nature
The registered company is Springer International Publishing AG
The registered company address is: Gewerbestrasse 11, 6330 Cham, Switzerland

Foreword

Professors Thilagaraj and Liu are to be congratulated for bringing together this collection on restorative justice in India by some of its most distinguished scholars. The editors are both great founding leaders of the Asian Criminological Society. This collection shows that restorative principles have ancient roots in India and that restorative principles have recently been recognized in the judgements of Indian appellate courts.

The Nyaya panchayat village courts were charged to resolve conflicts through dialogue, an idea advocated by the leader of the Indian Congress Gandhi and finally implemented by Prime Minister Rajiv Gandhi. This book shows that the disappointments of the Nyaya panchayats have been considerable in many states. But as several chapters point out, the Panchayats remain a space available to be invigorated by local democracy and local restorative justice. Moreover, there are places where this promise has been richly realized.

How do we distinguish the Nyaya panchayats that seize the opportunity to take restorative justice to new heights, to empower women, control corruption, enrich deliberative democracy, and those that do not? That is a great challenge that lies in the hands of empirical Indian criminology and in particular in the hands of the pioneers of the field who have contributed to this informative volume.

Large societies like India, the United States and China offer unusually rich opportunities for comparative research that compares many different parts of the same society, especially since on many matters these complex societies include the best and the worst of justice practices. Books like this one are important because restorative justice is a field dominated by the Western network of practice leaders and scholars. These Western leaders need to travel to India to learn more of the rich tapestry of democratic innovation that does survive in what Gandhi hoped would be village republics. India is a particularly interesting society because of its ancient and continuing history of punitive forbearance toward children. While this is forcefully contested today, there persists a reluctance to criminalize or incarcerate children.

On all the important strengths and weaknesses of Indian justice and its engagement with restorative ideals, this book lays valuable foundations. My warmest wishes to the Indian community of restorative practitioners and restorative justice researchers as they expand knowledge about how we can all continue to learn from India. And my thanks for the revealing window into Indian restorative justice offered in this collection.

June 2016 John Braithwaite

Contents

Editors and Contributors

About the Editors

Prof. R. Thilagaraj was former Chair and Professor in Criminology, Department of Criminology, University of Madras. Presently Director (Academic), Center of Excellence in Digital Forensics, Chennai and Chairman, Indian Society of Criminology. Recipient of ISC—Kumarappa Reckless Award and ISC—Prof. Sushil Chandra and Haikerwal Award for Senior Social Scientist.

Jianhong Liu is Professor at the University of Macau. He is the Winner of 2016 American Society of Criminology's Freda Adler Distinguished Scholar Award. He is the Founding President of Asian Criminological Society, the President of Scientific Commission of International Society for Criminology, and the editor in chief of Asian Journal of Criminology. He is an author of more than 100 research articles and author or editor of 29 books.

Contributors

Namrata Goswami Institute for Defence Studies and Analyses, Development Enclave-1, New Delhi, India

Rakesh Kumar Handa University of Delhi, New Delhi, India

Shiva M. Jaamdar School of Criminology and Criminal Justice, Rani Channamma University, Belgaum, Karnataka, India

Kaushikee Nelson Mandela Centre for Peace and Conflict Resolution, Jamia Millia Islamia University, New Delhi, India

Sarfaraz Ahmad Khan National University of Juridical Sciences, Kolkata, India

S. Latha Department of Criminology, University of Madras, Chennai, India

Subash C. Raina University of Delhi, New Delhi, India

V. Ramya Krishnan KIIT School of Law, Bhubaneshwar, India

Natarajan Ravi Dr. Ambedkar Government Law College, Kalapet, Pondicherry, India

R. Thilagaraj Department of Criminology, University of Madras, Chennai, India

Ramanathan Uma Madras High Court and Research Scholar, Madras School of Social Work, Chennai, India

D. Umamaheswari Labour Law and Administrative Law, The Tamil Nadu Dr. Ambedkar Law University, Chennai, India

A. Vijayalakshmi School of Excellence in Law, The Tamil Nadu Dr. Ambedkar Law University, Chennai, India

Introduction: Restorative Justice Practices in India, The Way to Develop A More Harmonious Society

A system of criminal justice plays a vital role as an important formal agency in any organized society. The objective of a criminal justice system is to preserve and protect the rule of law. This objective is achieved through maintenance of law and order, and fair trials with equity in justice. Equity in justice is considered a significant part of Indian Constitution but at the same time it is widely violated in practice. As a legal principle its declaration embellishes court house sentences, class rooms in law schools, ceremonial occasions and constitutional decisions. But it comes nowhere near to describing what actually happens in the legal system. We tolerate a system in which money often matters more than merit, and equal justice principle is routinely subverted in practice. This is not, of course, the only legal context in which rhetoric outruns reality. But it is one of the most disturbing, given its centrality as an issue of fundamental rights. A commitment to equal justice is central to the legitimacy of any democratic process. It is a really a shameful irony that India is proudly spoken of as the largest democracy in the world yet its inadequate legal system assures that equal justice is often just a dream beyond access for the majority. Issues of equity in justice arise in the treatment of offenders and victims in the criminal justice system. The rights of the accused are protected at every stage of the criminal justice process. On the contrary the victim is completely neglected and forgotten. The participation of victims remains at the periphery of the criminal justice system, at the time of giving a complaint and during prosecution as a witness. The victim is a completely neglected subject in the system. This imbalance is reflected in the constitution of India, various statutory provisions and apex court judgments. What is an alternative system that would protect the rights and the interests of both the offenders and the victims and would repair, restore, reconcile, and reintegrate the offenders and victims to each other and their shared communities? Currently, restorative justice has emerged as an alternative approach to minimize these imbalances in the criminal justice system.

The restorative justice alternative can transform the way we think of punishment for wrongful acts. It revolves around the idea that a crime or a serious deviant act affects the victims, offenders and the community at large. In restorative justice the primary concern is to make the offenders aware of the harm they have caused, to get them to understand that they must meet their responsibilities to repair such harm and to ensure such offences are prevented from reoccurring; the form and amount of reparation from the offender to the victim and the measures to be taken to prevent reoffending collectively by offenders, victims and members of their communities are arrived at through constructive dialogues in an informal and consensual process. This approach will improve the relationship between the offender and the victim and also contribute to the development of a harmonious society.

Restorative justice represents the latest approach to effective justice in democratic societies and develops hand in hand with structural reform to the existing legal system, without having to rely on the completion of that process of reform. The dual advantage of restorative justice is that it meets the needs of victims of crime by atoning physical and psychological harm, and it helps reform offenders by providing them opportunities for resocialization through acknowledging their responsibility and contributing towards restoration. While addressing the immediate needs of individuals, restorative justice also contributes to long-term societal change and to the development of civic values and faith in the rule of law when the legal system is continuing to undergo reform.

The term restorative justice has been defined in many different ways by different scholars and practitioners. The most succinct definition of restorative justice is offered by Howard Zehr, whom many consider the leading visionary and architect of the restorative justice movement and is the "father of restorative justice." His seminal book, *Changing Lenses* (Zehr 1990), provided the conceptual framework for the movement and has influenced policy makers and practitioners throughout the world. According to Zehr,

> *Restorative justice is a process to involve, to the extent possible, those who have a stake in a specific offense and to collectively identify and address harms, needs, and obligations, in order to heal and put things as right as possible*

According to Braithwaite (1998) restorative justice has been "the dominant model of criminal justice throughout most of human history for all the world's peoples," and that it is grounded in traditions from ancient Greek, Arab, and Roman civilizations and in Hindu, Buddhist, and Confucian traditions. Braithwaite emphasizes that restorative justice means restoring victims as well as offenders and the community. In addition to restoring lost property or healing personal injury, restoration means bringing back a sense of security. Essentially, restorative justice proponents emphasize the need to support both victims and offenders and see social relationships as a rehabilitative vehicle aimed at providing formal and informal social support and control for offenders (Bazemore and Schiff 2001).

Zehr (2002) has identified three principles of restorative justice. The first, harms and needs, focuses on the importance of identifying victims' needs first. The objective is to repair harm as much as possible using both symbolic and concrete methods. This means that victims' needs should be considered even when there is no offender identified. The second principle described by Zehr is that harm results in obligations, which means that the offender's accountability and responsibility should be the focus of restorative interventions. Rather than the retributive stance in which accountability equals punishment, restorative principles infer that offenders must be held accountable in order to better understand the harm caused so that they may take responsibility and make amends. Finally, the third restorative principle is that interventions should promote engagement by the stakeholders; those affected by the crime should have a role in the justice process. In some cases this means dialogue between parties; in others indirect communication or other involvement is suggested.

Restorative justice has its roots in a number of indigenous cultures, embracing traditions of "spirituality" and holistic healing, and aims to reconnect the offender with his/her environment and community (Sharpe 1998). Although restorative justice is an ancient concept (Zehr 1990), the restorative perspective gained impetus in the 1970s and 1980s from the victims' movement, from experiences with reparative sanctions and processes, and from the rise of informal neighborhood justice and dispute resolution programs (Galaway and Hudson 1990; Schneider 1985). The mid-1970s marked the birthing phase of what would become known as the restorative justice movement. The "child" of this birthing process was the first Victim Offender Reconciliation Program ("VORP") in Kitchener, Ontario, in 1974 (Peachey 1989). From the late 1970s to the early 1980s, a number of experimental programs based on restorative justice principles and modeled after the Kitchener program were initiated in several jurisdictions in North America and Europe, with the first VORP in the United States located in Elkhart, Indiana, in 1978 (Umbreit 1988). Through the mid-1980s, in many jurisdictions restorative justice initiatives remained small in size and number and continued to have little impact on the larger system. Since the 1980s restorative justice has become a significant element of criminal justice systems of many countries. It is found in Europe and far beyond, such as in Australia, New Zealand, Canada, South Africa, and the United States.

The restorative justice movement started to have a more clear delineation of its aims and to be articulated for the first time as a distinct paradigm of justice in the late 1980s–early 1990s, when the especially influential work of Howard Zehr (1985) *Retributive Justice, Restorative Justice* expanded later in his important book *Changing Lenses*. In this work he claimed that the current criminal justice system's "lens" is the retributive model, which views crime as law-breaking and justice as allocating blame and punishment, and he proposes seeing "crime" as a "wound in human relationships" that "creates an obligation to restore and repair" (Zehr, 1990).

Along the same line, Daniel van Ness published a book in 1986 pursuing the idea of a paradigm shift that would introduce restorative values into the justice system. The concept has been further expanded in John Braithwaite's important book *Restorative Justice and Responsive Regulation* (2002). There he attempts to locate restorative peacemaking efforts within the dynamics of globalization, i.e., within various social formations, private or public corporations as well as within large international organizations, linking top-down strategies of conflict regulation to bottom-up initiatives.

From the mid-1980s to the mid-1990s, the movement slowly began to be recognized in many communities as a viable option for interested crime victims and offenders, though still impacting only a very small number of participants.

Restorative justice is also developing in many other parts of the world, including Australia, Canada, numerous European countries, Japan, New Zealand, South Africa, several South American countries, South Korea, and Russia. The United Nations, the Council of Europe, and the European Union have been addressing restorative justice issues for a number of years. Meeting in 2000, the United Nations Congress on Crime Prevention considered restorative justice in its plenary sessions and developed a draft proposal for *UN Basic Principles on the Use of Restorative Justice Programs in Criminal Matters.* The proposed principles encourage the use of restorative justice programming by member states at all stages of the criminal justice process, underscore the voluntary nature of participation in restorative justice procedures, and recommend beginning to establish standards and safeguards for the practice of restorative justice. This proposal was adopted by the United Nations in 2002. The Council of Europe was more specifically focused on the restorative use of mediation procedures in criminal matters, and it adopted a set of recommendations in 1999 to guide member states in using mediation in criminal cases.

The implementation of restorative justice has been considered a priority component of world policy in modernizing criminal justice and has been incorporated to the legislation of many countries as a new and modern approach to criminal justice. Recent studies both theoretical and empirical indicate that its implementation may help official criminal justice to achieve its objectives much better in areas such as victim's satisfaction, increasing offender's responsibility for his/her actions, and reducing both recidivism and fear of crime in the community (Umbreit 1995). Restorative justice policies and programs are known to be developing in more than 45 nations. In July 2002, the UN Economic and Social Council adopted the *Resolution on Basic Principles on the Use of Restorative Justice Programmes in Criminal Matters*. It called upon member states to design strategies and policies aimed at the development of restorative justice.

The *Vienna Declaration on Crime and Justice: Meeting the Challenges of the Twenty-first Century* (2000) encouraged the "development of restorative justice policies, procedures, and programs that are respectful of the rights, needs and interests of victims, offenders, communities and all other parties". In August 2002, the United Nations Economic and Social Council adopted a resolution calling upon Member States that are implementing restorative justice programs to draw on a set of *Basic Principles on the Use of Restorative Justice Programmes in Criminal Matters* (hereinafter: the *Basic Principles*) developed by an Expert Group. In 2005, the declaration of the Eleventh United Nations Congress on the Prevention of Crime and the Treatment of Offenders (2005) urged Member States to recognize the importance of further developing restorative justice policies, procedures, and programs that include alternatives to prosecution.

Over the past decades, restorative justice initiatives have seen significant growth worldwide (Hughes and Mossman 2001). In India a restorative justice approach is found in a number of alternative dispute resolution methods such as mediation, lok adalats, arbitration, conflict resolution, plea bargaining, and the Nyaya panchayat.

One of the central insights of restorative justice is that the process itself may be more important than its direct outcome. It is important for the parties involved that they are treated in a fair manner, with attention paid to their particular needs. If the process is experienced as being fair and just, it is also easier to commit oneself to the outcome. Commitment and learning may also be facilitated by the feature that all those involved are able to participate in the decision-making and to share in the responsibility for the success of the endeavor.

The present book provides a plethora of issues pertaining to restorative justice practices in India. The book is divided into six parts; the first part comprises two chapters that deals with the restorative justice tradition in India. Chapter 1 explains the evolution, constitution, and functioning of the Nyaya panchayat system as a dispute resolution practice prevalent in the villages. Panchayat justice is a time-honored institution having its deep roots in the ethos of the country. The author explains the formalization of the Nyàya Panchayat Act which was enacted to revitalize the system of Nyaya panchayat. Chapter 2 focuses on the peace negotiations and dialogue between the Union Government of India and armed Naga groups. The Naga dialogue represents an "insider" prevention and management of violent ethnic conflicts. Ethnic conflict is a serious issue in the tribal areas of northeast India. Over the years, as the conflict has become more protracted and bloody, more and more Nagas have gotten involved in the process of consultation and dialogue through both traditional and institutional structures, with the goal of bringing about peaceful reconciliation. The Naga intra-community dialogue has an articulated vision for the future: a progressive, multi-linguistic, multicultural, unified *Nagalim* in which small Naga tribes as well as others will be given due recognition.

Part II traces the development of restorative justice in India. This section not only explains various kinds of restorative justice methods but also the transformations that Indian society has undergone during the British period through the present day. It consists of four chapters. Chapter 3 analyzes two parallel systems of dispute settlement in India with basic elements of restorative justice—one, the formal British-created criminal justice system dominant in urban India, and the other the informal traditional system prevalent largely in rural India. The author also examines various alternative dispute resolution mechanisms that exist in India. Chapter 4 examines the responses of the Supreme Court and the High Court towards the concepts of restorative justice. The criminal justice administration deals with the formulation of legislation, enforcing the law, the detection and prevention of crimes, trials of offenders and executions, but most of the time it does not try to alleviate the suffering of the innocent victims or their families. The duty of a welfare state is to devise ways and means to bring solace to helpless victim by way of payment of compensation on humanitarian grounds which would give some consolation to the distressed. The legislative framework in India regarding compensation to victims of crime can be traced through two major legislations, i.e., Code of Criminal Procedure, 1973 and Probations of Offenders Act, along with the Constitution of India.

The author of Chap. 5 highlights that restorative justice is a sort of crimino-victim justice system wherein equal justice to crime-doers and victims is ensured. In its most idealized form, there are four active features of restorative justice, i.e., to *repair*, *restore*, *reconcile*, and *reintegrate* the offenders and victims to each other and to their shared communities. Chapter 6 analyzes the concept of restorative justice through a theoretical framework and process practices. According to the author, adapting to the restorative system of justice requires certain spade-work to soften the ground and necessitates the need for certain changes in the legal framework pertaining to criminal justice that involve recategorizing crimes and decriminalization.

Part III of the book deals with restorative justice practices such as mediation and plea bargaining and the application of such measures to prisoners, juveniles, victims of rape, and communal violence. This part has six chapters. Chapter 7 is about the importance of the process of mediation through the amicable settlement of disputes. It attempts to empower the disputants to understand their part in the conflict, acknowledge responsibility, express appreciation of concessions made, and effectively assist parties to understand what they need. While mediation is at present resorted to only in civil cases, criminal actions also can be mediated when the situation reveals possibilities for reconciliation or restoration. The stakeholders in the dispute resolution process have to believe in negotiation, formulate areas that are possibilities for discussion, identify issues that will bring out mutual gain, and—not the least—not get lost in frustration with the progression of the litigation system. Chapter 8 is on the system of plea bargaining. The incorporation of a plea-bargaining principle in the Criminal Procedure Code has given a new dimension to the Indian Criminal Justice System and provided a scope for making restorative justice principles implicit in our administration of justice system. Chapter 9 attempts to show that in order to integrate this into the system there is a need to focus on improving measures which will facilitate a more flexible system where the involvement of the victim is held to be optional. The researcher also points out the idea that this process should ensure there is no opting to focus only on a single aspect while dismissing or downplaying issues of human rights of the offenders.

Chapter 10 concerns justice and reconciliation in the aftermath of mass level atrocities and collective violence; its restorative justice lens highlights the importance of restorative justice in communities recovering from genocide, war, violence, and trauma. This can facilitate individual healing, of both the victims and the perpetrators, and sustain the process of reconciliation. Restorative justice is not primarily about forgiveness or reconciliation but it does provide a context where this might happen. Chapter 11 is about the applicability of restorative justice for juveniles in conflict with the law. The wide and deep implementation of restorative justice principles, especially when dealing with young people, has been recognized as the "green" way to go. This is so because the principles of restorative justice do not, either actually or symbolically, reduce incidents otherwise recognized as offences/crimes and which give rise, due to societal reaction and censure, to a bundle of predefined and pre-structured rights relations. Chapter 12 is about the application of restorative justice for victims of rape. Restorative justice emphasizes important roles of crime victims and community members through more active involvement in the justice process, holding offenders directly accountable to the people and communities they have violated, restoring the emotional and material losses of victims, and providing a range of opportunities for dialogue, negotiation, and problem solving—all of which can lead to a greater sense of community safety, social harmony, and peace for all involved.

This book will be of immense use for practitioners to learn more about restorative justice practices in a developing country like India and also significant to students of law, criminology, and other related subjects. Deeply thankful to Remya Mariam Raju who provided valuable assistance at every stage of the progress of this book.

Chennai, India R. Thilagaraj
Macau, China Jianhong Liu

Part I
Restorative Justice Tradition in India

Chapter 1
Nyaya Panchayat

R. Thilagaraj

1.1 Introduction

India has a strong tradition of adjudication at the village level. Panchayat justice is not a novel idea but a time-honored institution having deep roots in the ethos of the country. It is village self-government in action at the level of administration of justice. It has helped both in involving people in dealing with law and justice and in the institutionalization of local resolution of disputes (Mathur 1997). The term panchayat literally means an 'assembly of five persons,' hence, the meeting, council, or court of five or more members of a village or caste who assembled to judge disputes or determine group policy. This body of five elderly, nominated persons, over the course of time, was vested with sacred and with judicial and executive powers. These village communities were the centers of administration and the custodians of social harmony. The panchayat is endowed with functions based on broad principles of natural justice and tends to remain procedurally as simple as possible. They can be given civil and minor criminal jurisdiction.

Since Indian independence almost all states have enacted village Panchayats Acts as guided by the directive principles. The village panchayat and nyaya panchayat existed as dual entities in order to have a separation of the judiciary from the executive. Nyaya panchayats are guided by local traditions; the culture and behavioral pattern of the village community instill confidence in the people about the administration of justice. The earliest nyaya panchayats were the village courts established under the Village Courts Acts of 1988. The Royal Commission on Decentralization of 1909 recommended the revival of nyaya panchayats having both criminal and civil jurisdiction within the village.

The law commission in its report in August 1986 indicated that Article 39-A of the Constitution of India directs the state to secure that the operation of the legal

R. Thilagaraj (✉)
Department of Criminology, University of Madras, Chennai 600005, India
e-mail: rthilagaraj@gmail.com

R. Thilagaraj and J. Liu (eds.), *Restorative Justice in India*,
DOI 10.1007/978-3-319-47659-9_1

system promotes justice on the basis of equal opportunity and shall in particular provide free legal aid, by suitable legislations and schemes or in any other way, to ensure that opportunities for securing justice are not denied to any citizen by economic or other disabilities. This is the constitutional imperative. All agencies of the government are now under a fundamental obligation to enhance access to justice. Article 40, which directs the state to take steps to organize village panchayat and endow them with such powers and authority as may be necessary to enable them to function as units of self-government, has to be appreciated afresh in the light of the mandate of the constitution. With the 73rd amendment becoming a part of the constitution, decentralized justice should have found renewed expression through nyaya panchayats.

1.2 Dispute Resolution Practices in Ancient India

Ancient India is the period of history in India from pre-historic period (i.e., the Stone Age) to the period when the foundations of Muslim rule in India were laid beginning from the Arab conquest of Sind. The people who lived in India before the Muslims invaded were Hindus and they were governed by their own laws called the Hindu law. A review of the ancient literary works of India such as the Vedas, Sutras, Epics, and Dharmashastras gives us very useful information about the dispute resolution institutions prevailing in ancient India.

Recourse to a village panchayat without court intervention was one of the natural ways for the ancient Hindus to seek resolution of their disputes. Village panchayats provided a means for villagers to mediate between contending parties within their own village. In some cases, the panchayat resembled a real judicial court because the panchayat could intervene on the complaint of one party and not necessarily on the agreement of both the parties, e.g., as in a caste conflict. Hindu civilization expressly encouraged the settlement of differences by tribunals chosen by the parties themselves, whose decision was to be accepted as final and conclusive by all parties. Apart from the courts established by the king, there were other tribunals recognized in the ancient texts and digests of Hindu law (Gavrielides 2011).

There were two popular institutions in Vedic times called *sabha* and *samiti*. The *sabha* was a house of elders or an assembly of villagers, while the *samiti* was the assembly of the whole people. The general tendency was to encourage the town councils and village panchayats (the assembly of elders and respected inhabitants of a village) to try local disputes. In the sutras age, there were parishads (assemblies of learned men who knew law) whose decisions on the interpretation of the Vedic texts were binding. The method of procedure generally adopted in the tribal meetings in the states was not by voting on a motion. The point at issue (dispute) was either carried unanimously or referred for arbitration to a committee of referees.

In the *Brihadaranyaka Upanishad*, Yajnavalkya states that village councils (kulani), corporation (sreni), and assemblies (puga) be used to decide lawsuits (Kane 1946). The decision of kula was subject to revision by sreni, which in turn could be revised by the puga. These arbitral tribunals assumed the form of "panchayats" in the villages, wherein the "panches" decided matters informally and untrammeled by the technicalities of procedure and evidence. The panches were village elders elected according to their wealth, social standing, and influence in the village. Fear of social ostracism corroborated the binding value of the decisions delivered by the panches in rural India.

However, with changes in social and economic conditions, the functioning of such arbitral bodies became inadequate and outmoded, although even today, in some form or another, variants of such arbitral bodies are still prevalent in some rural areas (Maholtra 2002). The panchayat system was thus one of the important natural methods of deciding many disputes in ancient India.

1.3 Formalization of the Nyaya Panchayat Act

The plan to formalize nyaya panchayats and to bring them within the ambit of organized justice in India was planned as part of the Panchayati Raj reforms of Rajiv Gandhi in the 1980s but was put on hold to coincide with broader reforms of the justice system. After the 73rd Constitutional Amendment, the states of Bihar, Himachal Pradesh, Punjab, Uttar Pradesh, Jammu and Kashmir, and West Bengal provided for nyaya panchayats in their new confirmatory laws or in their confirmatory amendments to old laws. The states of Andhra Pradesh, Gujarat, Haryana, and Karnataka made no provision for nyaya panchayats in their post-73rd amendment law, though they had the provisions in their earlier laws.

Any structure pyramidic in character must have a strong foundation and, therefore, the draft proposals centered upon restructuring the foundation. Accordingly, a forum for resolution of disputes emanating from rural areas and participatory in character was received. In reaching this tentative conclusion, the law commission took notice of the obvious fact that while the system of administration of justice in our country is one integrated whole, it ignores or overlooks the wide social and cultural divides between the rural population, urban population, and the metropolitan elite. This approach ignores the vital fact that the nature of disputes arising in rural areas is wholly dissimilar from those in metropolitan areas and both required an altogether different model for resolution. Commercial and mercantile litigation, enforcement of corporate laws, foreign exchange regulations, monopolies and restrictive trade practices, and complex constitutional issues figure in the litigation in metropolitan areas. Labor disputes dominate the courts in industrialized cities and towns. The disputes that arise in rural areas are largely related to ownership and possession of agricultural land, problems of cultivation, boundary disputes, land records, petty family and property disputes. Ignoring the stark difference between the natures of disputes, the present system requires complex voluminous procedural laws for the dispensation of justice at both levels. This realization dictated the approach of the commission to devise a different kind of forum for the resolution of disputes at the grassroots level. The nature of the dispute must

members of panchayats nominate a person from among themselves to membership of the nyaya panchayat; such nomination may also be consensus. The nominations are then screened by a sub-divisional officer and forwarded to the District Magistrate, who as a chairman of Advisory Committee established for the purpose shall ultimately appoint members of the nyaya panchayat.

Another combination of nominative and elective principles is furnished by the Bihar legislation in which the Panchayats Courts, comprising the sarpanch and 8 other panchas, are chosen in three different ways. The sarpanch is directly elected by the gram sabha; four nyaya panchayats are directly elected, but from wards into which panchayats are divided for election purposes; the remaining four are chosen from the gram panchayat by the nyaya panchayats sarpanch and four elected members in a joint meeting.

One might also mention the states of Kerala and the Union Territory of Delhi as furnishing extreme ends of the spectrum: in the former all nyaya panchas are nominated; in the latter all of them are directly elected.

One of the few empirical studies of nyaya panchayat discloses the dominant role of the sarpanch of the gram panchayat in the process of indirect elections of nyaya panchayats. Since each panchayat generally elects one nyaya pancha, politics and patronage do intrude in elections.

The dominance of panchayats by sarpanches has emerged as a general structure feature of PR in action. The recent report of a High Powered Committee on Panchayati raj in Rajasthan recommends the abolition of nyaya panchayats altogether, partly on the ground that they have "not been able to inspire public confidence." Similarly, The Maharashtra Evaluation Committee on Panchayati raj finds entrustment of judicial functions to nyaya panchayats "on the basis of democratic elections or otherwise" both "out of place and unworkable" and also recommends the abolition of nyaya panchayat.

1.6 Nature of Dispute and Quality of Justice

If available information on the organization and functioning of nyaya panchayat is meager, information on the subject matter of disputes and the quality of justice of nyaya panchayat processes and outcomes are virtually nonexistent. Aside from the statistical breakdown of disputed matters into the categories of "civil" and "criminal," neither the fourteenth Report of Law commission nor the 1962 study Team Report give us information relating to those two dimensions. But to comprehend nyaya panchayats we need to know about the types of disputes that reach them, the nature of their adjudicatory processes, and the outcomes they arrive at. An understanding of the interrelation of nyaya panchayat on the one hand and community dispute processing institutions on the other is inconceivable without a detailed grasp of the nature of disputes, sanctions, and incentives entailed in the functioning of nyaya panchayats.

Concern with the quality of justice administered by the nyaya panchayat system has been confined mainly to a theoretical and structural level. Considerable attention has been given to the issues of the constitution of nyaya panchayats and training programs for the nyaya panchas, but no existing literature probes the justice qualities of the functioning of nyaya panchayats.

1.7 Nyaya Panchayats—Jurisdiction and Authority

Nyaya panchayats have civil jurisdiction in pecuniary claims below Rs. 500 (unless both parties agree to submit a larger matter) involving money due on contracts not affecting interests in immovable property, compensation for wrongfully taking or damaging property, and recovery of movable property. Criminal jurisdiction is more extensive and covers a substantial range of offenses under the Indian Penal Code (e.g., criminal negligence, trespass, nuisance, including water pollution, possession or use of false weights and measures, theft, misappropriation, intimidation, perjury, attempt to evade summons) and specialized statutes (e.g., Cattle Trespassing Act, Gambling Acts, Prevention of Juvenile Delinquency Act). The nyaya panchayats are authorized to levy fines up to Rs. 100, but they have no power to sentence offenders to imprisonment, even for failure to pay a fine. They also have the power to admonish in some cases and can compensate the victim out of the fines collected. The state government retains the power to enhance nyaya panchayat jurisdiction as well as diminish it if there is "admission of miscarriage of justice" (Pillai 1977).

Two essential features of lay adjudication, simplicity of procedure and flexibility of functioning, are realized in the design of the nyaya panchayat. They are not encumbered by the need to follow elaborate rules of civil and criminal procedure or the law of evidence. Complaints may be made orally or in writing; no legal representation is allowed, although in some civil matters parties may be represented by an "agent." Witnesses, if any, are examined on oath or solemn affirmation. After the party's present evidence and informal arguments they are asked to absent themselves; panchas confer among themselves and arrive at a decision, which is pronounced in open court. A judgment is written and signed (or thumb printed) by the parties. Despite these informal attributes, NP does differ from traditional dispute institutions in several significant respects. Membership is fixed rather than flexible and based indirectly on popular election rather than social standing. Nyaya panchayat constituencies are territorial units rather than functional or ascriptive groups. They decide by majority vote rather than consensus. They are required to follow statutory law. Because they are supported by the government, they can assess minor court fees, issue a summons, proceed ex parte in the case of a recalcitrant party, and execute decrees by attaching certain movable property; they are required to maintain records of evidence, judgments, and all panchayat transactions, and are subordinate to higher civil and criminal courts through the sub-district magistrate; their decisions can be appealed in a few limited areas (Saxena 1971).

1.8 Functioning of the Nyaya Panchayat

The memberships of the nyaya panchayat are fixed and are based on popular election rather than social standing; their constituencies are territorial units rather than a functional or ascriptive group; they decide by majority vote rather than by rule of unanimity; they are required to conform to and apply statute law; and they are supported by the government in the compulsory execution of their decrees. Mysore, Madras, and Kerala had a nyaya panchayat system at the time of adoption of Constitution. Madhya Pradesh and Uttar Pradesh states implemented article 50. By introducing the nyaya panchayat system, the states made an attempt to replace existing dispute processing institutions such as caste institutions and other secular or special institutions by some social workers like Rangpur People's court.

The rules regarding appeals in disputed elections are the same as those which apply to gram panchayats. The nyaya panchayat has a chairman and secretary elected by its members; one-third of its members retire every second year. Almost all states have adopted election as a method of constituting nyaya panchayat. Each gram panchayat elects members for nyaya panchayat, and some states combine the method of elections with nominations. UP members of panchayats nominate a person from among themselves to membership in the nyaya panchayat. Such nomination may also be by consensus. A sub-divisional officer then screens the nominations, and forwards them to the district magistrate, who as the chairman of the advisory committee established for the purpose should ultimately appoint members of JP. In fact, the district magistrate relies on the advice of the sub-divisional officer, who in turn depends on the advice of minor government officials such as the village accountant and the panchayat secretary. However, such a procedure may result in favoritism.

1.9 Fundamental Duties of Nyaya Panchayats

1. All panchas shall, on the assumption of office, affirm their faith and allegiance to the Constitution of India and, in particular, shall adhere and follow Part IVA of the Constitution relating to Fundamental Duties.
2. It shall be the duty of the panch to discharge the functions assigned under this law in a fair and judicious manner without fear or favor, affection, or ill will.
3. The panch shall be vigilant in maintaining communal harmony and desist from taking any action which may directly or indirectly foment, provoke, promote, enhance, or sustain any disharmony.

1.10 Process of Conciliation in Nyaya Panchayat

According to the Act, the nyaya panchayat shall, upon receiving a complaint from a party, announce a date for conciliation proceedings in the matter and request parties concerned to be present at the nyaya manch or in exceptional cases at a mutually agreed public place at a suitable time.

1. It shall be the duty of the nyaya panchayat pramukh to attempt an amicable settlement of the dispute between the parties through conciliation.
2. If parties agree to conciliation proceedings, the nyaya panchayat pramukh shall give an opportunity to each such party to choose a conciliator from amongst voters resident in the area of the nyaya panchayat to represent them in the conciliation process.
3. The nyaya panchayat pramukh shall nominate two panchas to participate in the conciliation process.
4. The persons so selected shall together hear parties to the dispute and any member of the public who volunteers to assist the panchayat in attempting conciliation.
5. The nyaya panchayat may, on failure of conciliation or on the behest of the aggrieved party, take up a dispute for adjudication.
6. On the fixed date for hearing, the nyaya panchayat shall hear the parties and if needed call for evidence in support of their claim.
7. The nyaya panchayat shall, based upon evidence, decide the matter within three hearings or a period of 2 months of taking up of the matter, whichever is earlier.

The parties to any suit, proceedings, or dispute may enter into a special written agreement to refer any dispute of a civil nature to a particular nyaya panchayat falling outside its jurisdiction, provided that prior permission has been obtained in writing from the presiding authority.

1.11 Conclusion

The system of nyaya panchayat is indispensable because it ensures a participatory and people-oriented system of justice provides greater scope for mediation, conciliation and compromise, and encourages rendering justice with the knowledge of local culture, traditions of society, and behavioral pattern. It is close to the people geographically and psychologically, saves time, and the trouble and expense of the parties and witnesses and thus the Act should be utilized as a tool of empowerment for the rural masses.

References

Gavrielides, T. (2011). Restorative practices: From the early societies to the 1970s. *Internet Journal of Criminology*.
Kane, P. V. (1946). *History of dharmashastra* (Vol. III, p. 242).
Madabhushi, S. (2006). *Alternative dispute resolution negotiation and mediation* (1st Ed.). Lexis Nexis Butterworths.
Malhotra, O. P. (2002). *The law and practice of arbitration and conciliation*, ed. (p. 4).
Mathur, S. N. (1997). *Nyaya panchayats as instruments of justice*. Institute of Social sciences. Concept Publishing Company.
Myneni, S. R. (2004). *Arbitration, conciliation and alternative dispute resolution systems* (1st Ed.). Asia Law House.
Pillai, C. (1977). Criminal Jurisdiction of Nyaya panchayats. *Journal of the Indian Law Institute*, *19*, 443.
Rajan, R. D. (2005). *Alternative dispute resolution* (New Edition). Bharathi Law Publications.
Raju, K. D. (2007). *Alternate dispute resolution system: A prudent mechanism of speedy redress in India*.
Saxena, K. S. (1971). *The Political Movements and Awakening in Rajasthan (1877-1947)*. Delhi: S.Chand and Co. (Pvt.) Ltd.

Chapter 2
Peace Negotiations and Dialogue in the Northeast: The Naga Case

Namrata Goswami

The Northeast of India has suffered from multiple armed ethnic conflicts since India's independence. In 1946, the Naga National Council (NNC) was formed in order to provide a political platform for the Nagas to assert their demand for a separate state outside of India. In 1956, the NNC resorted to violence under the leadership of A.Z. Phizo, a charismatic Angami Naga rebel leader. This led to the deployment of the Indian army in the Naga areas and the Armed Forces (Special Powers) Act, 1958 was imposed. Over the years, the Naga ethnic conflict witnessed factionalism within the NNC which resulted in the formation of a breakaway group, the National Socialist Council of Nagaland (NSCN) formed in 1980. Due to leadership differences, the NSCN got further divided in 1988 into two factions: the National Socialist Council of *Nagalim* led by Isak Chisi Swu and Thuingaleng Muivah—NSCN (IM) and the National Socialist Council of Nagaland led by S.S. Khaplang—NSCN (K). In 2011, a new NSCN (Khole-Kitovi) group was formed as a breakaway faction of the NSCN (K). These three armed groups mostly operate in the Naga-inhabited areas in the Northeast. Manipur has also been deeply affected by ethnic violence after the formation of the United National Liberation Front (UNLF) on November 24, 1964. Another significant Manipuri separatist armed group is the Revolutionary People's Front (RPF) and its armed wing, the People's Liberation Army (PLA) engaged in armed struggle since 1978. The RPF and the PLA are suspected of being trained in Maoist guerrilla warfare by the Chinese in the 1960s and 1970s and both outfits aim at violent revolutionary change to bring about classless society in Manipur. Yet another armed group in Manipur is the *Kanglei Yawol Kanna Lup* (KYKL), which has taken up social afflictions such as fighting corruption, drug trafficking and sub-standard education practices as reasons for its armed struggle. Still another armed group, known as the Peoples'

N. Goswami (✉)
Institute for Defence Studies and Analyses, Development Enclave-1,
New Delhi 110010, India
e-mail: namygoswami@gmail.com

R. Thilagaraj and J. Liu (eds.), *Restorative Justice in India*,
DOI 10.1007/978-3-319-47659-9_2

Revolutionary Party of *Kangleipak* (PREPAK), was established in the 1970s with the objective of fighting for Manipur's independence from India.

Assam has also been plagued by insurgent violence since 1979 with the formation of the United Liberation Front of *Asom* (ULFA). Since the 1990s, the hills districts of Assam; namely, Dima Hasau and Karbi Anglong, also suffer armed groups like the *Dima Halam Daogah* (DHD) and the United Peoples' Democratic Solidarity (UPDS). The Bodo areas in Assam are disturbed by the existence of the armed National Democratic Front of Bodoland (NDFB). It is also important to note that most of these insurgent groups have thrived primarily due to strong external influences. Countries like China in the 1960s and the 1970s as well as Pakistan and later on Bangladesh have supported most of these armed groups by making available arms, training and most importantly, base areas for underground camps. Things have however improved with Bangladesh since 2008 with the coming of Sheikh Hasina to power. The ULFA leadership including Arabinda Rajkhowa, the Chairman of the outfit was arrested in December 2009 near the India–Bangladesh border. In 2010, Bangladesh handed over the leader of the NDFB, Ranjan Daimary, to India[1] (Bhaumik 2007).

In dealing with armed ethnic conflicts in the Northeast, besides the use of force, the signing of ceasefires and peace negotiations has always been a serious policy option for the Indian state. In the case of the Naga conflict, peace negotiations started early with the Akbar Hydari agreement in 1947, the civil society interactions in the 1950s, the Naga Peace Mission in 1964, and the Shillong Accord in 1975. At present, there are ongoing peace negotiations between the Union government and the NSCN (IM) and the NSCN (K), after the signing of ceasefires in 1997 and 2001, respectively. The Mizo armed conflict that afflicted the Lushai Hills from 1966 to 1986 got resolved through peace negotiations between the Union Government and the Mizo armed group, the Mizo National Front (MNF) (Goswami 2009).

At present, peace talks are underway between the ULFA and the Union government after the ULFA leaders including its Chairman, Arabinda Rajkhowa, its Deputy Commander-in-Chief, Raju Barua and others were arrested by the Assam police from the India–Bangladesh border in 2009. In order to facilitate peace talks between the Union government and the outfit, the Assam government released the leaders a year later. In 2011, the outfit submitted a 'Charter of Demands' to the Union government.[2] While the Charter listed issues like rehabilitation of the outfit's cadres, greater political autonomy for Assam, illegal migration from Bangladesh into Assam, etc., in return, the outfit agreed to give up its violent struggle and disarm.

---

[1]The Times of India. Bangladesh hands over NDFB Chief Ranjan Daimary to BSF. (May 10, 2010). Retrieved from http://articles.timesofindia.indiatimes.com/2010-05-01/india/28287637_1_d-r-nabla-ndfb-anti-talks-faction.

[2]The Times of India. ULFA submits its 'Charter of Demands' to Chidambaram. (August 5, 2011). Retrieved from http://articles.timesofindia.indiatimes.com/2011-08-05/india/29854318_1_ulfa-leaders-ulfa-team-top-ulfa.

In the light of this backdrop, this chapter focuses on the peace negotiations and dialogue between the Union government and the Naga armed groups. The significance of undertaking a detailed study on the Naga peace negotiations stems from the fact that the Naga armed conflict is the most critical armed movement in the Northeast. It has inspired the other armed groups in their demands for independence. Also, the Naga peace negotiations have involved not only the armed groups and the Union government, but also Naga society as a whole. The other important factor is that the negotiations are ongoing since 1997 and hence offers contemporary insights into the field of negotiations and dialogue. Most importantly, the Naga dialogue's wide-based representative character and legitimacy in Naga society classifies it as a fit empirical study to arrive at more causal generalizations at the abstract level of dialogue theory (Khatami 2000; Dallmayr 2002; Camilleri 2007; Saunders 2001; Tehranian and Chappell 2002).

This chapter is divided into six sections. In the first section, I provide a brief overview of the Naga ethnic conflict. In the second section, I identify the important actors taking part in the Naga dialogue process. In the third section, I dwell on the perceptions of these various actors on the conflict. In the fourth section, I discuss the key components of the Naga dialogue process. In the fifth section, I analyze the peace negotiations between the Union Government and the Nagas. In the last section, I offer certain prescriptions for a more optimal dialogue process.

2.1 Brief Overview of the Naga Conflict

The Naga ethnic conflict traces its roots back to 1918 with the formation of the Naga Club by 20 Naga members of the French *Labour Corp*, who had served in World War I (Nuh and Lasuh 2002). The wartime knowledge motivated the few who had come in contact with the European battlefield to politically organize themselves as a distinct ethnopolitical identity. The Club submitted a memorandum to the Simon Commission in 1929, in which it stated that the people of Naga areas, and that of mainland India, had nothing in common between them. Therefore, it would benefit both to stay separate and form their own political entities as and when the British left India. In 1946, the Club was further reinforced with the formation of the NNC under the leadership of Angami Zhapu Phizo. Phizo had trained with the British during World War II on the Burma Front against Japanese forces and he utilized that knowledge to impart training in guerrilla warfare to the NNC members.[3] Significantly, a Nine Point Agreement known as the Akbar Hydari Agreement was signed between the moderates in the NNC like T. Sakhrie and the Governor of Assam, Sir Akbar Hydari, on June 29, 1947. The Agreement gave the Nagas rights over their land as well as executive and legislative powers, but it was

[3]Chindits Special Force Burma (1942–44). Retrieved from http://www.chindits.info/ (accessed on April 22, 2008).

rejected by Phizo (Nuh and Lasuh 2002). On August 14, 1947, the NNC, led by Phizo, declared independence, a day before India attained its own independence from British colonial rule.

The 1950s, 1960s and 1970s were troubled periods in Naga history, with militancy on the rise and the state's military response based on acts like the Armed Forces (Special Powers) Act, 1958, amended in 1972.[4] The crossfire between the state forces and the NNC resulted in many non-combatant deaths as well as human rights violations. There were numerous efforts at peace by the Union Government, which resulted in the grant of statehood to Nagaland in 1963 and the establishment of a Nagaland Peace Mission (NPM) in 1964. However, it was the loss of bases in East Pakistan after the emergence of a new state, Bangladesh, as well as the constant pressure from Indian security forces, that coerced the NNC under Zaishe Huire to sign the Shillong Accord of 1975. The Shillong Accord, however, repeated the tragic story of the Nine Point Agreement in that it split the Naga rebel movement. The Shillong Accord was the proximate cause for the foundation of the original unified NSCN. Replicating Phizo's resistance to the Hydari Agreement, Thuingaleng Muivah, Isak Chisi Swu and S.S. Khaplang condemned the Shillong Accord as a sell out to the Union government, and they formed the NSCN in Myanmar in 1980. Subsequently, due to intense differences between Khaplang, Muivah and Swu, the NSCN split with Muivah and Swu, forming the NSCN (IM), while Khaplang formed the NSCN (K) in 1988 (Biswas and Sukhalabaidya 2008; Goswami 2007, 2008).[5]

Amidst these social and political complexities involving very stark issues of security in Naga-inhabited areas, the government of India signed ceasefires with the two main Naga militant actors, the NSCN (IM) and the NSCN (K) in 1997 and 2001, respectively. According to the terms of the ceasefire, both the Naga militant factions were to remain in the designated camps and could only move out by giving prior intimation to the Ceasefire Monitoring Group (CFMG). The CFMG was formed in 1997 and consists of members of the security forces, intelligence agencies, government officials, the NSCN (IM) and NSCN (K) (Haskar 2009). Significantly, both NSCN outfits agreed to refrain from collecting 'taxes' forcibly, as well as to refrain from recruiting new cadres into the outfits.[6] However, in reality, the NSCN (IM) and NSCN (K) do collect 'taxes' (extortions) and have also recruited new cadres. A glance at NSCN (IM) cadres will reveal that between 1997 and 2012, the outfit has increased its armed cadres from 1000 to nearly 5000.[7] Also, inter-factional violence between both outfits, aimed at establishing territorial

[4]The Armed Forces Special Powers Act (1958). Retrieved from http://mha.nic.in/pdfs/armed_forces_special_powers_act1958.pdf.

[5]Sashinunga. Nagaland: Insurgency and Factional Intransigence (2012). Retrieved from http://www.satp.org/satporgtp/publication/faultlines/volume16/Article4.htm.

[6]Revised Ground Rules for Ceasefire between Government of India and NSCN (IM). Retrieved from http://www.satp.org/satporgtp/countries/india/states/nagaland/documents/papers/revised_rules_cease_fire_goi_nscn_im.htm.

[7]Field observations by the author in Assam, Manipur and Nagaland from 2007 to 2012.

domination over the trade networks, especially in Dimapur (the main town of Nagaland) has resulted in both combatant and non-combatant deaths (Talukdar 2007). The level of violence between the factions was at its highest in the immediate aftermath of a split. In 1988, the split in the NSCN, propelled by differences between Thuingaleng Muivah and S.S. Khaplang, resulted in the killing of 200 of Muivah's men. It was subsequently followed by revenge killings, especially between the Thangkhuls, the tribe to which Muivah belongs, and the Konyaks, showcasing loyalty to Khaplang, who is a Hemi Naga from Myanmar. When the NSCN (IM) split on November 23, 2007, with the formation of a new outfit, the National Socialist Council of Nagaland (Unification)—NSCN (U), from within its folds, the violence threatened to 'spill over' into the tribal base. Significantly, Naga civil society actors controlled the violence through dialogue and consultations on the ground. This provided the much-needed hope that community-based processes for conflict prevention and management could have the legitimate capacity to handle violent ethnic complexities, especially when the legitimate state structures have failed in their law enforcement duties.[8]

2.2 Participants in the Naga Dialogue

The main participants in the Naga dialogue are: the Naga *Hoho* (Apex Tribal Council); Individual Tribal *Hohos* (councils); the Joint Forum on Gaon Burahs and Doabashis (JFGBDB); individual Village Council representatives; the militant actors like the NSCN (IM), the NSCN (K), the NNC, etc.; civil society actors like the United Naga Council (UNC); the Naga Students' Federation (NSF); the Naga Mothers' Association (NMA); Naga academics; NGOs; bureaucrats; Nagaland police; the business community; public intellectuals; church leaders; and the common people. The dialogue varies in participation from a minimum of 20 to a maximum of 10,000 people and the number of days reserved for the process ranges from two days to a month. The dialogue has been mostly facilitated by the Naga Hoho and the JFGBDB.

2.3 Actors' Perceptions of the Naga Ethnic Conflict

2.3.1 The Naga Hoho, the NSF, UNC, NMA and NSF

These multiple civil society actors view the Naga conflict as a response to the inadequate fulfilment of basic human needs in Naga society. Though Nagas rarely

[8]Namrata Goswami. A Way Out of Naga Factional Violence (2007). *IDSA Strategic Comments*. Retrieved from http://www.idsa.in/publications/stratcomments/NamrataGoswami230708.htm.

believe that the NSCN (IM)'s or NSCN (K)'s movements for independent sovereign homeland will succeed, they support the violent struggle as a fight for justice and ethnic lifeworlds (Biswas and Sukhalabaidya 2008). Here, I utilize one of the best known conflict theorist's, Edwar Azar's, 'theory of protracted social conflict [PSC]' as an explanatory framework to understand this support. In *Management of Protracted Social Conflict: Theory and Cases*, (Azar 1990), Azar argues that most individual loyalties and motivations to join armed groups and engage in violence arise in order to fulfil one's own societal needs—security, identity, recognition, economic fulfilment and so on. Drawing on a tradition of social anthropology and social psychology, Azar indicates that individuals will join armed groups that promise such benefits. The violent Naga ethnic conflict also enjoys cadre loyalty and support based on the deprivation of basic human needs.

While interacting with the *Naga Hoho* and Tribal Hohos, it is rather obvious that the Naga Hoho and Tribal Hohos realize that Naga sovereignty may be impossible in the context of a rising India that will never compromise its territorial integrity and sovereignty. The Naga Hoho and Tribal Hohos are therefore keen to bring about a 'Special Federal Relationship [SFR]' between India and *Nagalim,* resulting in a separate flag and army, and the unification of Naga areas within India.[9] However, their understanding of the SFR differs from that of the NSCN (IM). In an interview for BBC World, Muivah argued that SFR meant a special relationship with India but not 'within' India. He unequivocally asserted that 'SFR cannot be accepted within the framework of the Indian Constitution'.[10] The only areas that New Delhi will have control over are defence, external affairs, communication and currency. But while India will be obligated to defend *Nagalim* in the case of external threat, *Nagalim* will be under no such obligation concerning India's defence.

Despite being sympathetic to the NSCN (IM)'s stand on these issues, most of these social actors are acutely aware of the militant group's violent engagements, power battles and desire for territorial domination. Territorial domination is understood in the Naga narrative as the ability of the militant groups to run extortion networks and parallel governments in the area. In fact, over the years, the Naga Hoho, Tribal *Hohos*, the NSF and various village councils have openly condemned the violent means followed by the militant actors.

[9]Address of Mr. Isak Chishi Swu, Chairman, National Socialist Council of Nagalim at UNPO General Assembly (October 28, 2006), Taipei, Taiwan. Retrieved from http://www.nagalim.nl/news/00000487.htm. Also see The Hindu (April 29, 2005). Muivah talks of 'Special Federal Relationship' with India. Retrieved from http://www.hindu.com/2005/04/29/stories/2005042904201200.htm.

[10]Ibid.

2.3.2 *The NNC*

While being the descendent of the first Naga political organization, the Naga Club, the NNC became weak after Phizo's death in 1990. His daughter, Adino Phizo, who is the present president of the NNC does not enjoy the same stature that Phizo enjoyed in society. Nevertheless, the NNC views the Naga conflict as a struggle for independent homeland and sovereignty.[11] It is, however, against the NSCN (IM) being the sole representative of the Naga people in the Indo-Naga peace negotiations. To the NNC, the issue of Naga territorial integration in India is a 'red herring' used by outfits like the NSCN (IM) that deflects from the real issue of Naga independence.

2.3.3 *The NSCN (IM)*

The NSCN (IM)'s stated political objective is Naga territorial unification and sovereignty based on the historical narrative of Naga independence before British rule in the late nineteenth century. In his BBC World interview, Muivah stated that

> We can come as close as possible but it's not possible for the Nagas to come within the Indian Union or within the framework of the Indian Constitution. Why? Because it amounts to dismissing the whole history of the Nagas and the Nagas cannot do that… Nagaland was never a part of India either by conquest by India or by consent of the Nagas. This is very clear. This is the unique history and so according to this uniqueness a solution will have to be worked out.[12]

Since 1993, 'Nagaland for Christ' has been another important slogan of the NSCN (IM).

2.3.4 *The NSCN (K)*

The NSCN (K) aims to create an independent sovereign Christian Socialist Republic through the principle of people's supremacy, comprising all Naga-inhabited areas in Nagaland, and especially those in Myanmar. Interestingly,

---

[11]Okeet Jeet Sandham (2012), Core issue of Naga people is unequivocally upholding sovereignty of Nagaland: Adino Phizo. Retrieved from http://www.kanglaonline.com/index.php?template=kshow&kid=287.

[12]BBC Hard Talk. (April 29, 2005). Retrieved from http://www.youtube.com/watch?v=D4k0PgL1Kok.

the NSCN (K) views the Tangkhuls as Meiteis and not Nagas, and hence does not include the Tangkhul-inhabited areas in Manipur in its map of greater Nagaland.[13] The outfit has been issuing 'Quit Notices' to the NSCN (IM) and the Tangkhul Nagas from Nagaland for some years now. On January 29, 2009, it issued what it termed the 'final quit notice' to Tangkhuls living in Nagaland.[14] In reaction, however, the Naga Hoho asked the NSCN (K) to withdraw the notice and to work through dialogue to arrive at a mutually acceptable framework of living together peacefully in Nagaland. Also, socially influential public intellectuals like Charles Chasie argued strongly against such an irrational and absolutist posture on the part of the NSCN (K).[15]

Before we dwell on the Naga dialogue process, it is pertinent to conceptualize the meaning of dialogue and then locate the Naga dialogue within that framework.

2.3.5 *Definition of Dialogue*

The word 'dialogue' is a combination of the Greek words *dia* meaning 'through' or 'across' and *logos* meaning 'word' or 'reason'. Dialogue therefore implies 'a sense of creating meaning through talking or reasoning together' (Broome and Hatay 2006, p. 630). Dialogue deals with the challenge of understanding complexities at the social, political and cultural levels buttressed by differences in perceptions of the contextual situation, vagueness regarding causes of conflict, and ambiguity with regard to the future. Hence, the notion of dialogue, operating within the framework created by such antecedent conditions, is to squarely meet the challenge of coordinating meaning through participatory processes by bringing together diverse groups of actors with differences in personal experiences, perceptions and, at times, a history of violent conflict between them. The aim of most dialogical conflict resolution mechanisms is to create conditions for coordinated action towards a common goal: the end of violence and the emergence of an inclusive and peaceful society.

According to Hal Sanders, of the International Institute for Sustained Dialogue and the Kettering Foundation,

> Dialogue is a process of genuine interaction through which human beings listen to each other deeply enough to be changed by what they learn. Each makes a serious effort to take others' concern into her or his own picture, even when disagreement persists. No participant gives up her or his identity, but each recognizes enough of the other's valid human claims that he or she will act differently toward the other (Broome and Hatay 2006, p. 649).

[13]The Telegraph. Peace Rally to Support Naga Unification. (April 9, 2008). Retrieved from http://www.telegraphindia.com/1080409/jsp/northeast/story_9113678.jsp.

[14]NSCN (K) issues 'quit notice' to Thangkhuls. (January 30, 2009). Retrieved from http://www.zeenews.com/news351035.html.

[15]Charles Chasie. Quit Notice and the Deeper Issue. (2009). Retrieved from http://kanglaonline.com/index.php?template=kshow&kid=753&Idoc_Session=6580c6ea94011957d83ff68eb17b8d5c.

2.3.6 Components of Dialogue

Though the field of dialogue lacks substantial theoretical literature or conceptual mapping of dialogue processes, (Broome and Hatay 2006, pp. 649–652), the effectiveness of 'empathetic' and non-violent 'participatory' approaches in resolving disputes at the level of states or non-state actors, has given rise to strong supporters for this activity. Dialogue practitioners and academics (Camilleri 2009) have identified certain key components of dialogue (Pruitt and Thomas 2007, pp. 20–21; Camilleri 2009), which I argue is clearly present in the Naga dialogue. These are:

Inclusiveness: The process of dialogue is inherently informed by the element of inclusiveness based on a 'problem solving' approach. A number of stakeholders in a conflict with divergent or common interests and perceptions come together to work out a map for prevention, management and resolution of conflicts, both violent and non-violent. This inclusive base ensures that the support structure for a peace agreement is grounded on a solid legitimate social base undercutting the ability of peace-spoilers (Stedman 1997, p. 553), to sabotage the process. The element of 'inclusiveness' is also vital in a situation plagued by historical differences, violent conflicts and exclusion of imagined 'others'.
Joint ownership: The dialogue process must not be hijacked by a powerful actor (for instance, the state) who could utilize it to buy time to forward its own agenda. Instead, there must be joint ownership of the process in order to address problems and issues which have brought about social division.
Listening, learning, and adapting: Listening is of paramount importance to dialogue. Deep listening ensures greater understanding of issues at stake in a conflict, and helps in adapting one's own behaviour to bring about inclusive and pluralistic living. Judgements and preconceived notions are set aside in the act of listening, learning and adapting.
Empathy and humanity: Mahatma Gandhi, the leader of India's struggle for freedom and a champion of non-violent action, argued in the *Indian Opinion* that the 'most important requirement for any conflict resolution theory and practice is to find ways to not only understand one's own position but also empathize with the conflicting actor's point of view' (Goswami 2009). To Gandhi, it was mostly differences in positions or world views that created conflicts and hence one has to resolve differences at that level. In order to understand a conflicting other's worldview, one has to practice empathy for the position of the other without prejudice: recognizing the differences and yet finding common ground is the key to dialogue.
Notions of 'Self' and the 'Other': Dialogue aims to bridge the gap between the notions of 'Self' and the 'Other' and the constructed realities based on that distinction. Instead of billiard ball-like structures of 'Self', whose identity is defined based on a distinctive difference with the 'Other', or what is known as 'Othering', dialogue insists on the significance of accommodating the 'Other' into one's own identity construction and lifeworlds by focusing on the commonalities, shared

worldviews and ideas. Hence, it is not deemed imperative to construct one's own sense of nationhood and ethnicity based squarely on the linear notion of admission and segregation, but rather on ideas of tolerance and inclusion.

Understanding of context: The participants in the dialogue must have an understanding of the historical context leading to the conflict, and be sensitive to the changing political and social context. Cultural knowledge and understanding of the 'way of the land' is critical.[16] Political understanding should reveal the capacity to correctly gauge the power dynamics at play in conflict-affected societies.[17]

Transparency: Trust-deficit affects societies plagued by historical exclusivist narratives, conflict, and multiple violent actors. Hence, a level of transparency about the issues at stake, the problem areas and frank expression of one's position is important for dialogue.

A vision for the future: Any dialogue must have a long-term vision for the future propelled by the recognition that changed relationships hold the key to conflict resolution. Addressing the causes of the conflict takes time and patience.

2.3.7 Components of the Naga Dialogue

The Naga dialogue represents an 'insider' prevention and management of violent ethnic conflicts. Indeed, I argue that an in-depth analysis of the Naga dialogue reflects the eight components of dialogue identified above and is therefore a strong empirical case for dialogue literature.

Inclusive: The Naga dialogue is inclusive in character. The decision-making structures of the Naga *Hoho* and the various tribal councils are based on elected representation, with entire villages voting for representatives to their tribal Hohos like the *Ao* Hoho, Angami Hoho, Tangkhul Hoho, Konyak Hoho, and so on. The presidents of the *Hohos* thereafter represent the tribe in the Naga Hoho. Elections to *Hohos* are held every two to three years. The *Gaon Burahs* or village headmen council follows a slightly different procedure. Some of the chiefs are hereditary, for instance, the Sema, Konyak, Tangkhul, Chang and Yimchunger, whereas with regard to tribes like *Ao*, Jeme and Jeliangrong, the chiefs are elected by the village from among wise, elderly individuals. Family background matters to a large extent in this election procedure. There is also the *Doiabashis Hoho* (Village Elders Council). This body includes elected representatives from several villages with deep knowledge of Naga customs and traditions. The *Doaibashis* acts as a 'checks and balances' mechanism *vis-à-vis* individual Naga chiefs who may misuse power if left alone to their own volition. The *Doiabashis* also take part in the Naga *Hoho* where decision-making is based on consensus. The elections to the village councils

---

[16]Interview by the author with Temjenkaba, President, Ao Hoho, Dimapur, Nagaland, July 27, 2007.

[17]Ibid.

are held in every village. The day of election resembles a festival, with canvassing, speech-making and unfolding of agendas for the future by the individual candidates. Agendas can include basic issues like water, health, social service or political issues like Naga unification and India–Naga relations.

The Naga public sphere accounts for alternative voices, perhaps reflecting what Marc Lynch identifies as a global public sphere between Islam and the West or an 'Arab public sphere committed to open and critical public debate' (Lynch 2005). This social nature of dialogue aimed at conflict prevention and management after years of conflict appears promising. The effect of this was most apparent during the November 2007 split within the NSCN (IM), with the formation of a new militant outfit called the NSCN (U). Despite violent attacks by the former on the latter in the immediate aftermath of the split, the Naga dialogue successfully quelled the violence by enabling the two conflicting actors to come to the table under the aegis of the JFGBDB and the Naga *Hoho*. It must be noted here that the sensitivity of the NSCN (IM) to its reputation as a consulting actor in Naga society ensures the outfit's susceptibility to social pressures to forsake violent means to settle scores.

Joint ownership: The Naga dialogue is a jointly owned endeavour. The process started in the late 1950s after the Naga ethnic movement took on a violent turn under the leadership of A.Z. Phizo. Phizo established a Naga Army under the overall political structure of the *Khunak Kautang Ngeukhuma* (People's Sovereign Republic of Free Nagaland) in Tuensang district of Nagaland (Shimray 2005, p. 69). In August 1957, the Naga Peoples' Convention (NPC) was convened in Kohima under the leadership of Imkonglba Ao, one of the moderate members of the NNC sceptical about the utility of violence to fulfil Naga political aspirations. Significantly, the 1957 NPC involving participation by 1750 Nagas from across Naga-inhabited areas jointly agreed to seek a single Naga Hills and Tuensang district within the Indian Union, a setback to Phizo's call for sovereign independent homeland (Horam 1988, p. 84). Accordingly, on December 1, 1957, the Naga Hills–Tuensang Area (NHTA) was established as an autonomous district. However, violence between the Indian security forces and the extremist division of the NNC continued, and a second NPC was called in May 1958 by the moderate NNC leaders and the Naga Hoho (Horam 1988). Phizo, however, refused to take part in the process. Subsequently, a third NPC was called between October 22–26, 1959, attended by 3000 Naga delegates in Mokokchung, Nagaland. This convention was significant as it came up with the idea of a Nagaland state within the Indian Union. In July 1960, a Sixteen Point Agreement was signed between the NPC representatives and the Union Government (Nuh and Lasuh 2002). The Indian Parliament subsequently passed the 13th Amendment to the Constitution of India in 1962, and on December 1, 1963, Indian president Radhakrishnan inaugurated the State of Nagaland. Though statehood within India was the result of three separate NPCs, the limitation of the process was that Phizo was unwilling to take part in any of them and shifted his base to London in 1960. From London, Phizo continued to assert in his writings that nothing short of independence from India was acceptable to the Nagas, fuelling violence again (Luithai and Haksar 1984, p. 16).

In 1964, the NPM was established by the Union Government with Bimala Prasad Chaliha, then Chief Minister of Assam, Jaya Prakash Narayan, leader of the Sarvodaya movement and the *Shanti Sena* (peace army), and Rev. Michael Scott of the Baptist Mission of Nagaland as members. Jaya Prakash Narayan, while sympathetic to the cause of Naga independence bluntly stated in Kohima on August 12, 1966 that Naga 'leaders must understand that India cannot agree to anything that might cause disintegration of its territory' (Narayan 1994, p. 359). Significantly, both Narayan and Michael Scott expressed the view that the geographical location of Nagaland risked a direct threat from China to its future independent status. Scott went on to argue that Nagas should try working out a federal structure with greater autonomy within India (Nuh and Lasuh 2002, pp. 226–230 and pp. 319–323). In a document titled 'Nagaland Declaration for Peace' issued on April 13, 1965, the Naga Hoho acknowledged the efforts of the peace mission and expressed its desire to solve the Naga conflict through a process of dialogue (Nuh and Lasuh 2002, pp. 223–225). However, tribal differences within the NNC, buttressed by Phizo's resistance to the peace moves, resulted in heated arguments in the Hoho with Kughato Sumi, the Nagaland leader for peace negotiations with the Government being accused openly of a lack of commitment to an inclusive dialogue. Worse still, his younger brother, Kaito Sema, the so-called defence minister of the underground Federal Government of Nagaland (FGN), revolted against Phizo's leadership. These divisions along tribal lines led to a further deterioration of the situation, with Phizo removing the president of the FGN, Scato Swu, a fellow tribesman of Kaito, and replacing him with Rev. G. Mhiasiu, a Phizo loyalist (Goswami 2007, p. 295; Aram 1974, p. 137; Asoso 1974, p. 294). The assassination of Imkonglba Ao, the pro-dialogue NNC leader, further worsened the situation, with accusations against the NNC for playing along tribal lines and favouring the Angamis, Phizo's tribe (Shimray 2005, p. 86). However, at this critical juncture when the NPM appeared to be failing, the Naga Church under the leadership of Rev. Longri Ao, then executive secretary of the Nagaland Baptist Church, took the lead in the community-based dialogue while rejecting openly the extremist tactics adopted by Phizo (Shimray 2005, p. 45).

Due to intense social pressure, the moderate elements in the NNC led by Zaishe Huire signed the Shillong Accord on November 11, 1975 with the Union Government. Though Phizo was not present, his younger brother Kevi Yalley took part in the signing of the Accord. The Accord meant the NNC recognized the Indian Constitution and it agreed to surrender arms, while India lifted the Unlawful Activities Prevention Act from Nagaland (Nuh and Lasuh, pp. 344–356). However, an inability to jointly own the process of negotiation led many NNC cadres to condemn the Accord and to the formation of a new outfit in 1980 called the NSCN.[18] In 1988, the NSCN further split due to differences in the leadership, with Muivah and Swu forming the NSCN (IM) and Khaplang forming the NSCN

[18]NSCN Manifesto, GPRN, Oking. (January 31, 1980).

(K) (Verghese 2004, pp. 95–96; Nayar 2005, p. 38).[19] The subsequent years in Nagaland have been vitiated by inter-factional killings between these two outfits aimed at territorial and political domination. However, Naga society's enthusiastic participation in an informal yet structured dialogue based on their deep-seated desire for peace and progress in the Naga areas have strengthened the community-based peace movements. From the late 1980s, the joint ownership of the process facilitated by the Naga Hoho has taken on a mass participatory base, with participation increasing to an astounding 10,000 people since 2007.[20] In March, 2009, a 'Naga Convention for Reconciliation and Peace' was held in Kohima in order to send across 'a message of peace and an end to bloodshed and violence'.[21] The convention was attended by thousands of people from various Naga tribes, the militant actors, the church and the civil society. According to Vivi, General Secretary of the NMA, 'the convention is a positive attitude, everyone expressing the desire for reconciliation … and this is where we can build our hope'.[22] What is most refreshing to observe is that no single actor claims ownership of this process. Rather, it is viewed as a collective effort by all stakeholders to the conflict.

However, I would like to add a caveat so that we keep the 'politics of representation' in stark focus. Militant groups like the NSCN (IM) would ideally like to control the dialogue process. For instance, in 2001 the Naga Peace Reconciliation move under the joint ownership of the Naga Hoho, the Nagaland Peace Centre and the UNC proved so successful in addressing issues of violence, basic needs and political aspirations of the Nagas that the NSCN (IM) feared losing its dominant position as the sole peace negotiator with the Union Government. In reaction, it issued 'threat notices' to the leaders of the Reconciliation Committee forcing them to leave Nagaland.[23]

Learning a lesson or two about NSCN (IM) behaviour from these experiences, the later dialogues, especially from 2005 onwards, have involved both the NSCN (IM) and the NSCN (K) in the process of consultations. On July 24, 2007, when the JFGBDB issued an overall underground ceasefire, the NSCN (IM) and NSCN (K) representatives were present.[24] Moreover, the visible involvement of the JFGBDB in the dialogue since 2007 makes it difficult for the NSCN (IM) to issue similar notices to the Naga peace facilitators as it did in 2001 due to the social

[19]Joint Statement of Muivah and Swu, (July 7, 1989). GPRN.

[20]Field Observations by the author in Nagaland, 2007.

[21]Vibhou Ganguly. Peace and Reconciliation Convention Held in Nagaland'. (2012). Retrieved from http://www.thaindian.com/newsportal/india-news/peace-and-reconciliation-convention-held-in-nagaland_100163818.html.

[22]Ibid.

[23]Author's interview with Naga Peace Reconciliation Leaders, July 2007. Names not revealed due to protection of source.

[24]Nagaland Post, GBs and DBs Declare CFs Among Factions (July 25, 2007). The author was also present in Dimapur on that day to observe the process.

stature of the JFGBDB. The power of the present Naga dialogue was recognized by the NSCN (IM) General Secretary, Muivah in his speech at Camp Hebron, the NSCN (IM) headquarters, in July 2007.[25]

The issue of religion is another bone of contention between the NSCN (IM) and Naga civil society actors. Since 1993, the NSCN (IM) has declared 'Nagaland for Christ'.[26] This makes political sense since 90% of Nagas are Christians.[27] (Eaton 1997). However, according to Secretary of the Naga Hoho, Keviloto, the NSCN (IM) should refrain from using religion as a legitimizing tool for their militant activities as it is uncomfortably similar to the Taliban movement in Afghanistan and shrouded with dangerous consequences for Naga society.[28] This viewpoint is also supported by Rumpui Jeme, president of North Cachar Hills Heraka Association which has 56 Naga villages as members. He points out that most of these villages follow the old Heraka cult of the Nagas and are not Christians.[29] On many occasions Naga village headmen in North Cachar Hills have been threatened by the NSCN (IM) to convert to Christianity. The Naga Hoho's stand on religion is a sincere attempt to accommodate other faiths in a highly politicized context.

Listening, learning and adapting: Listening to the other side's viewpoint is an inherent feature of the Naga tribal councils. Discussion on the need for reconciliation takes centre-stage, with the Naga *Hoho* playing the role of the facilitator. Participation by Naga youths in these forums trains younger community leaders in the art of 'listening', even if the views expressed could be controversial or conflicting. The representation from the militant actors ensures that they are included in the process of learning, listening and adapting to the changing context. The detailing of the conflict, listing the root causes, enables informed dialogue on conflict prevention and resolution mechanisms. At the end of the consultations, the various tribal councils usually adopt a unanimous resolution based on consensus. Dissenting voices are also reflected to give due recognition to non-consensual views.[30] The opinion of the council is then made available to the society at large. The crucial aspect in this community-based dialogue is the notion of 'self-preservation and survival'. As violence is such an intrinsic aspect of their

---

[25]Speech by Thuingaleng Muivah, 6th Naga Peoples' Consultation Meeting (July 27, 2007), Camp Hebron, NSCN (IM) headquarters, Nagaland where the author was present as an observer.

[26]Annual Report of 1992–1993, *Nagaland for Christ*, Council of Nagaland Churches, Oking (30 June 1993).

[27]Richard Eaton indicated that Nagas represented the second massive conversion to Christianity, the first being Filipinos. Eaton estimated that 90% of Nagas were Christians, while the NSCN (IM) puts the figure at 95%. Hence, it is not surprising that the NSCN (IM) declared in the Free Nagaland Manifesto 'Nagaland for Christ' in 1993. The NSCN (IM) has a separate Ministry for Religious Affairs, and a council called the 'Council of Nagaland Churches'.

[28]Speech by Keviloto, Secretary, Naga Hoho, Camp Hebron, Near Dimapur, Nagaland (July 27, 2007).

[29]Interview by the author with Rumpui Jeme, President, North Cachar Hills Heraka Association, Lodhi Village, North Cachar Hills (July 18, 2007). Heraka is an animist religion of the Nagas, who primarily pray to the sun. It has been in existence for centuries.

[30]Based on field observation of the author from 2007 to 2012.

lives, the people inhabiting these violent spaces have worked out mechanisms to handle violence through dialogue (verbal communication for them) which are not always interest-based. While interviewing the actors in conflict, I realized that they viewed their evolution not always in competitive but in cooperative terms, unlike the *realpolitik* reasoning that the evolution of human beings has always been based on selfish competition (Brookes 2009).

Empathy and humanity: Empathy and humanity are paramount in any dialogue, especially in conditions where violence between communities and tribes is a recurring phenomenon, and where the structures of the state bureaucratic system are insensitive to the affected societies. The Naga dialogue is unique in its ability to offer a platform for developing empathy and respect for the other's point of view. The tone of the dialogue is respectful and accommodating. For example, the Ao Hoho in its meeting on July 27, 2007 at Camp Hebron, Dhansiripar assumed responsibility for the problems afflicting the tribe while offering concrete solutions after consultations with all the different village representatives to the Hoho.[31] In the larger setting of the 6th Naga Peoples' Consultative Meeting the same day, the views of all the Hohos like Ao, Angami, Thangkhul, Jeme, Konyak, Sema (and so on), and the NSCN (IM), were listened to with empathy by around 5000 participants from all the Naga-inhabited areas of the Northeast. By the end of the day, a common consensus was arrived at: indefinite extension of ceasefire between the NSCN (IM) and the Union Government; transparency in the functioning of the NSCN (IM); support for the peace negotiations between the Union Government and the NSCN (IM); more representations from the Nagas in the formal peace talks; infrastructure development; and improvement in the security situation in conflict prone areas (Van Ham and Saul 2008).

Notions of 'Self' and the 'Other': The Naga ethnic conflict has been afflicted by the distinction drawn between 'self' and 'other' based on tribal lines. Historically, tribes fought each other over land, village boundaries and natural resources, and practised 'head-hunting'.[32] The tribal identify was solidified by drawing a clear distinction, for example, between an Ao and a Konyak. These differences still exist and affect the violent militant actors. What the Naga intra-community dialogue has been successful in achieving over the years is to compel a large number of Nagas to give up rigid notions of 'self' and 'other' and converse together under a common banner on issues of critical concern. This has enabled many to think beyond a narrow tribal base and genuinely to engage so-called 'others'. In order to break down violent differences between militant actors aligned along tribal lines, the Naga dialogue participants utilize various means, including music and sports. In October 2008, a special football match was played between the NSCN (IM) and the NSCM (K) which brought together not only their cadres but, most importantly, their leaders, on a common platform. This was a unique move. As spelled out by Zhapu Terhuja of the Nagaland Christian

[31]Ao Hoho Meeting, Camp Hebron, July 27, 2007.

[32]Ibid.

Forum, 'It's an event which conveys a message to the people that something is taking place, which has never taken before'[33] aimed at peace and reconciliation.

Transparency: The level of transparency in the Naga dialogue has increased over the years, thereby increasing its credibility and level of sustainability in Naga society. Earlier, in the 1960s and the 1970s, the dialogue was limited to a few from the Naga Church, Naga politicians like S.C. Jamir and Hokishe Sema of the Naga Nationalist Organization, and militant leaders like Phizo, Muivah and Swu. The Union Government for its part was secretive about what transpired in the process of consultations. This lack of transparency left socially powerful groups like the Tribal and Village Councils with no space to offer their positions on the issues at stake in the overall situation. Over the years, as the conflict has become more protracted and bloody, more and more Nagas have got involved in the process of consultation and dialogue through both traditional and institutional structures, with the goal of bringing about peaceful reconciliation. The Nagaland Peace Centre, the Naga Hoho, the JFGBDB, the UNC, the NMA, the NSF (and so on) have taken up prominent responsibilities to bring about transparency in the dialogue with regard to issues intrinsic to Naga society like land, religion, infrastructure development, governance, militant extortion networks and agriculture. This transparency has been also possible due to the flexible nature of social bodies like the Naga Hoho and the tribal Hohos. Women, who were traditionally kept out of any serious consultation processes, are now strong agents for social change. An example is the involvement of the *Tangkhul Shanao Long* (Tangkhul Women's Organization) in averting a violent exchange between the Assam Rifles and the NSCN (IM) in Shirui Village of Ukhrul district, Manipur in January 2009 (Haskar 2009).

In direct contrast to the Naga civil society, my field experiences in Manipur and Nagaland have revealed that the NSCN (IM) functions through a highly centralized and hierarchical political structure known as Government of the Peoples' Republic of Nagaland (GPRN) (Shimray 2005, pp. 150–151; Horam 1988, p. 23).[34] The headquarters of the group is at Camp Hebron by the Dhansiri River in Nagaland, India. The GPRN has a president, vice president, prime minister, kilonsers (Ministers) and ministries.[35] The military wing consists of the People's Army of Nagaland with the chairman as the supreme commander, followed by the defence minister and the chief of army staff.[36] Among the leaders, Muivah is politically charismatic, articulate, and obviously wields the highest influence within the militant structure. The support of the NSCN (IM) for dialogue will therefore depend mostly on Muivah.

---

[33]Historical football match played by warring factions of Naga underground groups. (2009). Retrieved from http://www.thaindian.com/newsportal/india-news/historical-football-match-played-by-warring-factions-of-naga-underground-groups_100111268.html.

[34]Insights based on the author's visit to the headquarters of the NSCN (IM) in July 2007.

[35]Based on speech by Thuingaleng. Muivah, General Secretary of the NSCN (IM), Camp Hebron, Dimapur, Nagaland (July 27, 2007) where author was present.

[36]NSCN (IM). Retrieved from www.nscnim.online.

Understanding of context: The main participants in the Naga dialogue are local actors with a vital stake in the Naga conflict. Their deep understanding of the historical narratives and local politics increases their capability to resolve issues which appear incomprehensible to an outsider. The involvement of various actors in the dialogue, including Nagas from Arunachal Pradesh, Assam, Manipur and Myanmar gives a rich contextual basis to understand issues and is perhaps the best way forward for long-term conflict resolution.

A vision for the future: The Naga intra-community dialogue has an articulated vision for the future: a progressive, multi-linguistic, multicultural, unified *Nagalim* in which smaller Naga tribes as well as others will be given due recognition. Connection with a bigger tribe is also viewed as a 'security guarantee'. For instance, the Anal Naga tribe which inhabits the Chandel district of Manipur are only 13,853 compared to the larger Naga tribe Tangkhul in Manipur, numbering 112,944.[37] Since they fear the Meiteis, the Chandel Naga Peoples' Organization fully supports the NSCN (IM)'s agenda of a unified *Nagalim* and has sold land surrounding their villages to the Tangkhuls represented by NSCN (IM) for ensuring protection.[38]

2.4 Brief Overview of the Peace Process Between the Indian State and the Nagas

Before getting onto the section on prescriptions for a more inclusive dialogue between different actors affected by the violent Naga ethnic conflict, I offer a brief overview of the peace process between the Union Government and the NSCN (IM) as well as indicate the limitations in that process of consultation. While peaceful dialogue between the Indian state and the Nagas started way back in the 1950s when the three NPCs were convened in 1957, 1958 and 1959, respectively, followed by the establishment of the Nagaland state in 1963 and the NPM in 1964, these developments did not quell the violent Naga independent movement. Instead, it sharpened the divide between the pro-statehood (within India) and pro-independence groups with the pro-state (within India) Naga moderate leader, Imkonglba Ao assassinated in the 1960s. Subsequently, due to intense intertribal rivalry, the Naga independence movement suffered from splits with new armed outfits emerging from within the original NNC and trying to wrest control of the Naga ethnic movement. In this unfolding drama, the NSCN (IM), established in 1988, emerged as the most powerful Naga armed group and the Government of India, perhaps in recognition of that fact, has engaged the group in peaceful dialogue from 1997 till date.

[37]W. Nabakumar. The Inter Ethnic Relationship of the Different Communities of Manipur: A Critical Appraisal. (2012). Retrieved from http://www.manipuronline.com/Features/November2005/interethnicrelationship17_2.htm.

[38]Interview by the author with Chandel Naga Peoples' Organization (August 18, 2009) at Chandel Headquarters, Chandel District, Manipur.

2.5 Peace Negotiations Between the Union Government of India and the NSCN (IM)

On February 23, 1996, an offer for unconditional talks was put forward by the then Indian Prime Minister, P.V. Narasimha Rao to the NSCN (IM). In its response on July 31, 1996, the NSCN (IM) set three preconditions for talks:

1. Negotiations should focus on sovereignty,
2. Talks would be held in a third country,
3. A third party mediator should be included.

Rao's successor, Prime Minister H.D. Deve Gowda met the NSCN (IM) leaders on February 3, 1997 in Zurich. After a series of high-level meetings, a ceasefire agreement was signed on July 25, 1997 during I.K. Gujral's tenure as Prime Minister, which came into effect from August 1, 1997.[39] Then onwards, the ceasefire had been renewed either on a six-monthly or a yearly basis. Significantly, on July 30–31, 2007, the peace negotiations between both the sides was held for the first time in Dimapur, Nagaland, India, indicating that the NSCN (IM) had come down from its rigid stand of 'talks would be held in a third country'. Significantly, the ceasefire was extended indefinitely in that meeting, mostly due to the pressure from Naga civil society, who had expressed great dissatisfaction with the uncertainty of a six-monthly or yearly ceasefire extension in the Naga Peoples' Consultative Meetings.[40]

In the meantime, the NSCN (IM) has steadily extended its influence in the Northeast by setting up an umbrella organization known as the United Liberation Front of Seven Sisters. This overarching organization consists of the now surrendered Dima Halam Daogah-Jewel faction (DHD-J) of North Cachar Hills, Assam, the United People's Democratic Solidarity (UPDS) of Karbi Anglong, Assam, Arunachal Dragon Federation (ADF) of Arunachal Pradesh, People's Liberation Army (PLA) of Manipur and the Revolutionary Democratic Front (RDF). Earlier, on November 30, 1994, it formed the Self-Defence United Front of South East Himalayan Region in order to coordinate the activities of Hynniewtrep-Achik Liberation Council (HALC), National Liberation Front of Tripura (NLFT), Karbi National Volunteers (KNV), Hmar People's Convention (HPC) and Kanglei Yawol Kanna Lup (KYKL).[41]

---

[39]Nagaland. (2006). Retrieved from http://nagaland.nic.in/profile/history/peace.htm.

[40]Observations by the author based on her participation in Naga Peoples' Consultative Meetings (July 27, 2007) at Camp Hebron, Dhansiripar, Nagaland.

[41]National Socialist Council of Nagaland. (2012). Retrieved from http://www.satp.org/satporgtp/countries/india/states/nagaland/terrorist_outfits/nscn_im.htm.

2.6 India's Dilemma in the Peace Dialogue

Despite such disturbing developments, New Delhi has so far, failed to arrive at any substantial solution to the Naga movement for a unified homeland beyond the extension of the ceasefire. Perhaps, given the complexity of the Naga problem, which has been festering for the last sixty years, it might not be an easy task for either party to arrive at a mutually acceptable solution. The demand for sovereignty by the NSCN (IM) cannot be encouraged by New Delhi as it will stimulate further secessionist tendencies in other states, threatening the integrity of India. The NSCN (IM) is also perhaps right in its demands for a unified Naga homeland encompassing all Naga-inhabited areas in the Northeast. However, territorial demarcation is not an easy task and is forbidden by the Constitution of India unless the states are willing partners in the project. Neighbouring Assam and especially Manipur strongly resists Naga political and territorial unification within its borders. The path to peace appears more complicated than ever as a result of the ongoing contest between the NSCN (IM) and other groups with regard to territorial demarcation.

2.7 Contested Spheres of Territory

The NSCN (IM)'s demands in the peace process for a common unified Naga homeland are contested in the real world of interstate territorial discourse. The idea of *Nagalim*—seeking unification of all Naga-inhabited areas in Manipur, Assam and Arunachal Pradesh into a common politico-administrative unit—has exacerbated the situation. The NSCN (IM) has been demanding that the existing ceasefire agreement with New Delhi be extended to all Naga-inhabited areas in the region. This is a highly emotive issue with Manipur and Assam. In theory, a ceasefire automatically means the giving up of violence in favour of peaceful negotiations to a conflict. In this case, the extension of the ceasefire to Manipur and Assam would theoretically mean the end of a violent resistance by the NSCN (IM). However, a larger more 'diabolic' fear pervades the minds of the population of the other neighbouring states, especially Manipur. Any extension of the ceasefire to Manipur, with its large Naga population, is perceived to become a springboard of the Naga territorial unification process. The Meiteis fear that lurking behind the extension of the ceasefire is a legitimization of the NSCN (IM) demands on Manipur's territory. Such a move would also acknowledge the NSCN (IM)'s growing presence in the hills of Manipur. The NSCN (IM) too is caught up in a dilemma. A number of the NSCN (IM) cadres along with their leader Muivah belong to Ukhrul in Manipur. Therefore, in his inability to clinch an extension of the ceasefire to the Manipur hills, Muivah faces the possibility of being sidetracked. But an important part of the hills of Manipur seems to form the core of the Naga movement conducted by the NSCN (IM). Therefore, although the militant group has appeared silent on the sovereignty issue in recent years, it would be rather difficult for them to give up their demand for a unified Naga homeland. If the demand for unification is given up, the NSCN (IM) faces the fatal prospect of losing the reason for their existence. The militant group knows well that without the unification card New Delhi might not talk to them, their larger struggle based on a historical 'uniqueness' notwithstanding. Even more obvious is the fact that without including the Tangkhul Naga base in the larger *Nagalim* project, the present NSCN (IM) leadership possesses limited influence in Nagaland per se—particularly given the fact that these areas are dominated by the Ao, Angami, Chakesang and Konyak Naga tribes whose loyalty to the NSCN (IM) is rather suspect.

2.8 Manipur Raises the Ante

Under pressure from the NSCN (IM), in a joint statement issued on June 14, 2001 in Bangkok, the Indian government and the NSCN (IM) extended the Naga ceasefire 'without territorial limits'.[42] This led to violent protests in Manipur, with the state assembly building being burnt down and 13 protestors being killed on June 18, 2001. Meitei, Kuki and Muslim civil society organizations in Manipur were united in a mass movement against the decision to extend the Naga ceasefire to the Naga-dominated hill districts of Manipur—Chandel, Ukhrul, Senapati and Tamenglong. These protest groups included the All Manipur United Clubs Organisation (AMUCO), comprising 83 social and voluntary organizations across Manipur. Later, a new body comprising the AMUCO as well as All Manipur Students' Union (AMSU) was formed to carry forward the protests. Finally, New Delhi was forced to reconsider its decision, and on July 27, 2001, it revoked the new ceasefire arrangements, and restored the status quo of a territorially restricted ceasefire with the NSCN (IM) in Nagaland.[43]

The Meiteis are deeply apprehensive that the current peace process could end up in the balkanization of Manipur. Geographically, the hills constitute 70% of Manipur's territory and any further slicing of territory would leave Manipur at a disadvantage (Baruah 2005, p. 114). Meiteis also claim that their culture is a synthesis of Naga and Meitei cultures and are embittered by the identity and historical exclusivity discourse of the Nagas. Their narratives concentrate on the state's culture of pluralism. Meiteis point out that the term 'Naga' in a historical sense had never been applied to the hill tribes of Manipur by the Ahoms and the British, but

[42]For full text of the agreement see South Asia Terrorism Portal. Countries; India; States; Nagaland; Papers; Extension of the ceasefire with the NSCN-IM (2006). Retrieved from www.satp.org.

[43]The ULFA has said that the NSCN (IM)'s claim of eight Assam districts as part of Nagalim has 'neither credibility nor any historical basis'. Arabinda Rajkhowa, the ULFA chairman, has called upon the NSCN (IM) to remove the eight Assam districts from its Nagalim map. See Ajai Sahni. Survey of Conflicts and Resolution in India's Northeast. (2006). Retrieved from http://www.satp.org/satporgtp/publication/faultlines/volume12/Article3.htm.

was limited to present Nagaland. Indicating the state's historical cultural plurality and ethos, Manipuri narratives point out that Panheiba, a Naga, ascended the throne of Manipur in 1714. He later adopted Hinduism and also assumed the title Gharib Nawaz being conferred on him by the Meitei Pangals (Muslims) for his kindness towards them. Two Tangkhul Naga politicians, Yangmasho Shaiza and Rishang Keishing have been chief ministers of Manipur. Keishing, despite his Tangkhul lineage, passed a resolution in 1994 in the Manipur assembly upholding the territorial integrity of Manipur on the face of the Nagaland assembly adopting a resolution calling for unification of all Naga areas (Baruah 2005, p. 115).

2.9 External Linkages

Internal conflicts fought for local issues also involve a complex transnational network (Kaldor 2006, p. 2). External support is contingent on the geographical proximity and political relations maintained by the armed groups with external actors. These groups procure the hardware of violence and update their strategies through external support. Support from neighbouring areas could be political, moral, military, economic, territorial or cultural based on ethnic ties (Bajpai 2002, pp. 33–37). The NSCN (IM) is heavily dependent on external support for its violent movement. The northeastern states share a 4500 km highly porous border with China in the north, Myanmar in the east, Bangladesh in the southwest and Bhutan in the northwest. The NSCN (IM) has training camps in Bangladesh and Myanmar. Significantly, the unified National Socialist Council of Nagaland (NSCN) was formed in Myanmar on January 31, 1980.[44] The NSCN (IM) is also suspected to have a strong links with the Kachin Independence Organization and the Karen National Union (KNU) in Myanmar. The GPRN sends emissaries abroad to acquire funds for an annual NSCN (IM) budget of Indian Rs. 200–Rs. 250 million. Drug trafficking, arms procurement and intelligence from groups in South and Southeast Asia is vital for the group. Arms are purchased from Thailand and other Southeast Asian countries and transported through Myanmar and Bangladesh.[45] Unless these external linkages are thwarted by India, the militarization of the Naga ethnic movement will continue unabated.

A significant development that took place in the 1990s was the admission of the NSCN (IM) into The Hague based Unrepresented Nations and Peoples' Organisation (UNPO) on January 23, 1993. The admission elevated the Naga movement to the international arena (Nuh and Lasuh 2002, pp. 449–462). It is, however, surprising that apart from articulating a weak condemnation, New Delhi did not question the basis of the membership. Consequently, the internationalization

[44]See Nagalim. (2007). Retrieved from http://www.unpo.org/member_profile.php?id=41n.

[45]For more details on NSCN (IM) and (K) factions, see Nagaland Timeline. (2006). Retrieved from http://www.satp.org/satporgtp/countries/india/states/nagaland/timeline/index.html.

of the Naga issue perhaps drove home the inevitable truth for New Delhi—that in order to mitigate a growing crisis, a proposal for peaceful resolution must be negotiated with the armed group. The NSCN (IM) has also strong linkages with Kreddha—the International Peace Council for States, Peoples and Minorities based in Amsterdam which is involved in the prevention and resolution of violent conflicts between population groups and the government of states within which they live.[46] The role of Michael C van Walt van Praag, a lawyer and member, Kredda in the peace negotiations in a rather covert fashion on the side of the NSCN (IM) is a well established fact. The legal language of the NSCN (IM)'s text in its negotiating position with the Indian government is suspected to the handiwork of Praag. While it is interesting to observe this kind of third party mediation, it remains to be seen how effective it is going to be towards finding a final resolution to the Naga conflict unless support exist for such outside involvement from the Naga community.

The Naga Reconciliation process headed by Baptist clergyman Wati Aier has also received the support of the Baptist World Alliance and a UK-based Quaker group, which organized a reconciliation meeting of the Naga factions, community Naga organizations and tribal Hohos at Chiang Mai in Thailand in June, 2008. This kind of peaceful support is significant as it further vindicates the fact that community organizations possess the credibility to bring together warring factions for peaceful reconciliation.

2.10 Prescriptions for Better Dialogue Mechanisms

The Naga dialogue is a useful, solid base for informing the formal, official negotiations between the Union Government and the NSCN (IM). Negotiations are important to bring about a peace agreement but they have never by themselves succeeded in establishing peace. It has been observed that negotiations between two conflicting actors usually involve each side taking up strong positions on issues, thereby rendering the process incapable of reaching a consensus. Hence, instead of shared 'meaning-making' based on respect, listening to the other side and the articulation of divergent voices, negotiations tend to streamline various issues and voices into a structured decision-making process based on asymmetries of power.

The difference between negotiation and dialogue is that while negotiation aims at finding a concrete agreement, dialogue aims at a changed relationship. The Naga peace negotiations reflect a similar situation and hence have been stalled for decades due to their intense focus on dealing with rigid postures (the Union Government's position that India's territorial integrity and sovereignty are non-negotiable and that the Naga political resolution has to be squarely placed within the framework of the Indian Constitution; the NSCN (IM)'s insistence that

[46]Kreddha. (2012). Retrieved from http://www.kreddha.org/text/index.asp?text.asp?cat1=1&cat2=5&cat3=0&langId=1 ~ main.

resolution has to be outside the framework of the Indian Constitution). Therefore, a Naga community dialogue could perhaps be more successful in finding new ground for mutual respect and understanding. The government of India must while holding future peace talks go beyond its conceptual framework of conflict management to conflict prevention and resolution, giving due recognition to the informal yet very critical groundswell of Naga dialogue process. Since the entire Naga society is affected by violent conflict, representation must be accorded to various actors like the Naga Hoho, tribal Hohos, Village Councils, NMA, etc. The few prescriptions offered here are:

1. Reframe the negotiation framework between the Union Government and the NSCN (IM) to make it more inclusive, broad-based and socially viable.
2. The positive change that the Naga community dialogue has brought about in Naga society and its ability to control violent escalations between the militant outfits is truly remarkable. Therefore, the government of India and the Nagaland State government must take valuable inputs from these civil society actors to increase effectiveness of democratic governance and in bringing down the levels of bureaucratic corruption in Naga areas.
3. The *Naga Hoho* and the JFGBDB must be institutionalized and their informal dialogues recorded and widely disseminated to bring about greater awareness of these 'bottom up' approaches to conflict management and resolution.
4. The NSCN (IM)'s *Nagalim* map threatens the territorial integrity of states like Assam, Manipur and Arunachal Pradesh. The Naga militant actors are also instrumental in setting up other violent ethnic groups like the *Dima Halam Daogah* (DHD) in Assam. It is perhaps necessary that the Union Government involves people affected by the conflict in other states in the process of dialogue and negotiation in order to make the entire process of resolving the conflict a joint effort.

In conclusion, one can hope that the involvement of Naga society in the dialogue process and its support for the peace negotiations between the Naga armed groups and the Government of India provides the requisite legitimacy to these processes. The recent developments in the peace process are encouraging. In October 2012, the NSCN (IM) organized a people's consultative meeting at its headquarters, Camp Hebron, which was attended by top-ranking leaders as well as by members of Naga civil society. After this meeting, the group issued a statement to the effect that almost all present at the meeting backed the leadership's efforts to find an honourable solution through the ongoing peace negotiations with the Indian government.

On the Indian government's side, Union Home Minister Sushil Kumar Shinde was even more categorical; he has hinted that a solution is most likely by March 2013. The other significant development in this regard is the commitment reiterated by the representatives of the Joint Legislators' Forum of the Nagaland Assembly led by Nagaland Chief Minister Neiphiu Rio that they support an 'interim solution' and are ready to resign from their present positions in order to facilitate a final resolution to the Naga conflict by March 2013.

What could count as a feasible resolution package in this context? For one, it should not threaten the present territorial boundaries of the states of Assam, Manipur and Arunachal Pradesh. As is well known, the NSCN (IM)'s Greater *Nagalim* demand is based on the territorial unification of all Naga-inhabited areas in Nagaland, Assam, Manipur and Arunachal Pradesh. These include: Manipur's four hill districts of Churachandpur, Senapati, Tamenglong and Ukhrul; Assam's Dima Hasau and Karbi Anglong districts; and Arunachal Pradesh's Tirap and Changlang districts. Hence, any resolution based on territorial changes will not be acceptable to these states as was demonstrated by the violent protests in Manipur in 2001. However, what will work is a non-territorial resolution and this is what the Union Home Minister appears to be hinting at. That would mean greater autonomy for the Naga-inhabited areas in these other states. This would encompass separate budget allocations for the Naga-inhabited areas with regard to their culture and development issues. For it to be practically feasible, a new body should be constituted that would look after the rights of the Nagas in the other northeastern states besides Nagaland.

This is a resolution framework that is worth considering by the other states, especially Manipur as it would enable it to maintain its territorial *status quo* while only giving up developmental privileges in its Naga inhabited areas to a new Naga non-territorial body. This arrangement should serve Manipur well as, under the present circumstances, the ethnic divide and distrust between the Meiteis and the Nagas is so immense that most Nagas residing in Manipur believe that they are discriminated against when it comes to development packages by the Meitei dominated Manipur state assembly. It would also mean that Manipur can then concentrate on the development of its other ethnic minorities and not have to constantly worry about Naga dissatisfaction. A non-territorial resolution framework also favours the Nagas as their other core demands such as recognition of their 'unique history' and culture, Naga leverage over deciding the development path for the Naga-inhabited areas in the Northeast, etc., will all be met through greater autonomy based on a non-territorial resolution package. This is an optimal gain for all affected parties under the present circumstances. For the India government too, it would result in recognizing the Naga's 'unique' history and culture within the territorial integrity and sovereignty framework of the Indian Constitution. This is something worth working for in the near future.

References

Aram, M. (1974). *Peace in Nagaland eight years story 1964–1972*. New Delhi: Arnold Heinemann.

Asoso, Y. (1974). *The rising Nagas*. New Delhi: Vivek Publishing House.

Azar, E. (1990). *Management of protracted social conflict: Theory and cases*. Aldershot: Dartmouth.

Bajpai, K. (2002). *Roots of terrorism*. New Delhi: Penguin.

Baruah, S. (2005). *Durable disorder: Understanding the politics of Northeast India*. Oxford: Oxford University Press.
Bhaumik, S. (2007). *Insurgencies in India's North East: Conflict, co-option and change*. Washington D.C.: East West Center Washington Working Papers.
Biswas, P., & Sukhalabaidya, C. (2008). *Ethnic life-worlds in North-East India: An analysis*. New Delhi: Sage.
Brookes, D. (2009, April 6). The end of philosophy. *The New York Times*. Retrieved from at http://www.nytimes.com/2009/04/07/opinion/07Brooks.html
Broome, B. J., & Hatay, A.-S. J. (2006). Building peace in divided societies: The role of intergroup dialogue. In J. G. Oetzel & S. Ting-Toomey (Eds.), *The Sage handbook of conflict communication integrating theory, research and practise*. London: Sage.
Camilleri, J. A. (2007). Citizenship in a globalizing world: The role of civilizational dialogue. In F. Dallmayr & A. Manoochehri (Eds.), *Civilizational dialogue and political thought* (pp. 129–159). United Kingdom: Lexington Books.
Camilleri, J. A. (2009, March). Interfaith dialogue: The next phase. *AUSTRALIANmosaic*, *21*, 4–6.
Dallmayr, F. (2002). *Dialogue among civilizations some exemplary voices*. New York: Palgrave Macmillan.
Eaton, R. (1997). Comparative history as world history: Religious conversions in modern India. *Journal of World History*, *8*(2), 243–271.
Goswami, N. (2007, March). The Naga narrative of conflict: Envisioning a resolution roadmap. *Strategic Analysis*, *31*(2), 287–313.
Goswami, N. (2008, May). Unraveling insurgent groups' strategy: The case of the National Socialist Council of *Nagalim* in India. *Strategic Analysis*, *32*(3), 413–438.
Goswami, N. (2009). The Indian experience of conflict resolution in Mizoram. *Strategic Analysis, 33*(4), 579–589.
Haskar, N. (2009, April). Machiavelli's cease-fire and the Indo-Naga peace process. *Mainstream Weekly*, XL VII/16. Retrieved from http://www.mainstreamweekly.net/article1276.html
Horam, M. (1988). *Naga insurgency-the last thirty years*. New Delhi: Cosmo Publications.
Kaldor, M.(2006). *New & Old Wars*, p. 2 Cambridge: Polity Press.
Khatami, M. (2000, September 5). Speech at round table: 'Dialogue among Civilizations'. New York: United Nations, Provisional verbatim transcription. Retrieved from http://www.unesco.org/dialogue/en/khatami.htm
Luithai, L., & Haksar, N. (1984). *Nagaland file: A question of human rights*. New Delhi: Lancer.
Lynch, M. (2005, January). Transnational dialogue in an age of terror. *Global Society*, *19*(1), 5–28.
Narayan, J. (Ed.). (1994). *Nation building in India*. Varanasi: Navachetna.
Nayar, V. K. (2005). *The North East and Jammu and Kashmir: From Real Politik to Ideal Politik*. New Delhi: Shipra.
Nuh, V. K., & Lasuh, W. (2002). *The Naga chronicle*. New Delhi: Regency Publications.
Pruitt, B., & Thomas, P. (2007). *Democratic dialogue: A handbook for practitioners*. Washington D.C. and New York: GS/OAS, IDEA, UNDP.
Saunders, H. H. (2001). *A public peace process sustained dialogue to transform racial and ethnic conflicts*. London: Palgrave.
Shimray, A. S. (2005). *Let Freedom Ring Story of Naga Nationalism*. New Delhi: Promilla.
Stedman, S. J. (1997). Spoiler problems in peace processes. *International Security*, *22*(2).
Talukdar, S. (2007, September 7). Rebel rule. *Frontline*, 33–36.
Tehranian, M., & Chappell, D. W. (Eds.). (2002). *Dialogue of civilizations: A new peace agenda for a new millennium*. London: I.B. Tauris.
van Ham, P., & Saul, J. (2008). *Expedition Naga Dairies from the Hills in Northeast India 1921-1937 and 2002-2006*. Bangkok: River Books.
Verghese, B. G. (2004). *India's North East resurgent ethnicity insurgency governance development*. New Delhi: Konarak Publishers.

Part II
Restorative Justice Development in India

Chapter 3
Restorative Justice in India: Old and New

Shiva M. Jaamdar

Criminal justice systems in many developed countries today are witnessing a re-emergence of two often conflicting schools of thought: on the one hand, neo-deterrence seems to be sweeping mainstream criminal justice practices; on the other hand, restorative justice approaches are also emerging on the side-lines. As revealed by the US Bureau of Justice Statistics (2010) of all European countries and the US, the growing menace of terrorism, drug trafficking and violence are compelling them to take recourse to more punitive laws leading to unprecedented rates of arrest and imprisonment, notably in the US. Sentencing discretion of judges is being replaced by mandatory punishments; the death penalty has come back in many states; teenage delinquents are being increasingly imprisoned in the United States of America. Released offenders are being put on surveillance and registration. Homeland security is tightened and the parole system is either abolished or less used.

In contrast, one can also see a slow and steady growth in the number of victim–offender mediation projects (in England and Australia), victim–offender reconciliation efforts (in the USA and Canada), reintegrative shaming and community conferencing (in New Zealand) and more community policing schemes. More judges seem to be inclined today to impose on the first offenders a variety of community service sentences and orders for victim restitution (in England and USA). Victim compensation schemes and a variety of victim assistance agencies have proliferated in many developed countries (South African Law Commission report 97).

While crime rates are rising steadily in almost all countries of the world, the crime problem is more serious in developed countries than in developing ones. The miserable plight of crime victims and sensational media reports of violent crimes in

S.M. Jaamdar (✉)
School of Criminology and Criminal Justice, Rani Channamma University,
Belgaum, Karnataka, India
e-mail: sm.jamdar@gmail.com

R. Thilagaraj and J. Liu (eds.), *Restorative Justice in India*,
DOI 10.1007/978-3-319-47659-9_3

these countries are arousing alarming fear of crime and a threat to the safety of their citizens (Kania and Kuhnrich 2006). Crime fighting therefore frequently becomes a part of the electoral agenda and political rhetoric in power politics. The conventional approach of dealing with crimes and criminals in these countries does not seem to work. The futility of punishments in preventing crimes, the failure of correctional treatment in preventing recidivism and utopian solutions of radical criminology have created a vacuum in the practice of criminal justice (Braithwaite 2004). In this vacuum, restorative justice seems to be gaining increasing popularity, especially in the United States of America, Europe, New Zealand and Australia.

Restorative justice is not a new invention but a rediscovery of past practices which are simpler, local, informal and more effective in dealing with criminals and their victims. Primarily it holds that crime is a disruption in the normal relationship between two private individuals—the criminal and his or her victim—both of who operate in a given community (Zehr 2002). Strangely, the basic premise of the criminal justice system is that crime is an offence against state and not a private matter between the involved individuals. It is further argued that the state by intervening and usurping to itself the monopoly of punishing powers alienates the victims, demonizes the criminals, and endangers the safety of the society. It is true that the present state of criminal justice in developed countries seems to squarely fit into such argument. But the perpetual bloodshed between conflicting private parties made it necessary for the intervention of the state or religious authority which preceded it.

According to restorative justice the best way to settle crimes is by bringing the criminal and his victim together and encouraging them to sort out their problems amicably (Braithwaite 2004). The role of the society is to mediate, conciliate and facilitate such amicable settlement of conflicts between the victims and criminals. These methods are more emphasized.

It is asserted that the criminal must own up his responsibility for the crime and make adequate and proper amends to the victims. But if that were so easy there would have been no need for the whole process of adversarial or inquisitorial justice systems. It is further asserted that the victim should forgive, accept the recompense and adjust. But what happens to the victims' sense of outrage, injustice and spontaneous revenge against the offenders in an overwhelming majority of crimes?

The process of criminal owning his fault and making amends for it, and the victim accepting the apology and reparation by the criminal, it is claimed, satisfies the victims, reforms the criminal and reintegrates the criminal into the community. Consequently, it is presumed that there will be less crime, least recidivism, and greater peace and safety in the community.

These seemingly convincing arguments of restorative justice, viewed from the totality of the situation, sound overly simplistic. They take several things for granted which may not be operating in a real given context (Gregory and Takagi 2004). Undoubtedly, restorative measures can work effectively in some societies and for some crimes and criminals but not everywhere nor in every crime category or situation (Latimer 2005). This paper briefly examines the role of restorative justice in the traditional society of India and some emerging concepts and practices in that direction. It presents a broad overview of the traditional Indian systems of conflict resolution in comparison to the formal criminal justice system created by the British in India and how it is struggling to cope with the change.

3.1 The Indian Criminal Justice System

The formal Indian criminal justice system, as it stands today, has nothing 'Indian' in its form, content or practice except what has been developed in practice over the last 150 years by the lawyers and the Indian judiciary including the post-independence constitutional framework. An eminent jurist of India, M.C. Setalwad, who said in one of his public lectures in the Patna Law College, that the Indian judicial system did not suit India reversed his opinion when he became Chairman of the Indian Law Commission (Setalwad 1970). Under similar circumstances of a lawyer's private opinion conflicting with his professional opinion, Lord Kilbrandon in the Lynch case said: 'that law reform by lawyers for lawyers (unless in exceptionally technical matters) is not socially acceptable'. That is what the present Indian Criminal justice is! It evolved by superimposing an alien British system on a [preexisting Indian judicial system by the British colonial administration in the eighteenth and nineteenth centuries (Chandra 1990; Bhardwaj 2001). Excluding the revision of the Criminal Procedure Code in 1973 and a few amendments to the Indian Penal Code and the Indian Evidence Act, no major changes have been made to the criminal justice system in India in the last six decades since it got freedom from the United Kingdom (Bhardwaj 2001, p. 36).

3.2 Indigenous Justice Systems in India

Before the advent of the British era, being an ancient civilization, India had, and even today has, its own home-grown and parallel system of justice which settles disputes—civil or criminal—in traditionally acceptable ways (Chandra 1990). Nothing is more than just a third-party decision which is acceptable and satisfactory to the victim, the offender and the community in which they live. It may not be a 'perfect' system in comparison to its European and British counterparts. Judging from the standpoints of equality before law, the rule of law, and the prevailing sense of equity, the ancient Indian judicial systems suffered from caste-based discriminations which prescribed unequal punishments for equal crimes according to the status of the offender in the Varnashram system of Hindu social hierarchy. The colonial rulers did not like the discriminatory practices (Macaulay 1843, 1900). But the traditional systems of justice in India as laid down in the Smritis such as the most influential Code of Manu, or the much used Code of Yajnavalkya or the Arthashastra of Kautilya, excluding the inequality before law, had their own merits and major strengths in other respects. Instead of reforming the defects in the old system, the colonial rulers, misled by the egotists like Thomas Bobbington

Macaulay (who suffered from bloated notions of British superiority), chose to ignore the positive aspects and abolished the old systems altogether (Smith 2003). They threw the baby out with bath water.

3.3 Islamic Influences and Survival

The traditional system of criminal justice in India, as the British administrators found it during their empire building days, was somewhat influenced by the Islamic Juridical practices since the advent of Muslim rule in the thirteen century (Bhardwaj 2001, p. 21). Nonetheless, the Islamic and the native Hindu systems of justice in India did not disappear with the forcible introduction of alien British system of laws and justice. They survived due to the insulating nature of Indian society against the 'corrupting influences' from the intruding alien cultures be it Islamic or European (Smith 2003, pp. 50–64). Despite 500 of Muslim rule and 150 years of British domination the basic tenets of Hindu social traditions continued albeit with a few cosmetic changes.

3.4 Resilience and Change

During these 650 of history only 2% of Indians became Christians and ten per cent became Muslims. Among multilingual Indians about 20% speak Urdu and around 10% English (Census of India 2011). Men's dress changed to some extent but not the majority of women's dress. Despite the secularizing impact of British rule, the caste system has neither disappeared nor is it likely to do so. It cannot be said that India did not change at all but the change was not so dramatic as one finds in the American, Australian and African continents which were colonized for about the same period by European countries: Britain, Spain, Portugal, France and the Netherlands. As a subsystem of the overall social system, the indigenous traditional systems of settling criminal or civil disputes even to this day prevail to a considerable extent, in some mutant forms in the rural, informal and tradition-bound villages of India (Kidder 1978). The two competing systems coexist where the formal system of justice supersedes the informal system whenever they clash.

3.5 Conflicts Between the Native and Alien Systems

The superimposition of an alien system of justice on India has resulted in several maladjustments in the operation of the formal judicial system. First of all, a large majority of people being barely literate does not understand formal court proceedings and secular laws as they are in English, which is spoken by about 10% of the people largely in urban India (Census of India 2011). Too much formality of procedure and gruelling appearances of witnesses for several days spread over several months and quite often years spell disaster and dislike of the formal courts among the public. Appearing as a witness or complainant itself is disliked and avoided if possible.

Second, the concepts of 'rule of law' and 'equality before law' which were alien to the Indian tradition and Hindu psyche are often breached in real practice (Madhav Menon 2000). Caste loyalties, belief in primordial traditions and individuals' senses of duties according to his or her place in the society are strongly shaped and maintained by the caste system. The equality, as understood for centuries in the caste sense by the Hindus, is the equality within the caste and among the members of the endogamous clan. The caste loyalties in India are very complex (Hayden 1981; Kikani 1912). It is not uncommon for law enforcement officers, witnesses and experts, irrespective of which side of the law they are on, to help their caste men if they are likely to get into trouble with court outcomes.

Third, several reformative social laws (having support of enlightened Indians) sought to abolish traditional Hindu evil practices like sati, polygamy, dowry, untouchability, female infanticide, child marriage, prohibition of widow remarriage, animal sacrifices and so on. These measures went against the traditional Hindu society which considered such laws as intrusions of alien influences into their culture (Chandra 1990). The sati system has virtually disappeared except for a very rare occurrence in the Jat lands of North India. Polygamy has been transformed into concubinage. Widow remarriage is still rare. All other the social evils—dowry, child marriage, female infanticide, social exclusion of lowest castes, animal sacrifices, prohibition of inter-caste and intra-gotra marriages, though reduced considerably, are still in vogue (Madan 1966). The enforcement of most of the social reform laws is lopsided and unsatisfactory. Consequently, in the absence of social support, the court outcomes in these cases are generally disappointing.

Fourth, the formal courts are located in taluka, district and state headquarters not in the villages which creates problems for easy and quick access. Despite development of roads, not all villages are easily accessible for want of all-weather roads and transport facilities.

Fifth, the lawyers' fees for professional handling of litigation in the formal courts are high and often unaffordable for poor people. Most people do not understand the difference between court fees and bribes to the court staff or even the rates of lawyers' fees. Often they are left to the mercy of the lawyers especially in civil litigations. Prevailing poverty in rural areas discourages people from formal litigation (Viscount Buckmaster 2001). Several popular jokes about formal courts such as "winner has lost, loser is dead", "lawyers are liars" reveal the general abhorrence of the formal courts in India.

Sixth, the cases in the courts drag on for years which dampen the retaliatory spirit or search for prompt justice. Inordinate delays, generally for many years, betray the sense of justice and cause desperation among the victims as well as the law enforcement agencies (Madhav Menon 2000).

Seventh, the punishments awarded by the formal courts carry imprisonment or death or fines as against many other restorative forms of informal traditional penal practices. Indian penal laws in general do not leave much discretion to the judges in respect of sentencing alternatives. This was perhaps on account of the general distrust of Indian officers by the British. The British lawmakers in the past deliberately adopted a determinate sentencing policy in lawmaking which tradition has continued unaltered after independence. There is no jury system now in India. People's participation in court proceedings is virtually nil except as compulsory witnesses or compelled attendance of experts. The Indian Penal Code which uniformly applies to all Indians in 28 states and six federal territories clearly prescribes specific sentencing alternatives and puts limits on their quantum. All other minor criminal statutes follow the same general principle. Probation of Offenders' Act, 1958 whose use is very limited does provide for release of first and minor offenders on probation. It also provides for admonition and restitution. Recent amendment to the Criminal Procedure Code has introduced state-funded victim compensation or restitution by the offenders. However, a vast majority of criminal courts do not use these provisions. Indeed, many of the judges do not even know of these alternatives.

Eighth, imposition of punishment, if found guilty, is never prompt as trials take several years to conclude. Appeal after appeal to the Court of Sessions, the state High Court, and ultimately to the Supreme Court of India ensures long delays and possible overturning of the lower courts' judgements. This fact exacerbates the frustrations and desperation of the victims and the prosecution (Madhav Menon 2000).

Finally, there is no certainty of punishment since the standards of proof expected in formal courts are so high that it is very difficult to prove guilt "beyond reasonable doubt". The Committee on Criminal Law Reforms (Malimath Committee 2003) suggested that guilt "beyond reasonable doubt" should be replaced by "beyond preponderance of probabilities" which is yet to be accepted. The rules relating to 'relevancy' and 'admissibility' of evidence and reliability of witnesses in the Indian Evidence Act are said to be too rigid (Madhav Menon 2000). Indeed, in India even now, more efforts are put by defence teams into disproving guilt than the prosecution efforts at proving it (Bharadwaj 2001). Quite often, in this legal jugglery of extreme exactitude of procedure and evidence and fictional presumptions, the first casualty is the truth and miscarriages of justice perpetuated on illiterate masses ignorant of law. Perceiving this clash aptly, the Nobel laureate of Indian origin V.S. Naipaul writes "Her (India's) borrowed institutions have worked like borrowed institutions; but archaic India can provide no substitutes for press, parliament, and courts. The crisis of India is not only political or economic. The larger crisis is of a wounded old civilization that has at last become aware of its inadequacies" Naipaul 1979, p. 8).

3.6 Aversion to Formal Judiciary

These problems create an aversion to the British-imposed formal system of justice. The rural population has all along tended to turn hostile to the formal justice system in India. Most villagers prefer local traditional forms of settling disputes locally rather than approaching formal courts and the police. This aversion turns into attempts to escape from the clutches of formal justice, if one can, or defeat it at best if inevitable. Telling lies to the police as well as in courts by the witnesses is not condemned by the society. Witnesses willingly turn hostile to defeat conviction (Madhav Menon 2000). Consequently, most of the trials end in acquittal. Today, the rate of crimes in India for 2010 shows that the conviction rate in general is 30%, and in case of many social reform laws, it is as low as 3–5%. The police are often bribed to defeat prosecution (Law Commission of India 14th Report) and if possible attempts are also made to bribe judges and prosecutors to defeat prosecution so that the cases end in acquittal (for example, Janardhan Reddy Vs. ACB; Justice Nirmal Kaur in Punjab High Court).

Going to the police station or formal courts, even as witnesses, is stigmatized in the rural areas as an undesirable behaviour. Persons, particularly women, who appear in courts or before the police find themselves ridiculed, looked down upon and face several difficulties in the villages especially in respect of marriage. Village people feel the pride and honour of their village which depends upon the behaviour of all of its residents. Disregard or breach of age-old traditions and strong cultural norms about individual conduct is subjected to strong local criticism (Naipaul 1979). Approaching police or courts often is viewed as an insult or disrespect to the village elders. Consequently, derogatory comments relating to formal justice system such as "winner is a loser, loser is dead" reveal the popular aversion to it. Generally, reporting of crimes to the police or taking civil disputes to civil courts is avoided unless it is too serious. Instead, all efforts are made to settle the crimes or disputes locally in a majority of minor or moderately serious cases.

3.7 Unreported Crimes and Overburdened Judiciary

Consequently, the number of crimes reported to police officially is considerably very small in India. As revealed by the Crime in India, annual reports of the Ministry of Home Affairs, Government of India, the average number of all crimes reported to the police in India in the last 25 years varies between 500 and 550 per 100,000 population. In the European countries, the United Kingdom, the United States of America and Australia the annual numbers of crimes reported to police hover around 5000–7000 for every 100,000 people which figures are ten times higher than that of India (Interpol Crime Statistics 2002). For every crime reported to police, there probably are two to three more crimes in India which are not reported to the police but which are settled locally and amicably.

Though India is a low-crime country, its judiciary is overburdened. As of 2010, as noted by the Crime in India report, 0.8 million criminal cases were decided by the criminal courts in India starting from Judicial Magistrates to the Supreme Court, whereas 8.3 million cases are pending in these courts for final disposal. At the current rate, it will take more than ten years to clear the backlog, and in the meantime fresh cases will build up. In civil matters, the situation is even more serious as the number of cases pending is around 15 million. In the last 50 years, the conviction rates are steadily falling from 60% in the 1960s to 30% in 2010.

Huge backlogs of pending cases in courts, poor conviction rates, and rampant corruption in the process are indeed making a mockery of the sacred institution of justice, and the people are losing faith in its efficacy and its very relevance. Falling conviction rates and the piling up of a huge backlog of cases pending trial are inducing people to seek direct and quick redress by resorting to strong-arm methods such as engaging local goondas, thugs and crime syndicates in cases of recovery of loans, removal of encroachers on properties, prevention or elimination of tormentors and protection for persons and their property or premises in urban areas. Numerous crime syndicates and underworld dons are springing up in cities big or small (Katju 2006, p. 4).

Further, the European criminal justice system that was imposed upon India tends to alienate the victim from the offender, the offender from the society and the society from the state. The state with its monopoly of punishing powers over the criminals has usurped the victims' right to avenge the crime. Fines collected from offenders fill state treasuries and leave victims helpless. The forced labour of the offenders in the prisons has added further revenue to the state. Neither does the offender gain from the crime he or she has committed (if caught!) nor does the victim get any relief for the loss suffered. In the conflict between the two, the state as the third party is the one who has gained (Elias 1983). In this scenario, it is mind-boggling to think what would happen if all cases of crimes and civil disputes in India are reported to the police and formal courts for formal adjudication. It is obvious therefore that the traditional informal justice systems prevailing in India seem to serve a significant function.

3.8 Informal Dispute Settlement Systems

The indigenous Indian systems of justice were a matter of great debate between two opposing schools of thought among the colonial rulers and British intelligentsia. While a band of British administrators like William Bentinck, Richard Temple, Lord Dalhousie and Macaulay condemned anything Indian, there were others generally known as orientalists like John Shore, Charles Metcalf, Henry Lawrence, Malcom, Munro and Curzon who staunchly defended and praised native Indian systems (Keay 2001). They indeed sought during their times to retain, strengthen and confer formal powers upon them (Smith 2003).

India is predominantly a rural society. The Census of India 2011 reports that there are 640,867 villages as against 7742 towns in the country. While the pace of urbanization has increased steadily and the urban population in India rose from 15% at the time independence (1947) to 31.16% in 2011, the remaining 68.84% lives in villages of varying sizes. Eighty per cent of the villages have a population less than 1000 and 236,004 villages have less than 500 people in each.

Eighty per cent of Indian villages are primarily peasant communities comprising about 100–200 families. In such small well-knit, age-old habitats, which Ferdinand Tonnies described as "gemeinschaft" communities (1935), residents know each other since their birth and judge each other according to the codes of conduct imposed by the local customs, traditions, folkways and mores rather than the standards of behaviour imposed by the secular laws. They are irritated by those laws which seem opposed to the well-defined and long-standing traditions. That is where social legislations seem relatively weaker. In almost every such village, the common mode of dispute settlement is primarily local, informal and traditional—be it civil or criminal. In small, simple and traditional societies deviant behaviour is controlled through customary practices which are very effective and do not even look like punishments.

3.9 Integrative Shaming: Role of Gossip, Criticism and Ridicule

In the tradition-bound villages of India, informal social controls work more effectively than formal ones. In small, well-knit communities everyone knows every other person, his or her strengths and weaknesses, habits good or bad, friends and acquaintances since the time of their birth (or even before). There is a greater social visibility and social respectability which render the behaviour of individuals amenable to simple social controls (Berger 1963).

There are several subtle ways whereby small communities ensure compliance to the values, norms and standards of conduct. Gossip is one such small measure. In almost every Indian village there is a place—either a platform under the shade of a big banyan or neem tree or a building called Chaupal (different names in different regions)—where villagers come to while away their time, rest, chat or gossip daily. Senior citizens, idle young men and others during holidays spend their free time gossiping about the events, persons or new developments in the village or outside (Chandhoke 1990). Generally, gossip topics, among other things, include deviant and criminal conduct of someone in the village, dubious acts of the local rich and powerful, hypocritical conduct of the religious heads, hidden incidents of crime, celebration of village fairs and festivals and the individual domestic problems of the gossipers, etc. For the women, the common places for gossip are the village wells, tanks or community toilets where women meet daily morning and evening (Saini 1975). The common topics of gossip among village women pertain to, among other things, clandestine love affairs, extra or premarital sexual relations, illicit pregnancies of unwed girls and widows, dowry harassments, problems of their menfolk, quarrels with in-laws and the like. A large majority of people try to avoid being objects and subject of gossip by walking the narrow path of acceptable conduct in traditional communities.

Criticism and ridicule are the next stages of societal reaction to deviance once the deviant acts get out of the closet. It is interesting to observe in Indian villages people cutting coarse and ribald jokes, taunts and sarcastic remarks against some members who are found to be erring or wanting in something. Such ridicule borders on direct criticism and open indictment of the member in a friendly and witty style. It pinches the target person but does not damage him or her devastatingly. It is simple, quick and more effective. Ridicule is an aggravated form of humour. Those who ridicule are the social agents whose inherent motive is to induce the errant individual to comply with the social codes. The embarrassment-causing ridicule acts as an internalizing social control strategy that causes one to follow the normal course of social life (Billig 2005). If the person who is criticized or ridiculed realizes his mistake and makes corrections so much better, it helps him or her to regain slowly and steadily his or her stature in the community. It is like a period on probation.

A person of good reputation, though poor and of low caste, gets greater respect, love and affection from his or her villagers than a rich and powerful person of bad repute in Indian villages. One way to get recognition is by maintaining good behaviour in the eyes of his or her friends, relatives, neighbours, villagers and even the neighbouring villagers and townsmen. Reputation in itself becomes an object to achieve and in turn it paves the way for high self-esteem, social status and not infrequently the fame and power in Maslow's sense. On the contrary, the loss of reputation is very costly and multidimensional. There are instances of persons suddenly suffering loss of face committing suicide instead of facing insult, humiliation, ridicule and criticism.

The methods the villagers in India use to penalize wrong doers very much look like the emerging methods of restorative justice. Healing the wounds, soothing the hurt feelings, repairing the damage and compensating the loss caused by the conflict, confrontation or crime are among the main aims of restorative justice. Such an approach helps in restoring normalcy to the relations between the offender and the persons affected. At the same time, it should also protect the society from the serious, habitual or professional offenders while not totally destroying the lives of minor or moderate wrong doers (Dorne 2007). Let us take a closer look at some more institutional methods of restorative processes at work in Indian villages.

3.10 Dispute Settlement by the Family and Kinship

Family and kinship form the first level of dispute settlement in India. In these blood relations, interpersonal, intra- and inter-familial conflict management cannot be punishment oriented unless the conflict involves death or serious chronic violence. Conflict resolution among members of the family and kinship is almost always aimed at amicable conclusion satisfactory to all the parties to the dispute which is the cornerstone of restorative justice. Since conflicts within and between the families tend to be mostly resolved in their early stages by the timely and proper intervention of the other members of the families (Chadha 2012), such resolutions are more effective and lasting.

3.11 Support of Joint Family

The existence of a joint family system (with grandparents, parents, and often many of their adult brothers and sisters living under the same roof and sharing the same kitchen) provides timely intervention at the onset of disputes. It also provides proper advice and support in the hours of crises. It helps parents in the upbringing of children and in teaching them acceptable behaviour patterns. In the Northern states of India—Uttar Pradesh, Rajasthan, Haryana and the Punjab—about 25% of the population live in joint or extended families. In the Southern states—Karnataka, Kerala and Tamil Nadu—joint families comprise about 16% of all the families, while the national average is 18%. The fast-developing states show declining trends whereas the slow-growing ones show a higher incidence of joint families. This is an indicator of the future of joint families in India.

3.12 Decline of the Joint Family

The joint family system entails subjugation of individual freedoms to the wishes of the elderly members, which often breeds several problems for young couples especially if they are highly educated. Further, the sharing of income and assets earned by the working members with the nonworking members of the joint families involves sacrifice and an altruistic attitude which in the context of the changing society does not seem to be conducive to the survival of the joint family system. Migration of members of the joint families from villages for employment, higher education or business to towns and cities splits apart joint families. In urban settings, limitation of space and housing accommodation also does not allow large families to live under the same roof (Chekki 1996). Modern practices of child-rearing which are at variance with the expectations of elders often create tensions within the joint family. A growing number of inter-caste and inter-religious marriages also seems to upset the joint family system but their number is ignorable. While it is generally believed that urbanization tends to diminish joint families, the latest Census of India 2011 indicates that the percentage of joint families in cities and towns of India is growing. It is possible to infer that as the number of joint families decline, family-based dispute settlement practices would diminish.

3.13 Remote Control

However, it is the ingenuity of Indian society and Indian psyche that they effectively adjust to changing circumstances by assimilating new ideas and preserving what is good in the old. It is not correct to say that the members of the joint families who separate from the family of their origin are outside its influence. The influence of kinship, the family of origin and the caste group continues to operate to a large extent even if they migrate to remote cities in the country or abroad (Mullatti 1995). How does one otherwise explain the phenomenon of Indian immigrant families living in African countries for more than 200 years who continue to arrange marriages for most of their daughters and sons by selecting girls or boys of their own caste living in India? Similar are the trends of Indian immigrant families who have migrated in the last hundred years to the United Kingdom, the United States, Canada, European countries and Australia. Within the country, no matter whether the separating sons share their assets with the original family or not, they continue to be influenced in a large majority of cases by the wishes, opinions and decisions of their elders living in the remote villages or towns in respect of issues such as marital discord, partition, upbringing of children, marriage, conflicts with others, support in the hours of crises or celebration of collective events like festivals, marriages, other rituals and rites of passage. Settlement of disputes, civil or criminal, is very much a part of that general pattern.

3.14 Arranged Marriages

Another fact which encourages the practice of restorative justice within the family system is that almost all marriages in India are arranged, i.e. parents choose the life partners for their children and arrange their marriage incurring heavy expenditure. Indian marriages are known for their pomp and gaiety. The selection of a bride or a groom is a lengthy process involving a thorough and painstaking verification and scrutiny of the would-be spouse's family background and social status, religion and caste, occupation and income, his or her habits and friends, health and physical compatibility of the boy and the girl. Nowadays, the boy's or the girl's consent is obtained before finalizing the marriage. Thus marriage in India is not just between the girl and the boy, but primarily it is between two families either related earlier or new to each other.

The institutions of family and marriage ensure survival of caste traditions for all practical purposes. While the number of inter-caste or inter-religious marriages seems to be increasing with the government support in recent years, especially in urban areas, such marriages occasionally end up in great catastrophes of "honour killings" in rural areas. The fear of the violent Khap Panchayats in the Jat lands of Uttar Pradesh, Rajasthan, Haryana and the Punjab and the threat of local caste panchayats in Maharashtra, Bihar and Karnataka discourage any such liaisons outside the respective castes or religion (Vintner 2012). Consequently, not more than one per cent of all marriages in India are outside the caste or religion. More than 83% of the people are Hindus. The other two major religions are Islam and Christianity which comprise 12 and 2% of the population, respectively. All three are rigid religions: Muslim and Christian families generally insist on conversion before marriage of the persons of other religions marrying their members whereas no conversion is possible for Hindus. The rare cases of the so-called "love jehad" involving marriage of Hindu girls to the Muslim boys occasionally incite communal riots and violence in India. Strangely, the neo-converts to Islam or Christianity (largely people of the former untouchable castes) find it difficult to marry members of the mainstream Muslim or Christian families in India. However, inter-caste or inter-religious concubines even of low caste are tolerated. Since arranged marriages ensure preservation and continuation of religious and caste identity, the kinship bonds are safeguarded and continued. Commenting on this phenomenon V.S. Naipaul states "But for the Indian woman a foreign marriage is seldom a positive act; it is, more usually, an act of despair or confusion. It leads to castelessness, the loss of community, the loss of a place in the world; and few Indians are equipped to cope with that" (Naipaul 1979, p. 26).

3.15 Physical Proximity of Kinship Groups

Most marriages take place within a close cluster of villages or nearby towns. The physical proximity of families related by marriage within the same caste and religion in a cluster of villages helps in enlisting quick support and close interactions whenever needed at times of crises like death, disease, local conflict or collective functions like celebration of marriages, festivals and a number of similar occasions requiring assistance of large number of people.

In a social system marked by intra-caste marriages, joint family, strong family and clan influences most of the marital discords including separation or divorce, child custody or maintenance, negligence of elderly persons, disputes over division of family property, occasional cases of bigamy and common law wives, domestic violence, delinquent acts of children, cases of minor theft, assaults or ordinary hurt are settled within the family and kinship arrangements.

Property disputes between the members of the family, matters of succession, adoption and inheritance are also settled by the kinfolks. The joint family system is conducive to such dispute resolution. It is through the strong family-based social systems that the traditional and customary systems of India, its heritage, and culture propagate. Naipaul writes "My ancestors migrated from the Gangetic plain a hundred years ago; and the Indian community they and others established in Trinidad, on the other side of the world, the community in which I grew up, was more homogeneous than the Indian community Gandhi met in South Africa in 1893" Naipaul was born in 1932 in the present-day Tanzania. He grew up in the 1930 and 1940s. Remembering his childhood in a Hindu family which left India a hundred years ago, he writes "Because in myself, like the split-second images of infancy which some of us carry, there survive, from the family rituals that lasted into my childhood, phantasmal memories of old India" (Naipaul 1979, pp. x–xi).

3.16 Caste Panchayats

The caste panchayats provide the second level of dispute settlement in Indian villages. The disputes between two families in the same caste or sub-caste not related by marriage are usually dealt with by their caste panchayats. In the Hindu social structure caste as a defining feature consists of the four-fold hierarchy comprising of Brahmin, Kshatriya, Vaishya and Shudra. Each caste-class has a specific social status, status-related mutual duties and obligations to other caste groups in the society. Among these four caste classes, there are thousands of castes and sub-castes varying from one region to another. Caste is by birth only and marriage is permitted only within the same caste. The caste identity, purity and continuity are maintained by the caste-specific intra-caste authority structures called "caste panchayats" which are very powerful though unelected and non-statutory. They have the force of tradition which induces nearly blind compliance to their dictates by the caste members.

These informal panchayats, whether secular or caste limited, are different from formal and statutory village panchayats created for development purposes and village administration. The village panchayats elected by the local people hold office for fixed periods and they are expected to collect local taxes from the residents for the purpose of providing basic services to the people. Elected panchayats do not have judicial, quasi-judicial or general conflict resolution powers.

In the North India, informal caste panchayats are known as khap panchayats. They are very powerful. Their members are generally elders or influential members of the same community as that of the parties to the dispute. Their decisions have the same effect as that of Islamic fatwas (Raina 2012).

In other areas, these bodies are generally known as caste panchayats which decide cases affecting their caste or its members such as inter-caste marriages, sagotra marriages and sapinda marriages. They also decide minor family disputes, succession and inheritance, maintenance and adoption, division of property among family members. They deal with minor criminal conducts between the members and families belonging to their caste.

The caste panchayats generally impose hefty penalties on its erring members which is used for the common services to the caste group. It is also common to impose punishment in the nature of restitution, compensation or community service on the errant members. Community feasts are occasionally imposed as penalties. An extreme form of punishment involves excommunication of the delinquent family and its members usually for a fixed period. Once excommunicated, no other members of the said caste would talk, help, cooperate or otherwise have any link or relation with the punished family. No one in the same caste would marry the girls or boys of the defiant family. No one would come forward to perform funeral rites or participate in the funeral of the dead member. They are totally unwanted and uninvited for all social festivities or celebrations such as village fairs, sports, or festivals. Excommunication resembles banishment or exile practiced in the past. It is interesting to note that punished persons comply with the orders of the panchayats. Rare are the cases taken to the formal criminal courts against such decisions. But extreme forms of excommunication are sometimes reported to the police who find it difficult to prove since most people do not cooperate (Hayden 1983). Issues, crimes and disputes involving members of different castes are referred to more secular informal panchayats of the village.

3.17 Informal Village Panchayats

There are occasions when interpersonal or inter-family disputes or moderate or minor crimes that are not resolved by the family, its kinship and caste panchayats. Such cases may end up at the third level of dispute settlement in rural India called informal panchayats. These are committees consisting of village elders irrespective of caste. These institutions vary from region to region but they are all local, informal and have traditional authority structures. "Panchayat" literally means a team of five. They are not elected but they command much greater respect than the legally elected panchayats (Gnanambal 1973). These informal panchayats are more secular and they try to resolve issues, disputes or crimes involving different caste members (Khan 2012). They were more powerful during the feudal period and most of the feudal lords were themselves acting as heads of such panchayats (Khan 2012). The second Police Commission of 1902 had also recommended the use of the local community for resolving local crimes and delinquencies locally (Bharadwaj 2001, p. 59).

At the request of the disputing parties, or sometimes on its own (when the alleged violations affect the whole community) the committee meets at a convenient time and place and deliberates on the disputes or the issues involved. The elders hear both the parties and the witnesses if any (Bhardwaj 2001). There is no question of telling lies as everyone knows everyone else since their birth and they live together till their death in the tiny villages of 100–500 families. They analyze the issues in a traditional style and arrive at a decision (Hayden 1981). There are instances, though rare, where the guilty party does not own up the fault, mistake or crime, and is asked to prove his or her innocence by resorting to a trial by ordeal or trial by divine intervention, resembling the days of inquisition or witch-trials in Europe. The most common method of inquisition involves the accused being asked to hold the right hand over burning flames, or dip the hand in a pot of boiling oil. If the flames of fire do not burn, or the boiling oil does not scald the hand the person is presumed innocent and praised. Such cases are extremely rare these days though they occur occasionally. Extraction of confession through mild torture is not uncommon. Most of the decisions of informal panchayats tend to be middle paths or compromises between the disputing parties so that neither is harmed seriously, but the aggrieved party's interests are taken care of more or less to its satisfaction.

In most cases settled by the panchayats, punitive damages or fines are imposed, which are appropriated to the committee account used for the common services in the village. In civil matters, the guilty party is made to make amends or pay damages to the affected party. In some cases, the guilty party is also made to arrange for a community feast or contribute to a common cause. The most common punishment comprises an admonition of the erring party after a long sermon based on age-old value systems, mores, taboos and folkways. By their informal, moral and social sphere of influence, they bring about an amicable settlement to which both parties most often agree. In many cases, the religious leaders, local religious institutions and village headmen play major roles in dispute settlement.

In any informal dispute resolution situation in villages, the elders of the village know the character and background of the complainants, the accused and the local witnesses. They can judge the quality, reliability and truth of the evidence placed before them. Consequently, the decisions the local arbiters arrive at would be much more accurate and correct than the ones in the formal courts (Hayden 1983). Almost all such decisions would be acceptable to the parties and binding on them. There is no appeal. But the persons not accepting the local decisions can always approach the formal courts. However, such defiant conduct would be viewed seriously by the local people and often invite avoidable social consequences.

The modes of justice delivery described above are simple and direct, local and speedy, cheaper and effective, thus satisfactory to all parties to the dispute as well as to the village community. These systems are not things of the past but they survive even to this day to a considerable extent in rural India. Frequently, we come across extreme cases of decisions of the panchayats such as khap panchayats in Northern India which even award the death penalty to youngsters marrying outside their castes or marrying within forbidden gotras. We also come across cases of caste panchayats imposing punishments of excommunication or banishment from the village. It is in such cases that traditional dispute settlement systems come in direct conflict with the formal criminal justice system in India.

3.18 Socio-Religious Methods of Restorative Justice

Apart from informal panchayats dealing with dispute settlements in rural India, in some regions there are unique but well-accepted institutions effectively administering informal justice and settling numerous types of disputes. Three such institutions in Karnataka deserve a brief narration for the restorative justice they deliver.

3.19 Dharmasthala Manjunath Temple

Dharmasthala (literally meaning a religious place) is famous for the temple of Manjunath (Lord Shiva) managed by a well-known Jain family of Heggades, where priests are Shiva Brahmins. People of all creeds and castes congregate there. Thousands of people visit this temple daily where they are served free food and given some accommodation.

Quite a few of them come to settle their disputes in the presence of Lord Manjunath. The Heggade, the owner of the temple, mediates the parties in amicably settling their differences and disputes. His word is final. It is based on the robust sense of what is fair and proper in a given set of circumstances which vary from case to case. Unlike the Western style of fitting each case into the narrow confines of a secular law, the native system manages to customize the resolution to suit the circumstances of each case. For a secular lawyer or foreigner, this system may sound strange. But that was how the traditional system worked in India.

There prevails a strong belief among people coming to Dharmasthala for dispute settlement that Annappa, the demon servant of Lord Shiva in Dharmasthala, would punish those who tell lies, who refuse to accommodate legitimate claims of disputants, and those who having agreed to the settlement in the temple renege on their commitment later. This belief induces the fear of divine displeasure and automatic compliance to the commitment. Every day dozens of disputes are settled in this temple very effectively without any legal counsel, without any fees, without delays to the full satisfaction of the parties to dispute. Most of the disputes relate to marital discord, partition of property, succession and inheritance, child custody and maintenance, giving up bad habits, group clashes, etc. People of all faiths, castes and creeds flock to this place seeking justice understood as divine justice. The fear of God, the wrath of the demon if one reneges, belief in the traditional notions of what is right, what is wrong and what is just seem to be most effective.

3.20 Sirigere Math

The Sirigere Math is another religious institution serving the socio-religious and spiritual needs of the followers who belong to a Lingayat subsect called Saadars. Lingayats are a large, progressive, protestant Shivaite sect founded by the twelfth-century social reformer Lord Basaveshwar. He opposed orthodox Brahmanical practices such as Upanayan (ritual initiation of young boys into Brahmanism by tying a sacred thread), untouchability (social exclusion of lowest caste people), caste-based social stratification, the doctrine of karma (fatalism), rebirth (transmigration of soul), belief in hell and heaven, low and unequal status of women, the dowry system and animal sacrifices during yagna, homa and havan (sacrificial rites for the propitiation of Hindu gods). Lingayats follow most these principles.

The Sirigere Math is a major Lingayath monastery, rich and powerful, with a huge following of about two million people in Karnataka. The current swamiji is highly educated, holds a doctoral degree in philosophy from Vienna and is a prolific writer. This Math also runs several educational institutions including an engineering college, hundreds of high schools and some Sanskrit schools.

The followers of Sirigere Math take their disputes to the swamiji (the head of the Math) on a fixed day (generally one day every week). The swamiji hears disputes in the presence of all disputants; examines their claims and counter claims and witnesses on both the sides; he discusses with the parties separately and together; thereafter he arrives at a decision which is binding on all. The word of the Guru is final: his diktat is based on age-old notions of morality, justice and fairness but it may not be a strict judgement within the meaning of secular law. The whole exercise is not aimed at finding fault and fixing responsibility, rather it is an attempt to find what is fair under the given circumstances and who deserves what.

Every week the swamiji devotes a day or two for this work, dozens of disputes are settled effectively without delay, without legal assistance and without any fees. Disputes settled here generally relate to property matters, marital problems like divorce and separation, maintenance and child care, group clashes, electoral representations in local bodies, failure of minor contracts and the like. What works here is the leadership of the swamiji and his control over the community and the trust in his sense of justice fair and proper. Those who renege on their commitments would invite the wrath of their community and often excommunication. Swamiji sometimes imposes payment of damages or compensation to the affected party by the wrong doer.

3.21 Hinchigere Math

The Hinchigere Math was an influential socio-religious sect among Lingayats although it has followers from other castes and religions. It used to dispense justice and settle disputes brought before it. Over a period of time its ways of dispute settlement came in conflict with the law due to the use of violent means in settling disputes. If a party did not agree to settle the dispute as decided in the Math, he or she would be abducted, brought forcibly to the Math, kept in bondage and put to hard labour under threat to his or her life until the party agrees to the settlement. For a long time its influence prevailed and thousands of difficult disputes both civil and criminal were settled amicably or forcibly outside the formal judicial system quickly, freely and effectively. At present, the head of the Hinchigere Math is serving a jail term for murder when his decisions clashed with the norms of secular laws.

3.22 Summary

The foregoing analysis presents a unique combination of existence of two parallel systems of dispute settlement in India—one, the formal British-created criminal justice system and the other, the informal traditional system. When a clash arises between the two, the former prevails. The traditional system prevails largely in rural India which comprises a majority of the country's population and the formal system is dominant in urban India covering about one-third of the people.

The basic social institutions of family, marriage, religion and the local community in India are still robust and capable of controlling and by and large containing the deviant behaviours of their members informally without involving in a majority of cases the punitive agents of formal criminal justice system: the police, the courts and the prisons.

It is a traditional system founded on the basic elements of restorative justice. Whether it is family or kinship, caste panchayat or traditional secular panchayat, all of them settle disputes and crimes keeping in mind the long-term impact of their decisions on the offenders, victims and the community. While the victims must be compensated and consoled, the criminals should also be reconciled and reformed so that they would not menace society again. The indigenous systems of conflict resolution are simple, local and restorative, and therefore desirable in the long run. It is these systems which have made India a low-crime country.

However, as the traditional systems gradually decline owing to the influence of increasing urbanization, decreasing proportion of joint families, and steady weakening of the caste and religious influences, more and more people will take recourse to the formal institutions of justice—the police, the courts and prisons—to settle their disputes and crimes. Increasing politicization of multi-ethnic and multicultural and multilinguistic society of India in the guise of deepening democracy holds dangerous portents. There is a lurking apprehension that India will go the way that developed countries went in the last two centuries replacing their traditional systems of social control and conflict management with the formal institutions of police, courts and prisons which form the modern criminal justice systems in most parts of the world today. If that is the trajectory of development, as it is apparent now, we cannot wish it away.

The institutions of justice all over the world have evolved from local and indigenous roots. India all through its chequered history has shown an astonishing ability to absorb the best elements of thought and action from alien forces and the local protestant movements which have impinged on its social, economic and political systems. The hope lies in the liberalization and humanization of the excessively adversarial criminal justice system we have at the present. It has to take into account the plight of the victims and redress their suffering; it has also to treat criminals differentially depending upon their propensity to reconcile, repent and own up to responsibility for their crimes and make amends for the wrong doing. While punishments for serious crimes and professional and organized criminals are essential, there should also be greater scope for retrieving the first offenders and others involved in accidental or circumstantial wrong doing. All minor and medium intensity crimes should be settled more by involving the local community and through the use of more informal procedures of mediation, compromise and settlement. The non-judicial actors serving as mediators and conciliators between the offenders and victims have to be given their due place in the reformation of the criminal justice system. The excessive reliance on formal rules of procedure, precedence, presumptions and legal myths should be reduced. Thus it is inevitable to explore more ways of restorative justice within the existing formal criminal justice system. In recent years, the critical problems of delays, huge backlogs of cases and occasional instances of glaring corruption in the Indian judicial system are compelling some changes in the formal system. Let us take a look at some of these recent developments in the formal justice system of India.

3.23 Restorative Justice Measures in the Formal Criminal Justice System in India

The existing system of formal justice in India—civil and criminal—already has in it many elements of restorative justice. With a few enabling arrangements they can be effectively harnessed for the practice of a more balanced justice in place of a moth-eaten system of only retributive punishments. For instance, section 89 of the Civil Procedure Code recognizes mediation as an Alternative Dispute Resolution method. Its constructive use has begun recently. Many High Courts in India have taken initiatives to set up mediation centres under their direct guidance and supervision; they are showing encouraging results by quickly resolving the cases transferred to them from the regular courts. Second, the power of courts to award damages or compensation in some categories of civil disputes serves the interests of the affected persons and provides much needed relief while vindicating their rights and rightly penalizing the wrong doers.

Similarly, several provisions in the Criminal Procedure Code, 1973 provide scope for practice of restorative justice if certain institutional arrangements can be made without great changes in the existing system. For instance, the provisions in the Code of Criminal Procedure for withdrawal of complaint (Section 257), withdrawal from prosecution (Section 321), power of the magistrate to stop prosecution (Section 258), compounding of cases with or without permission of the court (Sections 320), plea bargaining (Sections 265A to 265L) and power of the courts to order restitution by the offender (section 357) and payment of compensation from state funds (section 357A) allow enough scope to orient our criminal justice system towards restorative practices if some more institutional arrangements are made.

It could be possible for the Legal Services Authority to evolve a system of screening all new cases filed in the courts of JMFC which seem to be amenable for amicable settlement and redress of victim grievances under any of the above provisions. During the screening, the cases found suitable for processing under any of the above-cited provisions of the Criminal Procedure Code may be referred for settlement by mediation. Adequate number of mediators and conciliators who could intervene in all such cases may be trained and posted in each JMFC courts. Once mediation reaches a settlement, such cases may be withdrawn from prosecution or compounded or prosecution stopped by the magistrate or plea bargaining may be done. This type of Victim–Offender Mediation (VOM) will help in removing or at least reducing the ill-will, animosity and bad blood between the offender and the victim which will enable restoration of normalcy in the relationship between the offender and the offended and the peace in the society.

The present system based on retribution and state-inflicted punishment either acquits the criminal (in a majority of cases) or punishes him (in just a few cases) according to law. It does not care for the victim or the community or re-establishment of strained relationships and broken peace or stability in the society. If the present system of justice has to change on the lines of traditional justice, it has to absorb some elements of informality. Additionally, through these arrangements, it could be possible to reduce crowding of cases in the courts, expedite early decisions and improve the faith of the people in the judiciary.

From the victim's point of view, the scope for restitution of victims of crime from offenders (under section 357) or state-funded victim compensation (under section 357A) can be effectively used to help the hapless victims of crime, particularly in cases of victims of serious bodily harm and sexual offences. The system of state-funded compensation for the victims of crime is relatively new to India and is yet to take off.

The relative ignorance of a large number of members of subordinate judiciary and the self-interest of lawyers seem to have hindered the constructive use of the above-cited legal provisions for the propagation of restorative justice in India. It may be said that the very concept of restorative justice, as it is emerging in developed countries, sounds quite new to the formal Indian judiciary. In the following sections, some emerging practices under the rubric of Alternative Dispute Resolution Methods in India are briefly discussed.

3.24 Alternative Dispute Resolution Measures in India

Overwhelming pendency of cases and long delays in the delivery of justice in the mainstream judiciary have compelled India to adopt several Alternative Dispute Resolution (ADR) methods in recent years. Most such measures are primarily diversions from the rigid formal judicial system. Some ADRs deal with more specialized fields which require the assistance of experts in the respective fields of knowledge. These ADRs are

(i) Family Courts,
(ii) Consumer Courts,
(iii) Lok Adalats,
(iv) Mediation Centres,
(v) Arbitration,
(vi) Nyay Panchayats,
(vii) Gram Nyayalayas, and
(viii) Victim Compensation Schemes

3.25 Family Courts

Family Courts were first established in the United States of America as Domestic Relations Courts in 1910 and the United Kingdom reformed its system under the new Family Law Act, 1996. India enacted the Family Courts Act in 1984. Family Courts have been set up in almost all states of India. These specialized courts have now taken over the burden of all family- and marriage-related cases from the civil and criminal courts. Generally, family courts decide cases of judicial separation, divorce, validity of marriage and restoration of conjugal rights. They also deal with other marriage- and family-related issues such as child custody, guardianship, alimony and maintenance, adoption, restraint orders, etc.

Significantly, the procedure adapted in family courts is simple: no lawyers are allowed (Section 13); the proceedings are held in camera (Sec. 11); irrespective of the rigid rules of admissibility and relevancy, any evidence, witness, document or opinion which the court considers important is admitted (Sec.14); in the decisions based on mutual consent of the parties no appeal is allowed; no interlocutory order is permissible; only appeal in other types of decisions of family courts is to the High Court; only a summary of witness statements may be recorded.

Most importantly, the family court has to endeavour to allow the couple to reach a settlement amicably and if necessary, the court may provide appropriate assistance of medical or welfare experts to the couple. Family courts rely upon mediation as a means of achieving a settlement. Once a settlement is reached, the court passes the decree which is binding and enforceable like any other decree of a civil court. Thus there is more freedom and participation of the litigants in the settlement of their disputes. This procedure is simple, direct and restorative.

3.26 Consumer Forums

Increasing numbers of consumer grievances against manufacturers and sellers of infinite number of goods and providers of numerous services compelled the Indian State to provide for separate consumers courts which were set up in 1988 under the Consumer Protection Act, 1986. A hierarchy of consumer courts is created: these are called Consumer Forums at the district level, State Commission for Consumer Protection at the state level and the National Commission for Consumer Protection at the national level. Each Forum or Commission comprises of a sitting or retired district judge and two non-judicial members who have expertise in consumer matters. Appeals are allowed in that order from the district forum to the state commission and from there to the national commission.

Like the family courts, the procedure in consumer courts is very simple: aggrieved parties can file their applications within two years of the cause of action arising directly or through an agent; no lawyers are allowed; no court fee is charged;

decisions have to be made within six months; appeals at various levels can be filed within 30 days.

District Forums have power to order reliefs of up to five hundred thousand rupees. Any claim exceeding five lakhs of rupees has to be filed before the State Commission. Consumer courts can order replacement or repairs of goods bought, refund of price paid, financial relief for the loss or injury suffered and any other cost. They are also empowered to order stoppage of production or supply of goods in question.

These quasi-judicial bodies, unlike regular civil courts, follow simpler procedures and by not allowing legal practitioners make it cheaper. Being a multi-member bench allows greater scope for varying opinions and improves quality of decisions. They deal with a specialized category of disputes and provide easier and more prompt justice compared to regular civil courts.

3.27 Lok Adalats

As an ADR, Lok Adalats are more popular and successful in India than any other measure. Lok Adalat simply means "Folk Court" or "Peoples'Court". However, it is a misnomer to call them folk courts since they are neither set up by the people nor adjudicated by them. The cases coming within the competence of these bodies are those which are already filed and pending for decisions in the regular courts. The referral courts transfer the cases for adjudication before the Lok Adalats.

Lok Adalats are set up under the Legal Services Authorities Act, 1987 at various levels starting from the Munsiffs' courts to High Court. However such authorities are functioning mostly at the civil and district court levels more successfully. Each Lok Adalat is presided over by a sitting or retired judge who is assisted by two other members (one being a social worker and the other a lawyer). They can decide land acquisition matters, land disputes, money-related disputes, matrimonial disputes, labour disputes, property disputes and especially disputes relating to public service utilities such as telephone companies, electricity or water supply companies.

The procedure followed in Lok Adalats is the simplest: no court fee is charged and if already paid in the referral court, it will be refunded if the case is settled in Lok Adalat, otherwise the case goes back to the original court. No appeal is allowed when the decision is arrived at by mutual consent; evidence rules are liberal and anything considered relevant by the court is admissible. These courts emphasize compromise, mediation and settlement. From that angle they are non-adversarial. The decisions are quick, cheaper and satisfactory to both the parties.

It is reported that so far in the last two decades since their creation nearly 200,000 Lok Adalats were held and 1,600,000 cases were settled, paying compensation worth US $ 1 billion (Karthaeni and Bhatt 2012).

3.28 Mediation Centres

Section 89 of the Civil Procedure Code in India provides for settlement of civil disputes through mediation. In civil litigation relating to maintenance of wives, child custody, marital disputes, breach of contractual obligations, recovery of money, etc. a new beginning was made recently in India to resolve the litigation through mediation. Some High Courts have taken the initiative to set up Mediation Centres under their guidance. Civil courts are authorized to divert the long pending cases to Mediation Centres to amicably resolve the disputes.

> "Mediation", as defined by Justice Markandeya Katju, "is a voluntary and confidential process by which through the intervention of a person called the 'mediator', who is a neutral and impartial person, the parties are helped to come to a voluntary mutually acceptable resolution of their dispute". As he says, "The mediator guides the process but cannot impose any decision on the parties. The parties remain in control of the process throughout, and they can terminate the mediation at any time if they feel it is not serving their interests. However, once an agreement is reached and signed by the parties, it becomes binding and then can be enforced by the legal process".

Mediation differs from arbitration in that the arbitrator gives the decision after examining and analyzing all the facts, circumstances, the procedure and the legal issues, whereas in mediation the mediator's role is to act as friend, philosopher and guide to both the parties and help them to help themselves by showing mutual respect, concern and understanding which will help in resolving the differences and disputes. If they fail to arrive at any such decision, the litigation reverts to the referral court for adjudication as per law.

Mediation also differs from Lok Adalat where a senior judge after an informal consultation and negotiation with the parties to the dispute gives his decision which will be acceptable to both. In case any party does not agree to the decision of the judge, the case reverts to the court which diverted it to the Lok Adalat. Generally, Lok Adalats are used for settling compensation claims in land acquisition matters and motor vehicles accidents cases. So far Lok Adalats, by and large, have limited themselves to settlement of such financial claims.

In mediation the role of the mediator is very important. He or she needs to have effective skills in analyzing the issues impartially, communicating with both the parties in a language which does not hurt feelings of either party and yet it makes them see the other point of view. As Justice Katju says "it is absolutely essential that the mediator is held in high esteem by the parties. This means that the mediator must be a person who has a high reputation in society.... He must be a person of high ethics and good reputation". His words sound as if he is referring to the role of members of informal panchayats in villages which settle disputes in similar ways.

Mediation, in India at present, is a court-referred process. The apprehension of delay and uncertainty of final decision motivate the parties to agree for mediation. It is also at the mercy of lawyers of the parties whose advice plays a crucial role.

Table 3.1 Mediation statistics in Bangalore mediation centre since 2007

Year	Cases referred	Cases mediated	Cases settled	Connected cases settled	Total cases settled	Success rate (%)
2007	2529	1428	0771	097	0869	54
2008	4404	3602	2222	189	2410	62
2009	4987	3958	2632	111	2743	66
2010	5250	4153	2660	322	2982	64
2011	5283	4528	2910	777	3687	64

Source Report of Bangalore Mediation Centre 2011

Quite often it is the lawyers who prevent amicable settlement for their own selfish gain. Within the ambit of formal judiciary, the scope for mediation and its success will remain somewhat restricted as it depends on the sweet will of lawyers. It is only a mode of diversion and reduction of work load for the formal judiciary.

Mediation Centres at the state and district levels have been set up in many states like Delhi, Karnataka, Tamil Nadu and Kerala. So far the success rates vary from 40 to 60%. More success in business and financial litigations is reported by many Mediation Centres. These Centres have also been organizing training programs for the mediators. The Mediation Centre at Bangalore has trained 473 mediators from all over the country and 105 from Karnataka since 2002. In the last nine years, 17,457 cases were referred for mediation by the civil courts in Karnataka. 13,290 cases were mediated but 8918 cases were successfully resolved by mediation as shown Table 3.1 (Report of Bangalore Mediation Centre 2011).

There is a greater need to create awareness about mediation in the public, the lawyers and the judges of subordinate judiciary. More trained mediators are also required and adequate incentives need to be given to the mediators. There is a feeling that a separate statute may be passed for wider proliferation of mediation.

3.29 Arbitration

In civil matters such as contract-related disputes, partnership disputes, marketing and money-related cases, arbitration is a common method. Adequate numbers of honest and competent arbitrators are necessary but lacking. In arbitration, the parties to the dispute themselves choose a third competent person as arbitrator whose decision may be acceptable to both the parties. The procedure followed and the rules of evidence are flexible according to the circumstances of the case. Arbitration is extensively used in India in many civil disputes.

3.30 Nyay Panchayats

The problem of rural people in India not reporting crimes to the police nor approaching formal courts for resolving their disputes was known to the British administrators and judges. The experience of Indian leaders was also that formal courts cannot satisfy the overwhelming majority of poor, ignorant and tradition-bound people of Indian villages. They felt a need to create institutions of justice resembling the traditional panchayats but not repeating their weaknesses. The institutions called nyay panchayats were accordingly created. Nyay in Sanskrit literally means "justice", panchayats means "coming together of five persons", in other words nyay panchayats meant "council of justice".

During the British regime there was a strong move to revive traditional village councils. Lord Mayo, the then Governor General in 1870 had emphasized local self-governments. Similarly, the Famine Commission of 1880, the Resolution of the then Governor General Lord Rippon in 1882 and the Royal Commission on Decentralization in 1907 had recommended the creation of local panchayats with judicial powers among other responsibilities. Eventually, after the enactment of Government of India Act of 1919, the responsibility for the creation and administration of panchayats and nyay panchayats was transferred to the provincial governments. Around 1921 the Central Provinces, Assam, Bihar, Bengal and Bombay provinces created panchayats along with some rudimentary judicial powers (Khan 2012).

After independence, the states of Rajasthan, Orissa, Andhra Pradesh and Kerala also enacted NP laws. They had generally powers to hear and decide cases of public nuisances, misappropriations, criminal negligence, minor acts of perjury, thefts, intimidation, false weights and measures, gambling, delinquent acts of children and cattle trespass.

Nyay panchayats (NPs) were indeed modelled after the traditional village councils. The NPs had elected members appointed by the sarpanch from among members of the formal village panchayats. They were like judicial committees of the local elected panchayats. Members of the NPs sat as adjudicators to hear and decide disputes brought before them. NPs differed from the traditional village councils in many ways as shown in Table 3.2.

The nyay panchayats (NPs) created as part of the formally elected village panchayats are an uneasy mixture of seemingly traditional and largely British patterns of adjudication: traditional in that they had local lay members sitting as arbitrators over the disputes brought before them and that they followed conciliatory compromises and settlements in their procedures to arrive at a decision. They were more British in that the offences they were to ascertain were defined by the British-enacted laws and that they imposed punishments straight-jacketed in those laws. Their powers were very limited. They could reprimand an accused or impose a small fine not exceeding generally a hundred rupees, whereas traditional panchayats enjoyed much wider freedom in respect of imposing punishments that would suit the circumstances of the crime. Some states did not empower the NPs to

Table 3.2 Differences between Nyay panchayats and traditional panchayats

Features	Nyay panchayats	Traditional panchayats
1. Membership	Elected laymen up to five	Unelected village leaders up to five and sometimes more
2. Nature of authority	Formal and legal authority as vested by law	Traditional and charismatic authority based on their standing in the local community
3. Jurisdiction	Minor offences listed in the statute	Any deviant act minor or major
4. Power	Warning or fine up to Rs. 100	Warning, shaming, fine, lashes, exclusion, exile or death by tradition
5. Procedure	Conciliatory, mediation and compromise	Informal hearing, analysis and proof; accused had the opportunity to be heard; compromise, or authoritarian imposition
6. Appeal	Court of JMFC	No appeal generally but in the olden days some of their decisions used to be questioned before the king or feudal chiefs
7. Records	Record keeping necessary	No records only oral hearing and decision
8. Prestige	Not much respect	High prestige and respect
9. Compliance	Difficult	Automatic

enforce their decrees on par with the civil courts. Elected members sitting in judgement of the conduct of their fellowmen did not command the respect and prestige which the members of the time-honoured traditional panchayats commanded. As electoral politics introduced partisan, factional and casteist bias in the functioning of NPs people began to lose trust in them. They also lacked funding and proper supporting staff.

Many Western scholars who studied the functioning of NPs compared them to the traditional panchayats. Hayden found that NPs cannot be the same as traditional panchayats (TPs) since the two follow different sets of laws, procedure and purposes (Hayden 1981, 1983). Galanter as well as his associate Baxi noted several deficiencies in the NPs (Galanter 1968, 1972, 1978; Baxi and Galanter 1979). Durrett (1968, 1971) noted the role of religion and caste and the most important role of age-old tradition in the system of traditional panchayats. Kidder (1978) compared the functioning Western law and native responses to it. No wonder therefore that NPs could not be effective, acceptable and successful in the long run.

The Law Commission of India in its 114th Report examined the working and effectiveness of NPs in the country. It was observed that over the years (since 1949) the workload of NPs had decreased significantly: in 1949–1950 in Uttar Pradesh a total of 1,914,098 cases were filed before the NPS whereas in 1972 there were only 17,789 cases. In Bihar, 15 NPs heard 202 cases over a period of 16 years. In West Bengal, 937 cases were filed in 1965–1966 before 46 NPs whereas in 1973 there were only 13 NPs with hardly any cases. In Rajasthan, just 121 cases were heard in 1961–1962. In the light of the observation that NPs in the country had failed, the

Law Commission recommended a new law to strengthen and popularise them. Based on these recommendations, the Government of India circulated a draft NP Bill to the states in 2009 which has not yet seen any finality. Since the enactment of Gram Nyayalayas Act 2008, there seems no great future for the proposed NP Bill.

3.31 Gram Nyayalay Act, 2008

The heavy pendency of criminal and civil cases in the regular courts of India and the long delays in their disposal has been causing concern for a long time. To expedite timely justice, the Parliament of India enacted a new law called Gram Nyayalayas Act in January 2009 which came into effect on October 2, 2009 (coinciding with the birth anniversary of Mahatma Gandhi). Gram nyayalaya means "village court". Notwithstanding the name, gram nyayalays (GN) by no stretch of imagination are village courts like the traditional village councils. They are primarily the intermediate courts of Judicial Magistrates of the First Class (JMFC) especially empowered to hold the court in the villages to try minor civil and criminal cases preferably using the state's language. There are some differences between GNs and the regular JMFC courts

- (i) The procedure in gram nyayalays (GN) is more liberal; they follow more of summary trials;
- (ii) The emphasis is on meditation, compromise and settlement rather than strict adversarial process;
- (iii) The GNs will be set up at village panchayat levels for a group of up to 20 villages;
- (iv) Evidence rules are liberal irrespective of the provisions of the Indian Evidence Act;
- (v) Plea bargaining would be given greater scope in criminal cases;
- (vi) Appeals are restricted to certain types of decisions only;
- (vii) Trials will be continuous and adjournment will be not entertained in general;
- (viii) Trial to be completed in is six months and judgement within fifteen days of closing the trial.

The GNs are welcome to provide timely justice. They are not comparable either to traditional village councils or less formal nyay panchayats. While it is a new experiment, too early to evaluate, conceptually we may differentiate GNs from NPs in respect of varying composition, jurisdiction, powers, procedure followed, place of hearing, language used, appellate authority and keeping of record as shown in Table 3.3.

Nyay panchayats have largely failed in the country due to various reasons. Gram nyayalayas are new experiments whose efficacy is unknown. Since the traditions and traditional systems themselves are undergoing far-reaching changes in the

Table 3.3 A comparison of Nyay panchayats and gram nyayalays

No	Features	Nyay panchayats	Gram nyayalayas
1	Composition	5 elected laymen	One JMFC: Nyayadhikari
2	Jurisdiction	Minor crimes listed in law	Almost all crimes triable by JMFC
3	Powers	Fine up to Rs. 100	Imprisonment up to two years or fine up to Rs. 25,000 or both
4	Procedure	Conciliatory, mediation and compromise	Summary procedure, more liberal evidence rules; lawyers allowed
5	Place	Village panchayat	Village panchayat, mobile court also
6	Language	Local language	State language
7	Appeal	JMFC court	Sessions court
8	Records	Summary records	Full records

country, it would be difficult to revive and enforce traditional type of informal councils. The gram nyayalaya law seems to be an attempt at greater simplification of and much needed improvement to the rigid laws of evidence and procedure in the mainstream judiciary.

3.32 Victim Compensation in India

The worsening crime situation in developed countries provided impetus in the 1960s to the rise of a variety of victim advocacy movements. Victim assistance programs such as rape crisis centres proliferated in many countries. Sporadic victim surveys by universities and private organizations revealed huge magnitudes of unreported crimes. Over a period of time, some governments themselves institutionalized systematic victim surveys for the purpose of assessing incidence of crimes in comparison to the magnitude of crimes reported to the police annually.

State sponsored victim compensation schemes first appeared in 1960 in New Zealand and later spread to England in 1964 and thereafter to Europe and the United States. Many other developed countries such as Australia, Japan have also adopted a variety of schemes to compensate victims of crime from the funds of the state. Neglected victims in the developed countries are receiving some attention now in the criminal justice arena though most of developing countries do not yet have any victim compensation schemes.

There is a provision under Section 357 of the Indian Code of Criminal Procedure to award compensation in the form of restitution by the offender. However, the efforts of the trial courts to award restitution as a part of the sentence is not practiced much in the Indian judiciary perhaps because of the very limited scope available in the determinate legal system in India which clearly lays down specific punishments and the range of their quantum against each crime. Thus the judges in India do not have so much discretion as is available to judges in many developed countries like the United States of America or the United Kingdom.

These international developments were noticed by the Indian higher judiciary. Over the years the High Courts and the Supreme Court of India are compelling the Indian state in a number of cases to adopt state-funded victim compensation schemes (D.K. Basu v. State of W.B.; Nilabati v. State of Orissa; State of Gujarat v. Hon High Court of Gujarat). The increasing number of court directions compelled the Government of India to amend the Cr. P.C. by way of inserting new section 357-A which mandates formulation of schemes for state-funded compensation to the victims of crimes irrespective of the offender being found or convicted. This is also a new law and not many states so far have formulated implementable schemes or implemented them.

Although India is a late comer in providing for victim compensation schemes especially for the victims of crimes, there are at least, five different victim compensation schemes in the country. The oldest of them is the compensation to the persons injured or to the dependent families of the persons who die in the road accidents involving motor vehicles. Since the world's largest numbers of deaths and injuries in road accidents take place in India (around 130,000 year) insurance-based compensation schemes serve a great need. Motor Vehicle Accidents Claims Tribunals and their Appellate Tribunals award reasonable amounts of compensation in most of the motor accident cases. As every motor vehicle has to be insured for the third-party liability at the time of purchase and registration, the claims of affected persons are paid by the insurance company where it is proved that the accident did not result from the affected persons' carelessness. They get sizeable amounts once the Motor Vehicle Accident Claims Tribunal decides the claims.

Recently, under the Prevention of Atrocities (on Scheduled Castes and Scheduled Tribes) Act, 1989, the government pays compensation to the persons belonging to the Scheduled Castes or the Scheduled Tribes who are injured or otherwise affected by the violence or atrocity committed by non-SC or non-ST persons or groups. In the tradition-bound society of India, social exclusion of some low castes is legally prohibited but socially still difficult to remove. Although the practice of untouchability has diminished significantly it has not disappeared totally. On certain social occasions instances of exclusion are reported and they often end up in varying degrees of violence. In such instances, apart from seriously punishing the wrong doers the government gives sizeable monetary compensation to the affected members of the Scheduled Castes in India.

Third, the Government of India has adopted another scheme to compensate any person who suffers due to communal riots and violence. This is available to all persons all over the country irrespective of their caste, religion or gender. In a multicultural society like India, communal riots and violence occur occasionally. Communal flare ups are more common between Muslims and Hindus in India and least between Christians and Hindus.

Fourth, compensation is also available if a person's human rights are violated. If a person can prove that police arrested him without adequate grounds, or that he was detained illegally, or that a false case was booked against him, or that his human rights were otherwise violated by the government, the National Human Rights Commission or the respective State Human Rights Commission awards varying amounts of reasonable monetary compensation to such persons.

Fifth, persons getting injured or dying in accidents occurring in workplaces and industrial establishments, railways, or airways get reasonable compensation from the owners or the company under the Workmen's Compensation Act or under the terms of contract. In cases of natural disasters like lightning, landslides, avalanches, deluges, earthquakes and tsunamis persons dying or getting seriously injured get humanitarian relief and compensation of up to two lakhs of rupees from the government directly.

Finally, the Code of Criminal Procedure was amended in December 2009 by inserting a new section 357A to provide for schemes for compensating the victims of crime in the country. This came after repeated directions of the Supreme Court in a number of cases. The schemes for compensating victims of crime will be implemented by the State Legal Services Authority. Most states are yet to formulate such schemes. So far the states of Tamil Nadu, Karnataka, the Punjab, Maharastra, Bihar and Madhya Pradesh have formulated varying schemes for compensating victims of crimes. Generally, the maximum amount payable as compensation by the state government is limited to 2–3 lakhs of rupees in case of death. These schemes are limited to crimes against the human body. A varying scale of compensation is prescribed for different offences and degrees of injury. Psychological/mental pain is not included in the calculation of compensation. No compensation is payable for property crimes for which people will have to depend on insurance claims only if the properties are insured.

3.33 Conclusion

In developed countries rising rates of crimes and recidivism, increasing fear of crimes and the consequent politicization of crime problems seem to have created a need for exploring the measures of restorative justice. In India neither crime rates nor rates of recidivism have shown any significant spurt in the last three decades. But the volume of crime has definitely increased over the years keeping in tune with the growing population. More people mean more crimes; more laws mean more crimes. Accordingly there should be more policemen, more courts and more jails. But the system enhancement to deal with the increasing volumes of crimes has not been commensurate with the increase. While the numbers of courts and judges, numbers of policemen and specialized police units and the number of jails have somewhat increased, such increases are not sufficient enough. Consequently, the workloads of the courts and the judges, policemen and jail staff have virtually crushed these systems. The pendency of cases has obviously led to long delays and frustration on all sides. The quality of disposals by the courts, the police and even by the jails has also suffered. The net result is the disappointment, frustration, desperation and disenchantment with the system. These circumstances have compelled the state to search for other alternatives to deal with increasing deviance and crimes.

The traditional systems of marriage and family, kinship and caste influences, traditional panchayats and religious institutions which control and contain crimes informally within their respective boundaries have definitely helped to keep the system safer from explosive consequences. But slowly and steadily the traditional systems are becoming weaker and weaker due to the far-reaching and fast changes that are taking place in the political, economic and cultural arenas within the country and outside. Consequently, informal traditional systems are getting slowly replaced by formal systems of justice. India is thus moving imperceptibly in the same direction that developed countries moved in the last 200 years. But the existing formal systems of justice in India, unless suitably adapted to the changing circumstances keeping in view the unique sociocultural legacies and traditions, will soon find themselves incapable of coping with the change.

Luckily, as discussed in this chapter, the formal justice systems in India are slowly but surely changing in the right direction. The Alternative Dispute Resolution methods such as Mediation Centres and Lok Adalats are definitely trying to imbibe the spirit of traditional systems by resorting to participatory methods of dispute settlement by directly involving the parties to disputes and enabling them reach amicable settlements. They follow simple rules of evidence and quick procedures which enable early decisions.

Family Courts, Consumer Courts and Nyay Panchayats also follow simple procedures, simple rules of evidence and do not allow legal practitioners to complicate ordinary problems for their own benefit. They also involve directly the parties to the dispute and try to settle the disputes early. Gram nyayalays, being the latest entrants, also follow more summary trials, simple rules of evidence and place more reliance on mediation, compromise and settlement. They conduct their hearings like the nyay panchayats at the village level making it more convenient for the litigant public. If these new systems succeed, the formal courts will be devoting their time to more serious crimes and criminals who seem to be unfit for restorative measures or civil disputes and which require more serious consideration. It is thus obvious that India need not emulate developed countries which are going back to the past to reinvent traditional systems of conflict resolution that were forgotten a long time ago. As explained in the foregoing sections of this paper, ancient Indian traditions of justice have some excellent elements worth noting which are still alive. The present formal judicial systems in India are trying to emulate the essential features of Indian traditions such as simplicity of evidence and procedure, participation of all disputants in the proceedings, compromise between the conflicting persons and groups ultimately leading to peaceful resolution of conflicts in most cases.

Finally, the interests of crime victims which formed the core of traditional justice in India that were ignored in the British-created system are being brought back in the form of varying schemes for compensating the victims of crime. Compared to the compensation schemes available to victims of ordinary crimes in developed countries, India has gone some steps beyond. The unique caste system in India has created a special category of victims. The state does not recognize caste-based discriminations and the practice of untouchability has been prohibited. But social traditions die hard. Quite a few discriminatory practices are still found in the country. What has been banned by law is not banned by the society at large. This duplicity often causes caste-linked violence. The government has provided special relief to all persons who get affected by caste-related violence against the members of the Scheduled Castes and the Scheduled Tribes. The compensation is paid directly to the persons within a few days of the occurrence of violence by the government irrespective of the outcome of the crime. Similarly, in the multireligious society of India communal violence is also common. The government compensates all persons affected by the communal violence in the country directly and promptly. Compensation to the victims of accidents in industrial work places and motor vehicle accidents have been in existence in India for a long time as hallmarks of modern technology and modern times. Victims of government systems are provided compensation of reasonable amounts by the recently created National and State Human rights Commissions in India. Victims of natural calamities like earthquakes, deluge, tsunami, floods and avalanche or wild animal attacks in the jungle also get compensation from the government promptly. The victims of ordinary crimes get a statutory compensation from the State Legal Services Authority. Though limited to the victims of bodily crimes, the amount of compensation paid to crime victims is on par with the amounts paid in other similar schemes. Under these schemes either a court can order payment of compensation or the victims themselves can apply for it to the Legal Services Authority directly irrespective of the outcome in the criminal cases. Thus crime victim compensation in India is a more comprehensive and complicated system of multiple schemes.

The developments explained in this paper make it obvious that not only traditional systems of conflict resolution in India are based on the essential elements of restorative justice but also the formal systems of justice are trying to actively adopt principles of restorative justice in India.

References

Bangalore Mediation Centre. (2011). *A Report of the Second Regional Conference of Southern States on Mediation: Future Predictions and expectations.*

Basu, D. K. v. State of West Bengal. 1997:1 SCC 416 (para 41).

Baxi, U., & Galanter, M. (1979). Panchayat justice: An Indian experiment in lagal access. In M. Cappelletti & B. Garth (Eds.), *Access to justice, vol. III, emerging issues and perspectives.* Alphen aan den: Sijthoff and Noordhoff.

Berger, P. (1963). *An invitation to sociology: A humanistic perspective.* Doubleday: Anchor Books.

Bhardwaj, H. R. (2001). *Crime and criminal justice & human rights.* New Delhi: Konark Book Publishers.

Billig, M. (2005). *Laughter and ridicule: Towards a sociological critique of humour.* London: Sage.

Braithwaite, J. (2004). Restorative justice and de-professionalization. *Good Society, 31*(1), 28–31.

Chadha, N. K. (2012). *Intergenerational relationships: An Indian perspective.* At www.un.org/esa/socdoc/family/docs/egm12/CHADHA-PAPER.pdf

Chandhoke, S. K. (1990). *Nature and structure of rural habitation.* New Delhi: Concept Publishing Company.

Chandra, B. (1990). *Modern india.* New Delhi: NCERT.

Chekki, D. (1996). Family values and family change. *Indian Journal of Social Work, 69,* 338–348.

Dorne, C. K. (2007). Restorative justice in the United States. Prentice Hall.

Durrett, J. D. M. (1971). Tradition in modern India: the evidence of Indian law. In R. Park (Ed.), *Change and the persistence of tradition in India.* Ann Arbor: University of Michigan Centre for South and Southeast Asian Studies.

Elias, R. (1983). *Victims of the society.* London: Transaction Books.

Galanter, M. (1968). The displacement of traditional law in modern India. *Journal of Social Issues, 24*, 65.

Galanter, M. (1972). The aborted institution of indigenous law in India. *Comparative Studies in Society and History, 14*, 53.

Galanter, M. (1978). Indian law as an indigenous conceptual system. *Items, 32*, 42.

Gnanambal, K. (1973). *Religious institutions and caste panchayats in South India.* Calcutta: Anthropological Survey of India.

Government of India, Ministry of Home Affairs, Crime in India. (2010). Annual report of the National Crime Records Bureau.

Government of India, Ministry of Home Affairs, New Delhi. Census of India. (2011). Population Tables.

Gregory, S., & Takagi, P. (2004). Critique of restorative justice. *Social Justice, 31*(3), 147–163.

Hayden, R. M. (1981). *No one is stronger than the caste- arguing dispute cases in an Indian Caste Panchayat* (Ph.D. dissertation). Department of Anthropology, the State University of New York, Buffalo.

Hayden, R. M. (1983). Excommunication as everyday event and ultimate sanction: The nature of suspension from an Indian caste. *Journal of Asian Studies, 42*, 291.

Interpol, International Crime Statistics. (2002). Lyons, France.

Kania, H., & Kuhnrich, B. (2006). European crime survey (ECSS) 2005. Max Planck Institute of Foreign and International Studies.

Karthaeni V., & Bhatt V. (2012). Lok Adalats and permanent Lok Adalats: A scope for judicial review. *Madras Law Journal.* www.legalservicesindia.com/Articles/lok-a.htm

Katju, M. (Justice) (2006). Mediation, a speech delivered in Allahabad at a function of Samvaad on 6 October, 2006 (written version).

Keay, J. (2001). India discovered, (2nd ed.). Harpercollins.

Khan, S. (2012). Establishment of Nyay Panchayat inUttar Pradesh and other states in India and its progress. www.articlesbase.com/national-state-localarticles/establishment-of-nyaya-panc

Kidder, R. (1978). Western law in India and local response. In M. Johnson (Ed.) Social system and legal process San Francisco, Jossey-Boss.

Kikani, L. T. (1912), Caste in court, Rajkot, self published.

Kilbrandon quoted in Bhardwaj (2001), p. 36.

Latimer, J. (2005). The effectiveness of restorative justice: A meta analysis. *Prison Journal, 85*(2), 127–144.

Law Commission of India, Fourteenth Report quoted in Bhardwaj (2001), p. 72.

Macaulay, TB (1843, 1900). *Miscellaneous writings and speeches.* London: Longmans.

Madan, G. R. (1966). *Indian social problems.* New Delhi: Allied Publishers.

Madhav Menon, N. R. (2000). "Criminal justice-I", The statesman. September 14, 2000.

Malimath, V. S. (2003). *Report of the committee on reforms of the criminal justice systems.* Government of India: Ministry of Home Affairs.

Muttatti, L. (1995). Families in India: Beliefs and realities. *Journal of Comparative Family Studies, 26,* 1–25.

Naipaul, V. S. (1979). India: A wounded civilization. Penguin Books.

Raina, P. (2012). Does India still need Khap Panchayats? *New York Times: Global Edition*. India. October 30, 2012.
Saini, B. S. (1975). *Social and economic history of the Punjab (1901–1939) including Haryana and Himachal Pradesh*. Ess Ess Publications.
Setalwad, M. C. (1970). *My life; law and other things*.
Smith, D. (2003). *Hinduism and modernity*. Blackwell Publishing Ltd.
South African Law Commission, Discussion Paper 97, A compensation scheme for victims of crime in South Africa (on the website).
Tonnies, Ferdinand (1887, 1935), Community and Society, Darmstadt.
United States Bureau of Justice Statistics reports of 2010 on Prisons, crimes in other countries, and Uniform Crime Reports of the FBI, Department of Justice.
Vintner, P. (2012). Indian village bans marriages that have not received parental permission. In Mail Online dated October 30, 2012.
Viscount Buckmaster quoted in Bhardwaj (2001), p. 39.
Zehr, H. (2002). *The littlebook of restorative justice*. Intercourse, PA: Good Books.

Chapter 4
Compensatory Jurisprudence in India

S. Latha

4.1 Introduction

Increasingly the attention of reformers of criminal justice system has been directed to Victimology, control of victimization and protection of victims of crimes. Crimes often entail substantive harm to people and not merely symbolic harm to the social order. Consequently, the needs and rights of victims of crime should receive priority attention in the total response to crime. One recognized method of protection of victims is compensation to victims of crime. The needs of victims and their family are extensive and varied.

One school of thought justifies compensation in the criminal process in terms of the aims of sentencing. The Widgery Committee in Britain (1872) has listed several views about the rationale of the concept of compensation, namely, "benefit to the victims, possible deterrent effect on the offender or on the public, the possible educative or preventive effect on public morality, the possible reformative effective on offender, its effect in depriving the offender of ill gotten gains and the view that compensation has an intrinsic moral value of its own". The Law Reform Commission of Canada also was of the same view holding that compensation was consistent with the 'core values' of the community.

The proponents of state compensation justify it as

i) another form of public assistance for the disadvantaged and
ii) a medium of fulfilment of neglected state obligation to its citizens. The state has a humanitarian responsibility to assist crime victims. The assistance is provided because of the social conscience of the citizens and as a symbolic act of compassion. The state is responsible to maintain law and order, ensure peace, harmony and tranquillity in society, to use force to suppress crime and punish

S. Latha (✉)
Department of Criminology, University of Madras, Chennai, India
e-mail: lathasubramaniam@gmail.com

R. Thilagaraj and J. Liu (eds.), *Restorative Justice in India*,
DOI 10.1007/978-3-319-47659-9_4

offenders, to protect people and their property. If the law and order machinery of the state police is negligent or unable to prevent crime the state is responsible to make preparation to the victims. In addition, state compensation is also considered as a matter of social justice to crime victims, as the state system namely, its political, economic and social institutions generate crime by poverty, discrimination, unemployment and insecurity.

United Nations General Assembly in November 1985 adopted the declaration of "Basic Principles of Justice for Victims of Crime and Abuse of Power". This declaration is the magna carta of the Rights of Victims globally. The declaration has made certain suggestions for dealing with the problems of victims of crime including victims of abuse of power. Some of the suggestions which deserve a special note are as follows:

(a) Victims should be treated with compassion and respect for their dignity. They are entitled to access to the mechanisms of justice and to promote redress, as provided for by national legislation, for the harm that they have suffered.
(b) Judicial and administrative mechanisms should be established and strengthened where necessary to enable victims to obtain redress through formal or informal procedures that are expeditious, fair, inexpensive and accessible. Victims should be informed of their rights in seeking redress through such mechanisms.
(c) Informing victims of their role and the scope, timing and progress of the proceedings and of the disposition of their cases, especially where serious crimes are involved and where they have requested such information.
(d) Allowing the views and concerns of victims to be presented and considered at appropriate stages of the proceedings where their personal interests are affected without prejudice to the accused and consistent with the relevant national criminal justice system.

4.2 Definition of Compensation

Compensation is defined as financial assistance paid by the government, or by another party unrelated to the offender, to the victims of crime (Van Ness and Strong 1997). The amount of monies paid typically reflects the nature and extent of the injury suffered by the victim.

The word compensation in literal sense mean a thing that compensates or is given to compensate (for); a counterbalancing feature or factor; amends, recompense; spec. money given to compensate loss or injury, or for requisitioned property. When we talk about compensation to the victims it means something given in recompense, i.e. equivalent rendered. It is to be noted that the whole purpose of compensation is to make good the loss sustain by the victim or legal representative of the deceased (Abhishek Anand 1999). Generally when we talk about compensation in the present context it only limits it self to monetary compensation which is calculated on the basis of two head, i.e. pecuniary loss and non-pecuniary loss.

4.2.1 Evolution of Concept of Compensation to Victim of Crime in India

The evolution of the concept can be traced both historically and theoretically. Historically the concept of victimology in crude sense was not only part of Hammurabi's code but also existed in developed sense in ancient Greek city-states. The concept of compensation was also not new to India and existed in more developed sense than the present. Manu in Chapter VIII, verse 287 clearly says that

> **If limb is injured, a wound is caused or blood flows, the assailant shall be made to pay the expense of the cure or the whole.**

He further in verse 288 says that:

> **He who damages the goods of another, be it intentionally or unintentionally, shall give to the owner a kind of fine equal to damage.**

The quotes regarding the same can be found even in the works of Brihaspati. This is in brief the law relating to compensation to the victim of crime that even existed in ancient civilization of east as well as west. As far as tracing of gradual evolution of the concept is concern the whole era till mid of 1900 can be generally divided into three parts. In initial year of human civilization when the human started living together especially after stone age, because of the absence of rule of law and authoritative political institution, right to punish or rather might to punish (in from of eye for eye or money) was with the individual and hence in crude sense the concept of compensation existed at that time even but line of caution that need to be bear in mind is the fact that in primitive society criminal victim relationship was based on brutal mentality of attack being the best defence. Then came the era in which the social control in terms of mechanical solidarity creped in the society and the offence against an individual lost its individualistic character and now the offence was considered to be against the tribe or clan to which individual belongs and from this era, due to advent of concept of collective responsibility clan or tribe started replacing the victim's right. The third stage started with the advent of strong monarch after mediaeval period. In this stage on one hand criminal law saw far reaching change in all its discipline, but on other the hand position of victim right to compensation remained unheard due to advent of more strong institution named state and crystallization of a notion that King/State is parent of his subjects and crime is breach of peace of King or State. So it was King/State who had the right to punish and get monetary compensation. This position remained as it is even with advent of democracy and the cause of victim remained unnoticed until 1950 and after that a movement stared in U.S. and European countries and the concept again got prominence. Theoretically, radical criminologist championed the idea of cause of victim, which was result of reaction against the then criminological thinking that was only concern with criminals and not the victims.

The UN Basic Principles of Victims of Crime and Abuse of Power states the following on compensation:

> "When compensation is not fully available from the offender or other sources, States should endeavour to provide financial compensation to:
>
> (a) Victims who have sustained significant bodily injury or impairment of physical or mental health as a result of serious crimes;
> (b) The family, in particular dependants of persons who have died or become physically or mentally incapacitated as a result of such victimization.
>
> The establishment, strengthening and expansion of national funds for compensation to victims should be encouraged. Where appropriate, other funds may also be established for this purpose, including in those cases where the State of which the victim is a national is not in a position to compensate the victim for the harm".

The criminal justice administration deals about the formulation of the legislation, enforcing the law and detection and prevention of crimes, trial of offenders and execution of the offenders but most of the time it does not try to alleviate the suffering of the innocent victims or their families. In a large number of cases untold misery to the victims and their family members ensues in the event of any crime. In many cases the victims are left in a chaos wherein they suffer due to post-traumatic stress orders, social stigma and various other economic and financial losses. The duty of a welfare state also devises ways and means to bring solace to the helpless victim by the way of payment of compensation on humanitarian grounds which would give some consolation to the distressed victims.

The importance of providing compensation to the victims of crime attracted the United Nations. The 7th United Nations Congress on Prevention of Crime and Treatment of Offenders brought out a declaration of Basic Principles of Justice of Victims of Crime and Abuse of Power, which was later adopted by the U.N. General Assembly. According to this declaration, a victim of crime is defined as follows:

1. "Victims" means persons who, individually or collectively, have suffered harm, including physical or mental injury, emotional suffering, economic loss or substantial impairment of their fundamental rights, through acts or omissions that are in violation of criminal laws operative within Member States, including those laws prescribing criminal abuse of power.
2. A person may be considered a victim, under this Declaration, regardless of whether the perpetrator is identified, apprehended, prosecuted or convicted and regardless of the familial relationship between the perpetrator and the victim. The term "Victim" also includes, where appropriate, the immediate family or dependants of the direct victim and persons who have suffered harm in intervening to assist victims in distress or to prevent victimization.

The UN General Social Council's draft "**Guidelines for Measures on behalf of Victims of Crime and Abuse of Power**" laid down the types of harm, injury, loss or damage caused by wrongful conduct. It was as follows:

> **"The loss of life or of support, impairment of health, including physical or psychological injury, pain and suffering both physical and mental, loss of liberty, loss of income or livelihood, loss of property deprivation of the use of property. Due account must also may be taken of the special damages or expenses and costs reasonably incurred by the victim or, where appropriate, by the victim's family, dependants of heirs, which resulted from the victimization, including medical costs, legal costs, treatment and rehabilitation costs, and similar and related costs and expenses".**

The necessity of compensating the victims of war was declared in the draft guidelines for Measures on behalf of Victims of Crime and Abuse of Power by the United Nations Economic and Social Council. The treaties following both the First and Second World Wars obliged the defeated powers to pay full compensation with respect to war crimes and crimes against humanity committed by their armed forces on the territories of the allied and associated powers.

On the above grounds, later in India, many laws started providing the room for compensation except that for the victims of crime. As such there is no single law for providing compensation or assistance to the Victims of Crime and Abuse of Power. **The Personal Injuries (Emergency Provisions) Act, 1962** and the **Personal Injuries (Compensation Insurance) Act, 1963** envisage that the Central Government has the power to make schemes for the grant of relief in respect of personal injuries sustained during the periods of emergency that were declared on 26 October 1962 and 3 December 1971. Payment by way of allowance, shall be payable only where the injury or disease cause serious and prolonged or permanent disablement or death as a result of war.

The legislative framework in India regarding compensation to victims of crime can be traced through two major legislations, i.e. **Code of Criminal Procedure, 1973 and Probations of Offenders Act along with the Constitution of India**. Under the provisions of Code of Criminal Procedure the power to award compensation is vested under Section 357. The plain reading of the section shows that sub-Sections(1) and (3) vests power on the trial court to award compensation and sub-Section(4) gives power even to appellant or revision court to order for compensation. Sub-Section(1) empowers the courts to appropriate the whole or any portion of fine recovered for the purpose mentioned in the clauses to the sub-section, under which Clause (b) is most important and of our use. It demands that claim of compensation must be accompanied by the following conditions:

1. Loss or injury suffered
2. Loss or injury must be caused by the offence
3. Such person can recover the compensation in a civil court

Sub-Section(3) empowers the court, in its discretion, to order the accused to pay compensation even though fine does not form a part of compensation and hence although inserted in 1973 added new positive dimension to Indian philosophy of compensation.

Probation of Offenders Act vide its Section5 empowers the trial court to order for compensation. This section clearly shows that the power in case of this act vests only with the trial court. The whole discussion about legislative framework is incomplete until Sections 431 and 421 of CrPC. are read with above two substantive sections. Section 421 provides for means to recover the fine by attachment and sale of movable property of the offender and also from both movable and immovable as arrears of land revenue. Section 431 empowers the courts to recover any money (other than fine) payable by virtue of any order made under as if it were fine if method for its recovery is not expressly provided. As far as the Constitutional scheme is concern it is to be noted that it is an outcome of various decisions of Supreme Court of India either by reading Part third of the constitution—rights (in some cases part four as well) with Art. 32, 136 and 142 of Constitution of India is to be given either by the state or accused. Hence, the whole gamete of the above legislative framework about compensation can be summarized in the following way:

(i) Compensation from State, which is outcome of Judicial Imposition or some times, even ex-gratia under Constitution of India.
(ii) Compensation from an offender which is outcome either as a part of fine or allocation of specific sum to victim either under CrPC. or Constitution of India.

In addition to the above, the following legislations have the provisions for providing compensation under various circumstances in India:

1. **Motor Vehicles Act, 1988 (Will be dealt in detail below)**
2. **Section 124 and the rules framed under Section 129 of the Indian Railways Act, 1989 provided for payment of compensation to the Railway accident victims.**
3. **Under Section 5 of the Carriage By Air Act, 1972, persons who are carried by aircraft are entitled to claim compensation in the event of the death or wounding of a passenger, if the accident which caused the damage so sustained took place on board aircraft or in the course of any of the operations of embarking or disembarking.**
4. **Under Regulation No. 5 of the Indian Airlines Non-International Carriage (Passenger and Baggage) Regulations, 1980, the Indian Airlines Corporation is liable for damage sustained in such event.**
5. **Under Section 346 of the Merchant Shipping Act, 1958 the owners of the ship shall be liable to pay compensation whenever loss of life or personal injuries are suffered by any person on board a ship owing to the fault of that ship and of any other ship.**
6. **Under Sections 3 and 10 A of the Workmen's Compensation Act, 1923 a workman is entitled to claim compensation in the even of death or bodily**

injury caused to a workman in the course of his employment or while discharging his duties as a workman.

The above legislations provide compensation when some injury or death or damage is caused due to various accidental reasons.

In addition to all these laws, the Government of India enacted **Bhopal Gas Leak Disaster (Processing of Claims) Act, 1985** to settle the claim of compensation for those who suffered due to leakage of lethal gas from the Union Carbide Corporation at Bhopal. On the night of 2 December 1984 there was massive escape of lethal gas from the MIC storage tank at Bhopal plant of the Union Carbide (I) Ltd. (UCIL) as a result of which 4000 human lives were lost and thousands of citizens of Bhopal were physically affected. Action was brought up by the Union of India as 'parens patriae' before the District Court, Bhopal pursuant to the statutory enablement in that behalf claiming 3.3 billion dollars as compensation against the company. When an interlocutory matter pertaining to the interim compensation came up for hearing there was a Court-assisted settlement between the Union of India and the Union Carbide Corporation (UCC—owning 50.99%, shareholders of UCIL). Under this settlement a sum of 470 US Dollars was agreed to be paid by the UCC to the Union of India in full settlement of all the claims of all victims of the gas leak against the UCC.

When so many legislations deal with compensation, as mentioned before ***there is no single law that deal with the Compensation to victims of crime and abuse of power,*** but, as a solace, in a number of cases, the ***Supreme Court has laid down sound guidelines with regard to assessment of just compensation to be paid the various types of victims.*** But such cases are in a very meagre numbers. To quote a few cases:

(a) **Under Cr.P.C. or P.O.A.:**

The first case in the line, which attracted the mind of the court, came way back in 1952 where the Court concerned connected general principle of sentencing, i.e. while passing a sentence the court must bear in mind the proportionality between the offence and penalty with granting of compensation and observed that while imposing the fine court must consider gravity of offence and the pecuniary condition of the offender. Then came the case of Prabhu Prasad Sha v State of Bihar where the Court not only uphold the conviction of 15-year-old boy (actually at the time of commission of crime the accused was 15 years) but also observed that although requirements of social justice demand the imposition of heavy fine but taking into consideration the condition of the accused awarded a fine of Rs. 3000 to be paid by him to the children of the deceased.

In another case of Palaniappa Gounder v State of Tamil Nadu Supreme Court following the same view as of earlier not only reduced the amount of fine imposed by the High Court from Rs. 20,000 to 3000 but also observed that

> "It appears to us that the High Court first considered what compensation ought to be awarded to the heirs of the deceased and then imposed by way of fine an amount which was higher than the compensation because the compensation has to come out of the amount of

fine. Apart from the fact that even the compensation was not fixed on any reliable data, the High Court, with respect, put the cart before the horse in leaving the propriety of fine to depend upon the amount of compensation. The first concern of the Court, after recording an order of conviction, ought to be the determining of the proper sentence to pass. The sentence must be proportionate to the nature of the offence and the sentence, including the sentence of fine, must be unduly excessive".

Yet another land mark case is Sarwan Sing v State of Punjab where supreme court not only retreated its previous stand point but also laid down, in exhaustive manner, that what all should be taken into account while imposing fine or compensation.

The Court Observed that

"The object of the section therefore, is to provide compensation payable to the persons who are entitled to recover damage from the person sentenced even though fine does not form part of the sentence. Though Section 545 enabled the court only to pay compensation out of the fine that would be imposed under the law, by Section 357(3) when a Court imposes a sentence, of which find does not form a part, the Court may direct the accused to pay compensation. In awarding compensation it is necessary for the court to decide whether the case is a fit one in which compensation has to be awarded. If it is found that compensation should be paid, then the capacity of the accused to pay compensation has to be determined. In directing compensation, the object is to collect the fine and pay it to the person who has suffered the loss. The purpose will not be served if the accused is not able to pay the fine or compensation for, imposing a default sentence for non-payment of fine would not achieve the object. If the accused is in position to pay the compensation to the injured or his dependents to which they are entitled to, there could be no reason for the court not directing such compensation. When a person, who caused injury due to negligence or is made vicariously liable is bound to pay compensation it is only appropriate to direct payment by the accused who is guilty of causing an injury with the necessary mens ready to pay compensation for the person who has suffered injury.

And also it is the duty of the court to take into account the nature of the crime, the injury suffered, the justness of the claim for compensation, the capacity of the accused to pay and other relevant circumstances in fixing the amount of fine or compensation. After consideration of all the facts of the case, we feel that in addition to the sentence of 5 years' rigorous imprisonment, a fine of Rs. 3500 on each of the accused under Section 304(1), I.P.C. should be imposed".

The next important case is of Bhuperndar Singh v State of M.P. which was an out come of a quarrel between college students where the Court although allowed the compounding of offence but did not forget the cause of victim and granted the compensation of Rs. 3000.

The Case of Harikishan and State of Haryana v Sukhbir Singh and others is the second most important case after Sarwan Singh where court repeated its firm understanding once again in the following words:

"The payment by way of compensation must, however, be reasonable. What is reasonable may depend upon the facts and circumstances of each case. The quantum of compensation may be determined by taking into account the nature of crime, the justness of claim by the victim and the ability of accused to pay. If there are more than one accused they may be asked to pay in equal terms unless their capacity to pay varies considerably. The payment may also vary depending upon the acts of each accused. Reasonable period for payment of compensation, if necessary by instalments, may also be given. The court may enforce the order by imposing sentence in default".

In the case of Balraj Singh v State of U.P. the court stated the same point as discussed above but in most appropriate word by saying that the power to award compensation is not ancillary to the other sentence but in addition thereto.

(b) Under Indian Constitution:

The principle of payment of compensation to the victim of crime was evolved by Supreme Court on the ground that it is duty of the welfare state to protect the fundamental rights of the citizens not only against the actions of its agencies but is also responsible for hardships on the victims on the grounds of humanitarianism and obligation of social welfare, duty to protect its subject, equitable Justice, etc. It is to be noted that compensation by the State for the action of its official was evolved by the Court against the doctrine of English law: "King can do no Wrong" and clearly sated in the case of Nilabati Behra v State of Orissa that doctrine of sovereign immunity is only applicable in the case of tortuous act of government servant and not where there is violation of fundamental rights and hence in a way stated that in criminal matters (of course if there is violation of fundamental rights) this doctrine is not applicable.

Rudal Shah v State of Bihar is the most celebrated case where the Supreme Court directed the state to pay compensation of Rs. 35,000 to Rudal Shah who was kept in jail for 14 years even after his acquittal on the ground of insanity and held that it is violation the of Article 21 done by the State of Bihar. The case of Bhim Singh v State of J&K is another important case where Bhim Singh an MLA was arrested by the police only to prevent him to attended the Legislative Assembly, the Court not only entertained the writ petition of his wife but also awarded the compensation of Rs. 50,000 to be paid by the state. The case of Meja Singh v SHO Police Station, Zira is another case where the High Court of P&H took the cause of victim and awarded the compensation of Rs. 25,000 for illegal detention of son of the petitioner. This time it was High Court Bombay, which took the cause of the victim in the case of Ravikant Patil v DG Police, State of Maharashtra where the petitioner was taken handcuffed to court in clear violation of Judgment of Supreme Court that is law, as decided in the case of Prem Shanker Shukla v Delhi Administration. Custodial Death is another burning issue where the courts have awarded compensation to the victims of crime and the most important case under this heading is of Mrs. Cardino v UOI where although the accused was arrested on the charge of misappropriation of some plastic ware and hospital utensils worth Rs. 1500 but tortured like hard core criminal and hence he succumbed to the torture. Here when the matter was brought before the High Court of Bombay which gave the compensation of Rs. 2,00,000 to be paid by the state. In the case of Nilabati Behra v State of Orissa where the son of petitioner was arrested by the police and next morning his body was found laying down with several injuries on the railway track, the Supreme Court awarded the compensation of Rs. 1,50,000 that is to be paid by the State. On the issue of brutal use of force and misuse of authority by the police out side the police station case of SAHELI v Commissioner of Police is a land mark case where the son of Kamlesh Kumari died due to ill treatment by a Sub Inspector of Delhi Police, the Supreme Court directed the Delhi Adm. to pay the compensation of Rs. 75,000. The next important case is of Gudalure Cherian v UOI where Supreme Court following an innovative approach first directed the whole matter to be investigated by the CBI afresh and completion of investigation directed the Govt. of U.P. to first suspend the police officials and medical officers who tried to save the accused but also directed the state to pay compensation of Rs. 2,50,000 to the victim of rape and Rs. 1,00,000 to victim of other crime. The next in the line is the case of Bodhi Satta Gautam v Subhra Chakraborty where the Hon'ble S.C. invented the concept of interim compensation and enforced the part third right against an individual by saying that:

> "This decision recognizes the right of the victim for compensation by providing that it shall be awarded by the Court on conviction of the offender subject to the finalization of Scheme by the Central Government. If the Court trying an offence of rape has jurisdiction to award the compensation at the final stage, there is no reason to deny to the Court the right to award interim compensation, which should also be provided in the Scheme. On the basis of principles set out in the aforesaid decision in Delhi Domestic Working Women's Forum, the jurisdiction to pay interim compensation shall be treated to be part of the overall jurisdiction of the Courts trying the offences of rape which, as pointed out above is an offence against basic human rights as also the Fundamental Right of Personal Liberty and life.

The court also stated that

> "Having regard to the facts and circumstances of the present case in which there is a serious allegation that Bodhisaltwa Gautam had married Subhra Chakraborty before the God he worshipped by putting Vermilion on her forehead and accepting her as his wife and also having impregnated her twice resulting in abortion on both the occasions, we, on being prima facie satisfied, dispose of this matter by providing that Bodhisattwa Gautam shall pay in Subhra Chakraborty a sum of Rs. 1000/-every month as interim compensation during the pendency of Criminal Case......... in the Court of Judicial Magistrate, 1st Class, Kohima, Nagaland. He shall also be liable to pay arrears of compensation at the same rate from the date on which the complaint was filed, till this date.

In practice, the highest number of cases where compensation is paid is only in the cases of accidents. Even Supreme Court has laid down many guidelines with regard to the assessment of just compensation to be paid to the victims of accidents. Though in some hard cases, either no compensation was paid or inadequate compensation was paid, yet it is generally found that the Courts and tribunals have been liberally granting compensation to such victims in accordance with the observations made by the Supreme Court.

References

Abhishek, A. (1999). Compensation to the Victim of Crime: Assessing Legislative Frame Work and Role of Indian Courts, available at http://www.legalserviceindia.com

Amir, M. (1971). *Patterns in forcible rape*. Chicago: University of Chicago press.

Anitilla, I. (1974). Victimology: A new territory in criminology. In I. Drapkin & E. Viano (Eds.), *Victimology: A new focus*. (Vol. 1, pp. 5–8). Lexington: Lexington Books.

Arthashastra, K. (1915). I, II & IV (7). Translated by R. Shamasastry. Bangalore: Government Press, 245–246..

Arumugaswamy, S. (1997). Victim of Crime & Criminal Law: An Analysis. *Indian Journal of Criminology*, 25(1).

All India Reporter (1965–2003), Supreme Court Weekly, Delhi.

Chakraborty, N. K. (1999). *Compensation to crime victim*. Kolkata: Deptartment of Law, Calcutta University.

Cri. L.J. (1999). *The Law Declared by the S.S. in Vishakha V. State of Rajasthan*, by Dr. Y.F. Jaya Kumar Lecturer. Hyderabad: University College Law, Osmania University.

Galaway, B. & Rutman, L. (1974). Victim compensation an analysis of substantive issue. *Social Science Review 38*(1), 60–74.

Henting, H. V. (1949). *The criminal and his victims*. New Haven: Yale University Press.

Siddique, A. (1993). Criminology, Problems and Perspectives, II edn., Eastern Book House, Lucknow.

Van Ness, D. & Karen Heetderks Strong, (1997). Restoring Justice, Cincinnati, OH: Anderson Publishing Co.

Chapter 5
Restorative Justice in the Indian Context: Some Views and Thoughts on the Framework and Process

Natarajan Ravi

In any society with complex and multifarious interactions, interrelations and interface, both legal and nonlegal, conflict of interests in some extreme cases results in verbal altercation or physical assault, individual rivalry or group clash, invasion and encroachment of personal or property rights, and attack on life and liberty. Traditionally and conventionally, to regulate these and to bring social order, there has been a criminalization of such events and they are categorized as crimes of different orders. It is the duty of the state to maintain social order and peace through the instrumentality of law and its machineries viz. the police and judiciary.

In the contemporary criminal justice system, with all its systemic constraints and processual complexities, courts are overburdened, trials are protracted, witnesses turn hostile, prosecution fails, victims and their rights are forgotten, and justice is unduly delayed and thus denied. Above all, the focus is on punishing the offender; law breakers sometimes face long periods of trial, ending with imprisonment him behind the tall dark wall as forgotten damned souls. This system does little to prevent the recurrence of crimes or repair the damage they cause. All these exercises impose heavy costs on the state and raise serious concerns about resource management. A cost–benefit analysis would reveal a high level of waste of scarce resources and few benefits, if any, to both the parties involved and society. Much manpower is used and many hours of labor spent in the administration of justice, which escalates the cost. Long trials, extended pendency of cases, and the cost of imposing punishment, all impact negatively on scarce resources.

Due to hasty arrests and ineffective and delayed investigations the numbers of those in jail awaiting trial, a majority of whom latter turn out to be innocent, is escalating. The prisons serve as breeding grounds of criminality, doing further damage to society and facilitating recidivism. The phrase "law runs after the

N. Ravi (✉)
Dr. Ambedkar Government Law College, Kalapet 605014, Pondicherry, India
e-mail: dr.nr_lawprof@yahoo.com

R. Thilagaraj and J. Liu (eds.), *Restorative Justice in India*,
DOI 10.1007/978-3-319-47659-9_5

criminals" is perceived by the police to be a directive that they wait till the crime occurs or the criminals strike and then swing into action to bring them to book.

The paramount consideration of criminal justice should be the protection and promotion of the interests of the parties involved, the society and of course the state. The upholding of rights and recompensing victims, and the reintegration of offenders into society by avoiding, as far as possible, incarceration and consequential stigmatization would do a lot of good to the victim, the society and as well the offender, rather than viewing the latter as an ailing deviant. "The society prepares the crime and the criminal does it", so goes a saying to mean that the factors facilitating the crime are self-existing in society and are dynamics to which the unfortunate deviant falls prey. Hence the facilitating factors are to be checked, the deviance to be prevented and the deviant to be repaired and socially reintegrated. This is precisely what is understood to be the objective of restorative justice.

Restorative justice is a theory of justice that emphasizes repairing the harm caused by criminal behavior. With a more comprehensive view of crime than simple criminalization, restorative justice recognizes that offenders harm victims, the community and themselves. In responding to crime, restorative justice involves many parties, including victims and the community, quickens the process of justice administration, cuts costs and saves resources which could otherwise be better and effectively utilized.

Though it is claimed that, in the West, officially recognized forms of restorative justice are only approximately thirty years old, the annals of history reveal traditional practices of restorative justice in India at different points of time and historical periods. Those were the days when victims of offences could get better justice than they do today. Minor conflicts, wrongs, crimes and disputes were handled by village headman or groups of elders who commanded strong social support and esteem. Through conciliation and negotiation, they settled conflicts in a restorative manner, involving the wrongdoer, the wronged, their families and the community. The offenders were asked to pay compensation to the victims or render community service[1] in proportion to the damage or injury caused. The verdict was naturally and understandably binding and acceptable since it had the force of social sanction behind it.

Kautilyan jurisprudence contains much about restorative justice. Kautilya[2] held that the damage or loss caused by the commission of a crime had two dimensions, viz. the harm caused to the victim or wronged and the wastage of the potential of the wrongdoer invested and spent in performing the crime which otherwise could

[1]The wrongdoer is made to clean and maintain public places/portals and private premises as well, to collect, carry and supply water to the public and to houses and other such physical and domestic works as to serve the public.

[2]Vishnu Gupta, the less-known original name of Kautilya ('the cunning'), also commonly referred to as Chanakya, was the most scholarly pundit of the Mauriya Dynasty, known for his wisdom and cunningness.

have been applied to something constructive. Arthasasthra[3] contains a strong campaign for 'community service' as an alternative to institutional or corporeal punishments. It was considered to have a strong effect of expiation and realization on the part of the offender. In the course of rendering effective and sincere community service, as a measure of punishment, the wrongdoer earned the sympathy and appreciation of the society. That paved way for better resocialization and quicker reformation.

The invasion of India by the Moguls and the advent of British rule have transformed our traditional legal system, one that now claims to be modern, and this is what stands today as the contemporary criminal justice system. It is accused-centric and not victim-oriented. It defines crimes simply as law-breaking and gives key roles to the state and to the offender and measures success in terms of how much punishment is inflicted.

In the present-day Indian context, steps have been taken to integrate restorative ideas and ideals into the criminal justice system. Attempts are being made to incorporate certain restorative policies and programs on lines with models[4] found or adopted in some foreign countries, notable among them are alternative dispute resolution involving mediation, arbitration and conciliation, the concept of plea bargain, Lok Adalat, provision for compounding, compensation, probation, etc. The concept of restorative justice involves a certain theoretical framework and processes that need exploration as well as suggestions for necessary and appropriate changes.

Adapting to the restorative system of justice requires certain spadework to soften the ground. This necessitates certain changes in the legal framework pertaining to criminal justice and involves a re-categorization of crimes and decriminalization. In cases of serious or hardcore conventional crimes affecting public and social interest, which constitute comparatively a lesser percentage in crime statistics, the process of criminal justice should justifiably be as presented by law involving arrest without warrant, directed investigation and prosecution, warrant trial at full length ending in imposition of long-term imprisonment, or any other hard punishment as prescribed. Apart from that, in all other kinds of lesser crimes or crimes of lesser gravity, not involving serious violence or affecting public interest or social interest, at the first instance, the tendency to go for voluntary settlement between the parties, viz. the victim and the offender, should emerge and be encouraged. This necessitates a re-categorization of offences into two types. The first category could be named or referred to as 'crimes or delicts' comprising offences punishable, as per the substantive law in vogue or any special laws, with a death sentence, a life sentence or imprisonment above seven years. The second category is referred to as deviance or violations comprised of offences punishable with imprisonment below seven years

[3]The *Magnum opus* of Kautilya contains rich jurisprudence on economic, public, political, legal and other areas of administration.

[4]Victim Offender Reconciliation Programmes, Victim Offenders Community Meetings and Victim Reparation Programmes in Western Criminology, Victim Mediation Programmes and Victim Offender Encounters in Europe, Truth and Reconciliation Commission in Africa and Family and Community Group Conferencing in New Zealand and Thailand.

and or fines[5]. Offences in the second category which are punishable with less than two years of imprisonment or with a fine only can be grouped and addressed as 'civil offences' that can proceed to compensatory settlement[6]. Making necessary changes in the substantive law to this effect should be given a serious consideration. The parameter for categorization must be the social harm, public welfare, degree of violation, etc., and the feasibility of repairing and restoring. Similarly in tune with this categorization, the procedural law should provide for the nature of trials to be adopted and the powers of the police to arrest. An example is a provision restraining the police from making arrests in cases of offences that can be treated as civil matters. In other cases involving offences that can be considered civil offences, a summons trial could be employed and arrest should be allowed only on a warrant.

The settlement mechanism could be viewed possible and feasible at various levels/stages. First, the wrongdoer and the victim or the affected, without registering a complaint and on their own volition, may go for an interface and agree to make a settlement over the loss or damage caused or the impact of the crime on the victim by way of compromise, forgiveness, or suitable compensation. This would pave the way for resurrecting trust and good neighborliness as the victim is compensated for the damage and the wrongdoer gets repaired, re-socialized, and reintegrated. The process of settlement negotiation or conciliation can be assisted by local bodies or citizen groups.

If there is no motivation at the first stage as above, the next strategy could be tried at the level of the police. When a complaint is preferred by the victim or any other on his behalf, the police can motivate the parties toward a reconciliation which certainly should not contain any element of compulsion. Leaving it completely voluntary to the parties and their free decision to opt or not for reconciliation, the police may suggest, assist, and facilitate conciliation by enlightening the parties about its positive and beneficial outcome.[7] At this stage, agencies like NGOs, legal service authorities, and local bodies could be invited to facilitate conciliation and settlement. If the matter is conciliated and settled, the police does not proceed to prosecute and attaches no stigma to the offender. This necessitates prescribing or circumscribing the powers of police in this regard and incorporating changes accordingly in the procedural law that would enable them to initiate and assist.[8] As voluntariness and the absence of compulsion is a precondition, the police should be required to record in writing the voluntariness and willingness of the parties to conciliate, the initiative role played by police, and the settlement arrived at. The recording shall be signed by the parties and attested by two neutral

[5]This corresponds to the category of offences that are compoundable and offences where a plea bargain is permissible.

[6]In some of the foreign countries, mainly western and European, the offences that can go for compensatory settlement are decriminalized and treated as civil matters like torts or misdemeanors to enable settlement without police intervention.

[7]Such a scheme seems to be existing in the British model of restorative justice.

[8]This is similar to the legal provision enabling the police to release an arrested person on bail at their level.

witnesses, preferably any social assistance group or other agencies, if involved. This would ensure fair-play, lest it would turn a police Kattapanchayat.[9]

The emphasis should be on settlement without trial in cases of offences which could be categorized as civil offences, which are punishable under substantive criminal law and special laws with imprisonment for less than two years or with fines. On the failure of or unwillingness to pursue a settlement, if the matter reaches the portals of the court, the trial should be a summary trial ending in punishment which is compensatory without stigmatization of the offender except in repeat cases.

Lok Adalats play a vital role in promoting restorative justice. Taking up on their record only compoundable criminal cases, the Lok Adalats use the alternative tools of mediation and conciliation and eventually reach a compromise and settlement. This ambit is to be widened by suitable and necessary changes in concerned substantive and procedural laws to bring more offences under the category of compoundable offence.[10]

In cases of offences punishable with imprisonment of above two years and below seven years, the arrest must be with warrant and when the police initiate prosecution, the trial should be that of a summons case. At this stage, encouraging a plea bargain and arriving at a settlement in terms of winding up a trial and in terms of punishment and recompensing the victim would effectively activate the process of restorative justice.

Another aspect of justice reform in India is the concept of the plea bargain. By way of Amendment to Criminal Procedure Code in 2005, the plea bargain was introduced into the Indian legal system and incorporated under Chapter XXI-A of Cr.P.C.[11] The introduction of this is intended not only to expedite speedy disposal of cases but also to enable the victim of the crime to bargain with the accused along with the prosecutor. However certain offences[12] under a list of statutes are kept away from the preview of plea bargain.

Plea bargaining is hailed to be a device to resolve matters quickly, speed up court proceedings, guarantee conviction, reduce overcrowding in jails, and to enable case-load management for the prosecutor and cost management for the state. Yet there are potential risks involved in this system of plea bargain and its application. The outcome of plea bargains depends on efficient negotiation, which requires an efficient counsel who can be afforded only by the rich. Further

[9]This indicates a practice existing in different corners and places of many states, a kind of coercive, ruffian justice administered by local bigwigs or dadas.

[10]Such offences that are so recognized and named by the Criminal Procedure Code, vide Section 320 are essentially of a private nature and are relatively not quite serious. The Code considers it expedient that a compromise between the wrongdoer (accused) and the individual victim could be arrived at.

[11]Incorporated under Sections 265-A to 265-L, vide central Act 2 of 2006, with effect from July 5, 2006.

[12]These offences are those affecting the social-economic condition of the country that have been committed against a woman or a child below the age of 14 years.

involvement of police in the meetings might lead to coercion and the involvement of the victim in corruption. The plea should be made on the basis of one's own volition and free will. To reasonably compensate is a precondition for accepting the plea bargain process and this should be on persuasion and not coercion.

In the existing framework[13] there is ample provision for enabling the parties, viz. the offender and victim, in a pending proceeding, before final disposal, to go for settlement or adjustment by agreement, referred to as compounding of offence. This process is considered to absolve the accused from criminal responsibility. The complainant victim, on receiving compensation or gratification from the accused or even without any consideration or gratification but with some understanding to compose the difference, agrees not to prosecute the accused. This mechanism is to be effectively utilized for successful implementation of restorative justice.

Yet another scheme in our legal framework is the provision for victim compensation. Apart from the Criminal Procedure Code that provides for compensation under Section 357,[14] other cases where a legislative compensation scheme is provided are motor accident claims, violations under the Protection of Civil Rights Act, human rights violations, communal violence, and rape cases. However the scheme of compensation under Cr.P.C. has not often been pressed into service by the lower judiciary, and even if invoked, as in stray cases, very meager amounts have been awarded after the conclusion of the trial. The trial courts should be cognizant of the safeguards under Section 357 and should freely apply the provision. The Malimath Committee vociferously voiced out that Section 357 is to be broadened and amplified to cater to the needs of the victims. It requires much sensitizing for the judiciary and committee to be more cognizant of the provision for compensation and to invoke and apply it in more cases. However, responding to strong recommendation of the Malimath Committee and as expressed strongly by the Supreme Court in a number of decisions, legislative change to incorporate a specific provision is made in CrPC[15] enabling the creation of a victims' compensation scheme which would certainly be a tool for restorative justice in India.

An issue that needs to be addressed and stressed as an essential precondition for the successful implementation of restorative justice is the victim's response to the call for reconciliation. The response of the victim will certainly be varied in nature and degree and this variation is found in all societies. In our society, more than any other, there is a natural skepticism and hesitancy on the part of the victim to confront the person who perpetrated the injury or caused loss or damage. It is questionable why anyone should be subject again to an emotionally charged situation that has the potential to revive all the pain and feelings that the crime caused and to re-invoke the trauma. In a cost–benefit analysis, the psychological cost of

[13]Sec. 320 of Criminal Procedure Code, 1973.

[14]Sec. 357 of Criminal Procedure Code, 1973, empowers the courts to order payment of compensation to the victims of the offence, from the fine amount required from the accused.

[15]A new section 357-A is inserted by CrPC Amendment Act, 2008 (5 of 2009), with effect from December 31, 2009.

re-encountering the offender may weigh more than any benefit resulting from such an encounter. Although restorative justice would view both the victim and offender as active players in responding to and resolving the criminal conflict, often the victim, when and if he or she comes for reconciliation, would prefer that the offender be treated differently from a weaker standpoint and with lesser say than the victim. A high-degree persuasion is necessary to overcome these challenges and motivate victims toward reconciliation.

In the exercise of conciliation, either personal or institutional, or in the process of mediation, or in deliberations in the Lok Adalat or court, the real human impact of the deviant behavior should be impressed upon the offender participant. He or she must be made to feel repentant and accept the sanction, if any. This would facilitate the contriteness and remorse of the offender eventually leading to reform and reparation. Resourcefulness and an ability of the participants to create a meaningful response to the injury caused by the crime should be given serious thought and consideration.

Institutional motivation for the parties to prefer compensatory reconciliation, at any stage, seems more effective that individual motivation because of its tendency to be impersonal.

Lastly, as restorative justice seeks to restore social harmony by encouraging the society to embrace the victim and the offender who gets repaired and reintegrated, its viability depends on public participation in criminal justice. Public participation can be motivated by emphasizing certain duties to be imposed on various parties, as strongly suggested by the Malimath Committee; these parties include the general public, the victim, the accused, the witnesses, the police, the prosecution, the defense, the judge, the informant, and the complainant, calculated to bring about maintenance of fair criminal justice.

Chapter 6
A Justice that Heals: Restorative Justice from an Indian Perspective

Subash C. Raina and Rakesh Kumar Handa

6.1 Introduction

The element of crime is present in the nature since the birth of the cosmos, and therefore, it has been coexistent with that of humanity. It has also been co-extensive. Crime symbolizes a major form of conflict in society. It deprives the victim of fundamental human rights especially those pertaining to life, liberty, and safety.

Poor victims in India suffer because of two reasons. One is their ignorance and the second is lack of resources to approach the appropriate authorities (Sen et al. 2007). The criminal justice system is cumbersome, expensive and cumulatively disastrous. The poor can never reach the temple of justice because of the heavy cost of access and the mystique of legal ethos. The hierarchy of courts with appeals after appeals puts legal justice beyond the reach of the poor.

The grand corruption that pervades the highest levels of the national government leads to a broad erosion of confidence in good governance, the rule of law and economic stability. The criminalization of politics gains much importance nowadays. Elected representatives have a criminal past which results in the establishment of monarchic form of government (Vittal 2000). This type of system gives impetus to the rule of the jungle with all its signs of bravery, indecency, immorality and no question of right and wrong.

The whole scenario indicates that we are passing through a precarious period of world history under the shadows of catastrophic and impending dangers. Never before did we feel more strongly that we are leading a nefarious and neglected life. Is it a defective legal system; the corrupt role of police; the unfair use of the

S.C. Raina (✉)
National Law University, Himachal Pradesh, India
e-mail: scrainaclc@gmail.com

R.K. Handa
University of Delhi, New Delhi, India
e-mail: rakeshhanda_1976@yahoo.co.in

R. Thilagaraj and J. Liu (eds.), *Restorative Justice in India*,
DOI 10.1007/978-3-319-47659-9_6

legislative acts; the weak economic or political perspectives or the prevailing corruption in the judicial system that gives thrust to the administration of criminal justice and devours everything worthwhile in humanity? Do we have to still retain old concepts in this criminal justice system? How should we as a society respond to wrongdoing? When a crime occurs or an injustice is done, what needs to happen? What does justice require? Should we not think about a system in which equal justice to crime-doers and victims is ensured so that it minimizes the chances of recidivism and reoffending? Can we not welcome a crimino-victim justice system to ensure repair, restore, reconcile, and reintegrate the offenders and victims to each other and to their shared communities?

In recent years, a new way of thinking about how we should view and respond to crime has emerged and is beginning to make significant inroads into criminal justice policy and practice and that is less destructive and more effective responses to crime. This new approach is called restorative justice.

Restorative justice reflects a sort of crimino-victim justice system wherein equal justice to crime-doers and victims is ensured. In its most idealized form, there are four potent features of restorative justice: repair, restore, reconcile, and reintegrate the offenders and victims to each other and to their shared communities.[1] Thus, restorative justice seeks to repair the harm done by a criminal act by bringing together those most affected by the crime. Meaningful conferencing may change the offenders thinking and allow him or her to take responsibility for the behavior and the effect that it has had on the victim. Restorative justice is an alternative means of redressing the imbalance that may arise from adversarial systems where both victim and offender may feel that their needs have not been adequately serviced.

6.2 Definition of Restorative Justice

It is difficult to arrive at a single definition of restorative justice, because it is a deeply contested concept. It is a complex idea, the meaning of which continues to evolve with new discoveries. Some definitions focus on the elements of restorative processes (i.e., repair, restore, reconciliation, and reintegration) (Zehr 2002). Others begin with the idea that crime causes harm, and justice should promote healing (Sawatsky 2009). Others build on restorative values, such as respect for others. Still others suggest that restorative justice is a holistic approach to life and to relationships, one that has far-reaching effects beyond simply the issue of crime or rule-breaking. The idea of restorative justice typically centers on three basic conceptions: the encounter conception; the reparative conception; and the transformation conception.

[1]European Forum For Victim-offender, Leuven University Press, *Victim-Offender Mediation In Europe: Making Restorative Justice Work*, (2000), (Revised Edition), New York City: Cornell University Press, p. 44.

6.3 The Encounter Conception

The encounter conception focuses on the importance of stakeholder meetings and on the many benefits that come as stakeholders[2] discuss the crime, what contributed to it, and its aftermath. It helps identify one of the key differences between restorative processes and criminal justice processes (von Hirsch et al. 2006).

In restorative processes, the victim, offender, and other interested parties are free to speak and to decide what to do in a relatively informal environment and through that come to terms with what happened. In court, on the other hand, the active participants are generally professionals who have only a professional connection to the crime and to those who were touched by it. Decisions are not made by the parties, but by the judge. While the defendant generally has a lawyer, the victim does not; instead, the victim's interests are considered to be identical with society's interests, which the prosecutor represents.

6.4 The Reparative Conception

The reparative conception focuses on the action of repairing. "Crime causes harm; justice must repair that harm (Harcarik 2009)." The harm is at many levels, as we see, and it can often be addressed most fully when the parties meet in a restorative process to explore and respond to those. However, this conception is not limited by the inability or unwillingness of the parties to meet. In those circumstances, it would insist that court proceedings focus on identifying and taking steps to repair the harm caused by the crime. The reparative conception would not describe something as restorative if it did not provide some sort of redress to direct victims, communities, and offenders as well (Brophy et al. 2008).

6.5 The Transformation Conception

The transformation conception focuses on the marked change in nature, form, or appearance. This is far more expensive than the other two because it has to do with broken relationships at multiple levels of society. It addresses not simply individual instances of harm but goes beyond to structural issues of injustice such as racism, sexism, and classism (Mclaughlin and Hughes 2003). Each of these prevents people from living in whole, harmonious, and healthy relationships with others and with their social and physical environments. Restorative justice is therefore a way of life

[2]The word 'stakeholders' comprises of victim, offender, family members of both victim and offender (including those who may be similarly affected), neighbors, and other important members of the society.

because it addresses all of our relationships, and it offers a way in which broken relationships can be repaired (often through challenging existing societal injustices). The transformation conception would not describe something as restorative if it did not address structural impediments to wholesome, healthy relationships (Weitekamp and Kerner 2002).

The three conceptions are closely related, and most proponents would find themselves at home in each of the three depending on the context of the conversation. The concept of restorative justice falls within the reparative conception, with one important proviso: repair is most fully accomplished when it results from an encounter of the parties. Following my discussion, the definition of restorative justice can be summed up as follows:

> Restorative justice is a theory of justice that emphasizes repairing the harm caused or revealed by criminal behavior. It is best accomplished through cooperative processes that include all stakeholders. It is an invitation to join in conversation so that we may support and learn from each other. It is a reminder that all of us are indeed interconnected (Strang and Braithwaite 2001).

Sharpe (1998) summarized the goals and tasks of restorative justice as follows. Restorative justice programs aim to: put key decisions into the hands of those most affected by crime; make justice more healing and, ideally, more transformative; and reduce the likelihood of future offences. Achieving these goals requires that: victims are involved in the process and come out of it satisfied; offenders understand how their actions have affected other people and take responsibility for those actions; outcomes help to repair the harms done and address the reasons for the offence (specific plans are tailored to the victim's and the offender's needs); and victim and offender both gain a sense of 'closure,' and both are reintegrated into the community.

6.6 Restorative Justice of Restorative Practices?

As restorative processes have increasingly been applied in educational and business settings, some have suggested that the term 'restorative justice' is inappropriate because it implies that such processes can only be used when the culpability of one party is clear and conceded. In fact, conferencing and other restorative encounters can be very useful in addressing many kinds of conflicts, whether or not they stem from misbehavior. In other words, 'justice' seems to narrow the use of restorative practices to situations that would ordinarily be handled by the justice system. This has practical consequences in advocacy: should proponents promote restorative practices and encourage their application in multiple contexts, one of which would be in dealing with crime? Or is it better to focus attention on wrongdoing and in particular, criminal wrongdoing?

This is both a strategic and principled question. Those who support use of the term 'restorative justice' agree that restorative processes are effective in other settings and that increased use of them anywhere creates a 'restorative-friendly' context that might increase their use in criminal matters. So some organizations promoting restorative justice are asking whether they should expand their scope to all applications of restorative practices or maintain the focus on criminal and juvenile justice (Umbreit et al. 2010).

That is the strategic issue. The question related to principles has to do with what is lost by using the term ‘restorative practices’ rather than restorative justice. An obvious answer is that justice is lost when responding to crime or other rule violations. One of the needs of victims is to hear that this was not their fault (to the degree that is true). One can argue as well that offenders need to hear that they were wrong, and certainly society expects that there will be denunciation of certain kinds of behavior (Cragg 1992). It is clear that there is a huge overlap between restorative practices and restorative justice in terms of world view, values, principles, and methods. But the similarities are not complete, and the discussion is likely to continue.

6.7 Restorative Justice from India’s Perspectives

The restorative justice system and its practices are of great relevance in India. One of the major benefits of such programmes is its potential for flexibility: it can he adapted according to the needs of particular communities. It is also about having the capacity to change even before the case for changes becomes obvious. But in the case of having to deal more effectively with crime, the case for change is staring us in the face. Therefore, we should explore a paradigm shift from a retributive justice system to a system in which there is a balance between restorative and retributive justice. The numeric shadow of restorative justice can be found under the following heads.

6.8 Panchayati Raj System

The Indian heritage has much testimony to offer that its socio-cultural fabric contains an intrinsic mechanism to bring conflicting people together and settle their disputes in a highly informal manner. The Panchayati Raj System and other social institutions in the countryside have been effective in dispensing justice. The verdict delivered by these bodies is by and large acceptable to everyone. The interests of the victims are considered to be supreme. Many times the offenders are directed to compensate or restore the harm done to the victims. To encourage this practice, the Law Commission of India in its 114th report on “Gram Nyayalaya,” kept in mind the first and foremost objective of reviewing the system of judicial administration in order to ensure that it is responsive to the reasonable demands of the times. The aim was the elimination of delays, speedy clearance of arrears, and reduction in costs so as to secure quick and economical disposal of cases without affecting the cardinal principle that decisions should be just and fair as well as the simplification of procedure and elimination of technicalities. Gram Nayalaya Act, 2008 and Nayaya Panchayat Bill, 2009 were introduced by the government of India to revitalize the centuries-old concept of "panchayat" at the participatory grassroots level of dispute resolution through mediation, conciliation and compromise outside the formal judicial system.

6.9 Juvenile Justice (Care and Protection of Children) Act, 2000

In the Juvenile Justice (Care and Protection of Children) Act, 2000, we can find a glimpse of the restorative justice ideology behind its provisions. The law provides for separate treatment for children in need of care and protection and juveniles in conflict with the law. Juveniles in conflict with the law are kept in the observation home during the pendency of an inquiry under this act, care and classification is made giving due consideration to age group, physical and mental status and degree of offence committed by the juveniles for their further induction into the observation home.[3]

Children in need of care and protection are sent directly to the children's home during the pendency of any inquiry and provisions are made for their care, treatment, education, training, development, and rehabilitation.[4] The law has made for the establishment of special homes for the reception and rehabilitation of juveniles in conflict with the law.[5] These homes are of a custodial nature with regard to children in need of care and protection. The distinction between the children's home and the special home is illusory as the law treats both categories by prescribing custodial care as one of the options. The innovation the law makes with respect to children in need of care and protection is the conceptualization of restoration for the child as the focal point, with restoration being conceptualized as restoration to parents, adopted parents or foster parents.[6]

The juvenile home and special home are conceptualized as a crèche which is basically a sort of nursery for very young children. The law outlines four options for children living in juvenile homes and special homes; these include adoption, foster care, sponsorship, and aftercare. Care is needed in the procedures to regulate adoption and foster care (Kumari 2010).

---

[3]Section 8 of the Juvenile Justice (Care and Protection of Children) Act, 2000.

[4]Section 34 of the Juvenile Justice (Care and Protection of Children) Act, 2000.

[5]Section 9 of the Juvenile Justice (Care and Protection of Children) Act, 2000.

[6]Section 39 of the Juvenile Justice (Care and Protection of Children) Act, 2000.

6.10 Restorative Practices in Domestic Violence in India

The Protection of Women from Domestic Violence Act, 2005 was introduced to provide for effective protection of the rights of women,[7] guaranteed under the constitution,[8] who are victims of domestic violence[9] of any kind occurring within the family and for matters connected therewith or incidental thereto. The basic presumption behind the enactment of this act was the conceptualization of restoration of secure housing and protection for the aggrieved woman as being the first priority. The act provides for the right of a woman to reside in her matrimonial home or shared household whether or not she has any title in such a home. This right is secured by a residence order, which is passed by the Magistrate.[10]

The act empowers the magistrate to pass protection orders in favor of the aggrieved women to prevent the respondent from aiding or committing an act of domestic violence or any other specified act, entering a workplace or any other place frequented by the aggrieved woman, attempting to communicate with her, isolating any assets used by both the parties, and causing violence to the aggrieved woman, her relatives or others who provide her assistance from the domestic violence.[11] The act also provides for appointment of protection officers[12] and registration of nongovernmental organizations as service providers[13] for providing assistance to the aggrieved woman with respect to her medical examination, obtaining legal aid, safe shelter, etc. The magistrate may, upon an application being made by the aggrieved woman, pass an order directing the respondent to pay compensation and damages for the injuries, including mental torture and emotional distress.[14]

[7]The term "women" refers to sisters, widows, mothers, single women, or living with the abuser are entitled to legal protection under the proposed legislation.

[8]Articles 14, 15, and 21 of the Constitution of India provides remedy under the civil law which is intended to protect the woman from being victims of domestic violence.

[9]The term "domestic violence" is defined under Section 3 of The Protection of Women from Domestic Violence Act, 2005, which includes actual abuse or threat. Actual abuse may be physical, sexual, verbal, emotional, or economic.

[10]Section 19 of The Protection of Women from Domestic Violence Act, 2005.

[11]Section 18 of The Protection of Women from Domestic Violence Act, 2005.

[12]Section 8 of The Protection of Women from Domestic Violence Act, 2005.

[13]Section 10 of The Protection of Women from Domestic Violence Act, 2005.

[14]Section 22 of The Protection of Women from Domestic Violence Act, 2005.

6.11 Alternative Dispute Resolution (ADR)

ADR in India, unlike several foreign countries, is only applicable in civil disputes.[15] We have the Arbitration & Conciliation Act, 1996 to deal with civil matters. The ADR refers to any ways and means of resolving conflicts and disputes outside the courtroom. ADR includes arbitration, mediation, early neutral evaluation, and conciliation. Due to burgeoning backups in the courts, rising costs of litigation, and time delays that continue to plague litigants, many countries of the world have institutionalized ADR programs, including in criminal matters.[16] These programs operate on both voluntary and mandatory bases.

Keeping in mind that the pendencies of criminal cases have gone through the roof, the Law Commission of India in its 142nd report suggested reform, which included implementation of plea bargaining as one of the potent tools of ADRs in India. Further, in its 154th Report, the Law Commission reiterated the need for remedial legislative measures to reduce the delays in the disposal of criminal trials and appeals and also to alleviate the suffering of under-trial prisoners. The 154th Report of the Law Commission points out that an order accepting the plea passed by the competent authority on such a plea shall be final and no appeal shall lie against the same. The 177th Report of the Law Commission, 2001 also sought to incorporate the concept of plea bargaining which found a support in the Malimath Committee Report, 2003.

To give effect to the recommendations, the draft Criminal Law (Amendment) Bill, 2003 was introduced in the parliament. Despite a very huge hue and cry against it, the amendment was accepted and with the effect of same, Chapter XXIA was added to the Code of Criminal Procedure, 1973. The said chapter contains Sections 265 A to 265L, which deal with the concept of 'plea bargaining.'

6.12 Plea Bargaining in India

Plea bargaining can be defined as pre-trial negotiations between the accused and the prosecution during which the accused agrees to plead guilty in exchange for certain concessions by the prosecution. Notice is required to be given to the victim to participate in the meeting to work out a mutually satisfactory disposition of case,

---

[15]There are various criminal ADR programmes that are running throughout the globe. Some of these are: *Victim-Offender Mediation Programs (VOM)*; *Community Dispute Resolution Programmes (CDRP)*; *Victim-offender Panels (VOP)*; *Victim Assistance Programs (VAP)*; *Community Crime Prevention Programs (CCPP)*; *Private Complaint Mediation Service (PCMS)* and *plea bargaining*.

[16]Some criminal ADR programmes like Victim-Offender Mediation Programs have been successfully mediating to bring justice between crime victims and offenders for over 20 years. There are now over 300 such programs in the U.S. and Canada and about 500 in England, Germany, Scandinavia, Eastern Europe, Australia, and New Zealand.

including payment of compensation to the victim. This is a welcome step in direction of a victim-oriented approach to criminal prosecution.

The defense counsel's function in plea bargains is identical to that of a mediator, seeking to reconcile the positions of the defendant and the prosecution. Within this framework, the plea bargain should be seen as part of the broad conception of Alternative Dispute Resolution (ADR). The tactics of influence and use of an impression of force employed by the defense attorney in plea bargains are identical in every way to those used by mediators.

In the wake of restorative justice theory, a prototype shift has been made from an emphasis on retribution to one of restoration of good relations for those who admit their guilt. Plea bargaining provides for pre-trial negotiations between the defense and the prosecution during which an accused might plead guilty in exchange for certain concessions by the prosecution. There cannot be plea bargaining for offences where punishment above 7 years is prescribed. There will be no plea bargaining in three exceptional cases, namely offences against women, children below the age of 14 years and socioeconomic offences (like offences under the Food Adulteration Act, etc.). The basic purpose behind plea bargaining is to obtain important information from a defendant by the prosecutor, to avoid a long and costly trial, and to give a role to the victim in the negotiation, leading to settlement of criminal cases.[17]

6.13 Open Prison System in India

The open prison system is the most recent development as far as the prison system in India is concerned. It manifests the reformative aspect of the Indian prison system. Open prison is a system where there are no armed guards, no confining walls and locks. The prisoners are allowed to move freely and to maintain self-discipline and make a livelihood by means of labor. This creates an atmosphere which is congenial for reformation and rehabilitation—social, economic and moral—and helps to prevent recidivism to a large extent. It develops trust and builds up self-respect among prisoners and equips them with all the capabilities need for re-socialization once they are released.

[17]In recent case of *Vijay Moses Das* Vs. *CBI* (Criminal Misc. Application 1037/2006), Uttrakhand High Court (Justice Praffula Pant) in March 2010 allowed the concept of plea bargaining, wherein accused was charged under Section 420, 468, and 471 of IPC. In the said case, Accused supplied inferior material to ONGC and that too at a wrong Port, which caused immense losses to ONGC, then investigation was done through CBI by lodging a criminal case against the accused. Notwithstanding the fact that ONGC (Victim) and CBI (Prosecution) had no objection to the Plea-bargaining Application, the trial court rejected the application on the ground that the Affidavit u/s (265-B) was not filed by the accused and also the compensation was not fixed. The Honourable High Court allowed the Misc. Application by directing the trial court to accept the plea-bargaining application.

There are nearly 27 open prisons of different sizes in different states in the country. They are:

1949 Semi-open camp annexes attached to a model prison, Lucknow, U.P.
1954 Maula Ali Colony, Hyderabad, A.P.
1955 Prison Farm Yeravada, Maharashtra.
1955 Open Air Camp, Durgapur, Rajasthan.
1956 Open Air Prison, Singanallur, Tamil Nadu.
1960 Open Air Jail, Bilaspur, H.P.
1962 Open Prison Nettukheltheri, Kerala.
1963 Sampurnand Bandi Shivir, Rajasthan.
1964 Open Air Colony, Jorhat, Assam.

The advantages of open prisons in India are both practical and philosophical. From a practical standpoint, they are less costly than traditional prisons and often profitable for the state. They could help reduce crowding since they are relatively easy to establish and require few staff. Philosophically, open prisons are more humane and reduce the time inmates spend in locked rooms. They are much more effective in keeping families together and help give offenders a sense of social responsibility, which in turn helps to reintegrate them into the community in the future. The open prison system demonstrates that the presence of family has a moderating effect on the offender and that offending, punishing, restoring and compensating are all part of the social process.

6.14 Lok Adalat in India

Lok Adalat is a special kind of people's court in which some particular kinds of disputes are heard and efforts are made to solve disputes by direct talk between the litigants. The specialty of these courts is that in these courts the cooperation of social workers, workers, and the students of law is also procured, who seek to decrease the difference of opinion between the litigants. It is very difficult to contain and restrict the jurisdiction of the Lok Adalat, as matters can be settled easily through these courts. The following are the categories of cases where the functioning of the Lok Adalats can be most effective, fruitful and desirable.

Landlord–Tenant disputes relating to the enforcement of rent and vacating of premises.

Compoundable offences.

Cases arising out of motor accidents.

Matrimonial cases including cases relating to property given at the time of marriage, debts, securities, guardianship, custody of children, and divorce.

The system of Lok Adalats is a success of democracy and is a most up-to-date and cheap method of providing justice locally. It is justice visiting your location to shower blessing. The feeling of a Lok Adalat is a feeling of compromise, and it is a philosophy which strikes a balance and encourages the spirit of the philosophy of restorative practice. So far as the cases not arising out of dealings with the state are concerned, the results have been wonderful; they have been held in Delhi, Gujrat, Jaipur, Jodhpur, and Udaipur and in certain parts of U.P., where they have proved their role and success. In one Lok Adalat, about 8000 cases were reported to be solved. People feel a sense of relief and calm. If they do not get decision in their favor they have no grievances since the system of Lok Adalats is free from prejudice, bias and revenge.

6.15 Restorative Practices to Victims of Rape in India

One of the heinous crimes against women is rape, in which the victim suffers mentally, physically, psychologically, socially, culturally, and economically for the rest of her life. A victim of rape is victimized repeatedly, initially in the hands of the police when a complaint is lodged or an investigation is ordered, second, when the trial of the case starts, and lastly, which may never be the least, is when society behaves like a beast against the victims of rape. The net result is defamation and degradation of the victim of the rape in particular and womanhood in general, which contingencies have to be faced by the victim throughout her life.

The ministry of women and child development came up with a scheme to compensate the victims of rape by providing them financial assistance up to Rs.2 lakh but can it be enhanced up to Rs.3 lakh if the victim gets pregnant or is a minor, differently abled, mentally challenged or infected with STD (including HIV/AIDS as a consequence of rape) or in any other case where the designated authority finds it necessary. Depending upon their needs, the victims will also be provided various support services such as educational and vocational training so as to help them overcome the trauma and lead independent lives. This scheme, however, does not prevent an affected woman from seeking relief from the courts under Section 357, as well as applying under Section 357A of the Criminal Procedure Code (CrPC).

Rs. 20,000 will be given to the victim in the event a rape case is prima facie made out. The district board shall order the assistance as far as possible within 15 days and, in any case, not later than 3 weeks from the date of receipt of the application. Rs. 50,000 is the maximum amount the victim will receive as further aid after giving due consideration to her physical injury and emotional trauma.

Rs. 1.3 lakh will be given to the victim as final assistance within one month from the date on which the victim gives her evidence in the criminal trial or within one year from the date of receipt of the application in cases where the recording of evidence has been unduly delayed for reasons beyond her control.

6.16 Relief Available to the Victims of Rape

Section 327 of the Cr.P.C., provides the relief of conducting trial in camera while dealing with a rape case.[18] In *S/o Maharashtra* v. *Chandraprakash Mewalchand Jain*, AIR 1990 SC 658, the Supreme Court expressed the view that.

> The court must not be oblivious of the emotional turmoil and the psychological injury that a prosecutrix suffers on being molested or raped. She suffered a tremendous sense of shame and the fear of being shunned by society and her near relatives, including her husband. Instead of treating her with compassion and understanding as one who is an injured victim of a crime, she is, more often than not, treated a sinner, and shunned. It must therefore, be realized that a woman who is subjected to sex-violence would always be slow and hesitant about disclosing her plight. The court must, therefore, evaluate her evidence in the above background.

In *Shri Bodhisattwa Gautam* versus. *Miss Subhra Chakroborthy*, AIR 1996 SC 922, the Supreme Court held, inter alia, that a large number of women still fail to report rapes to the police because they fear embarrassing and insensitive treatment by the doctors, the law enforcement personnel or the cross-examining defiance attorneys. The fear has to be allayed from the minds of women so that if and when this crime is committed the victim may promptly report the matter to the police and on a charge-sheet being submitted, the trial may proceed speedily without causing any embarrassment to the prosecutrix who may come in the witness box without fear.

In *State of Punjab* v. *Ramdev Singh*, AIR 2004 SC 1290, the Apex Court opined that the name of the victim of rape should not be printed or published in the judgments. In this case, the Hon'ble Supreme Court further held that the courts are expected to deal with cases of sex crime against women with sensitivity. Such cases need to be dealt with sternly and severely.[19]

Article 21 of the Constitution of India provides that the right to "live" is not merely confined to physical existence but it includes within its ambit the right to live with human dignity.[20] In a landmark case, *Delhi Domestic Women's Forum v. UOI,*[21] the court reiterated some guidelines for trial of rape cases:

1. The victim of rape must be well acquainted with criminal justice.
2. Legal assistance will have to be provided at the police station since the victim of sexual assault might very well be in a distressed state at the police station.

---

[18]Sub-Section (2) of Section 327 specifically contemplates that "Notwithstanding anything contained in sub-sec. (1) the inquiry into and trial of rape u/s 376 of the Indian Penal Code shall be conducted in camera …."

[19]Sub-Section (3) of Section 327 of the Cr.P.C., reads as follows: "Where any proceedings are held under sub-Section (2), it shall not be lawful for any person to print or publish any matter in relation to any such proceedings, except with the prior permission of the court."

[20]*Maneka Gandhi* v. *Union of India* AIR 1981 SC 746.

[21]*Delhi Domestic Working Women's Forum* v. *Union of India* (1995) 1 SCC 14.

3. The police should be under a duty to inform the victim of her right to representation.
4. A list of advocates willing to act in these cases should be kept at the police station for victims who did not have any particular lawyer in mind.
5. In all rape trials anonymity (name not to be disclosed) of the victim must be maintained, as far as necessary.
6. It is necessary, having regard to the directive principles contained under Art. 38 (1) of the constitution, to set Criminal Injuries Compensation Board.
7. Compensation for victims shall be awarded by the court on conviction of the offender and by the Criminal Injuries Compensation Board whether or not a conviction has taken place.

In *Chairman, Railway Board* v. *Chandrima Das.*[22] The Supreme Court held that where a foreign national, a Bangladeshi woman, was gang raped, compensation can be granted under Public Law (Constitution) for violation of fundamental rights on the ground of domestic jurisdiction based on constitutional provisions and Human Rights Jurisprudence. Accordingly, she was awarded a compensation of Rs.10 lakh.

6.17 Restorative Practices to Victims of Child Abuse in India

Child abuse and neglect can be viewed as the intentional, non-accidental injury or maltreatment of children by parents, caretakers, employers or others including those individuals representing government/non-government bodies which may lead to death or temporary or permanent impairment of their physical, mental, psychosocial development or disability.

The term ‘child abuse’ has different connotations in different cultural milieux and socioeconomic situations. According to WHO (Gaur 2008) it can be physical abuse (i.e., inflicting physical injury upon a child); sexual abuse (i.e., inappropriate sexual behavior with a child); emotional abuse (i.e., verbal abuse, mental abuse, and psychological maltreatment); neglect (i.e., failure to provide for the child’s basic needs), etc.

India is home to almost 19 percent of the world’s children. More than one third of the country’s population, around 440 million, is below 18 years old. According to one assumption 40 percent of these children are lacking care and protection, which indicates the extent of the problem.[23] In a country like India with its multicultural, multiethnic and multireligious population, the problems of socially

[22]In *Chairman, Railway Board* v. *Chandrima Das* AIR 2000 SC 988.

[23]World Health Organization (1999): Report of the Consultation on Child Abuse Prevention; Geneva, http://www.who.int/%20violence_injury_prevention/violence/neglect/en/.

marginalized and economically backward groups are immense. Within such groups the most vulnerable section is always the children.[24]

Independent India has taken large strides in addressing issues like child education, health and development. The Ministry of Women and Child Development (MWCD) has taken significant steps to address the issue of child protection by setting up a National Commission for the Protection of Child Rights, amending the Juvenile Justice (Care and protection of Children) Act 2000 and the Child Marriage Restraint Act 1929, launching the Integrated Child Protection Scheme (ICPS), 2006 and proposing amendments to the Immoral Trafficking Prevention Act (ITPA), 1956 and draft Offences against Children (Prevention) Bill.

6.18 Restorative Practices in the Criminal Justice System in India

The applicability of the concept of restorative justice has been very limited in the Indian criminal justice system, which is largely a holdover from colonial times and is hardly victim oriented. The progress made in the spheres of victimology is yet to reach to the criminal justice practices in this country. There is no separate law in this country enabling the victim to have their say in the criminal justice process. Compensation, restitution and restoration are still not very common in the criminal justice system. The main reason is perhaps that the procedural law in the country does not provide much scope for these practices. As regards compensation, some highly inadequate and restricting provisions are available in the Sections. 357-58 of the Criminal Procedure Code, 1973. The procedure to get the prescribed compensation is too cumbersome to practically help the victim. The amount of fine imposed on the offender, the main source of compensation, has remained unrevised since 1860, the year when the Indian Penal Code was enacted.

6.19 Compoundable Offences

The victim and offenders can reach settlement in accordance with Section 320 of the Criminal Procedure Code. This procedural law allows the parties to undergo what is called "compounding of cases" in certain offences without the permission of court and in some cases with the approval of the court. The compounding of offences has connotations to what is now popularly being voiced as restorative justice. There are some offences which affect individuals but do not affect the society. This type of offence can be compounded without the permission of the

[24]The ministry of Women and Child Development in India has conducted a "Study on Child Abuse: India 2007" avail able at http://wcd.nic.in/childabuse.pdf.

court under sub-Section (1) of 320 of the Criminal Procedure Code, 1973. The offences in this category are: hurting the religious feeling of a person, hurt, confinement, mischief, criminal trespass, adultery, defamation, etc. The offences under sub-Section (2) of this law contains those offences which are of a grave nature and likely to affect people at large. These cannot be compounded without the permission of the court. The offences under this class include: grievous hurt, wrongful confinement, misappropriation of property, breach of trust involving heavy amounts, fraud, counterfeiting, indecent behavior towards women, etc. The offences reaching successful compounding always result in acquittal. This procedure is merely a way to dispose of the case. It does not attach any condition of restoration/reparation of harm afflicted. In the name of restoration, higher courts in India have recently given verdicts in favor of the victims.

6.20 Recent Verdicts of High Courts in Favor of the Victims

In the case of *State of Gujarat* vs. *Raghavbhai Vashrambhai and Ors.*[25] the honorable Justice J.N. Bhatt of Gujarat High Court opined:

> "In a realm of victimology the decision is one of the aspects towards fulfilling the design and desideratum and restorative justice to the victims of crime….."

In the case of *Bhagwan Kaur* vs. *State of Punjab*,[26] the honorable Justice Viney Mittal of Punjab and Haryana High Court observed:

> Compromise in modern societies is the sine qua non of harmony and orderly behavior. It is the soul of justice and if the power of the court is used to enhance such a compromise, which in turn, enhances the social amity and reduces friction, then it truly is the "finest hour of justice.

In a recent judgment, in the case of *Anupam Sharma* versus *NCT of Delhi and Anr.*,[27] the honorable Justice Pradeep Nandrajog of Delhi High Court observed:

> Restorative justice may be used as a synonym for mediation. The object and nature of restorative justice aims at restoring the interest of the victim. Involvement of the victim in the settlement process is welcome in the process of restorative justice. It is a process of voluntary negotiation and concentration, directly or indirectly between the offender and the victim.

Thus, various judges of High Courts in India have realized the importance of restorative justice which is a non-stigmatizing, economically viable and socially practicable process. In the words of Albie Sachs, a former judge of the

[25] *State of Gujarat* Vs. *Raghavbhai Vashrambhai and Ors.*, (2003) 1 GLR 205.

[26] *Bhagwan Kaur* Vs. *State of Punjab and another.*, RSA, 2701–2001, [2006] RD-P&H 723.

[27] *Anupam Sharma* Vs. *NCT of Delhi and Anr.*, 146 (2008) DLT 497.

Constitutional Court of South Africa, "Restorative justice is a system of justice which restores harmony in society; it is a system where everybody lives together and it happens to fit comfortably with Gandhian philosophy." Until recently, the criminal justice system was all about crime and punishment. The concept of restorative justice is helpful in that there is an insistence that the causes and effects of crime be addressed.

6.21 Barriers to the Adoption of Restorative Justice

While highlighting the apathy of our criminal justice system J. Krishna Iyer, in the case of *Rattan Singh* v. *State of Punjab*[28] aptly remarked that it is the weakness of our criminal justice system that victims of crimes do not attract the attention of law. In fact, victim reparation is still the vanishing point of our criminal law. The existing criminal justice system could have become a viable mechanism of restorative justice but there are impediments in the way; these include:

Political corruption. The ultimate and enduring solution to the growing problems of crime and criminality in our society would hinge on the political will and initiative to evolve and implement an alternative model of socioeconomic development aiming at the creation of a just and orderly society. Corruption is rampant among the Ministers (M.L.As and M.Ps) and other highest levels of the national government, leading to a broad erosion of confidence in good governance, the rule of law and economic stability. As a result there is huge pendency of cases and high rates of acquittal in the criminal justice system which indicates lots of barriers to prevent innovation of any kind.

Induced Exacerbation. It becomes a matter of interest to many that the conflict between the victim and offender should not subside. Lawyers from both side, for instance, are often said to exacerbate the conflict.

Inability to Foresee. Because of not being able to foresee the implications of this process the victim and offender do not take much interest in the process.

Fake Compromise. The compromise which takes place between the victim and the offender by way of middlemen and others is generally not in the interest of the victim. At times the victims are forcibly compelled to undergo the compromise. In fact, in some areas this has become a profitable business for many who, by inducing fear among the parties, try to settle the matter and charge large amounts of money.

[28]*Rattan Singh* v. *State of Punjab* (1979) 4 SCC 719.

6.22 Benefits of Adopting Restorative Justice

The search for effective and viable alternatives for the criminal justice process in India is no longer a matter of choice. Hundreds of reports from bodies like the Law Commission, National Police Commission, and several studies by organizations and individuals are testimony to the fact that the system of criminal justice in the country is virtually collapsed. Justice loses its basic purpose if only twenty percent of people get justice and millions remain in the queue for decades and if litigation is so costly that the victim continues to be sidelined and the accused manages to get all the procedural benefits. But by applying alternative dispute resolution and similar techniques, many crippling problems of the justice process have been overcome. If implemented systematically, the restorative model of justice in India can offer highly imperative results. The following are some of the things it can do:

Initiate a Crimino-Victim Justice System. Restorative justice is a type of crimino-victim justice system that ensures equal justice to crime-doers and victims.
Strive toward Repairing, Restoring, Reconciling, and Reintegrating. Restorative justice seeks to repair the harm done by a criminal act by bringing together those most affected by the crime. Its basic purpose is to repair, restore, reconcile, and reintegrate the offenders and victims to each other and to their shared communities.
Prompt Healing. Restorative justice absorbs all the weaknesses of the trial process based on an adversarial system and ensures prompt relief to both victim and offender. It seeks to repair the harm done by a criminal act by bringing together those most affected by the crime. In this way, the trial process cannot be delayed, prolonged, and costly.
Focus on Causes and Effects of Crime. Until recently, the criminal justice system was all about crime and punishment. The concept of restorative justice has changed that focus, causing the courts to address the causes and effects of crime also.
No Chance of Faulty and Slipshod Investigation. Restorative justice provides equal opportunity to the victim to participate in the entire process, which ensures no chance of faulty and slipshod investigation. Police cannot adopt differential attitudes. There is no violation of equality and human dignity.

6.23 Conclusion

There are multiple conceptions of restorative justice. For some, its essence lies in the encounters that take place during restorative processes through which the parties may find healing. For others, it is a view of justice that insists that the harm caused by crime be repaired to the extent possible. For still others, it is a way of living that transforms relationships with others and with the social and physical environment. We hold to the reparative conception and the understanding that repair is best accomplished when the parties themselves participate cooperatively in determining how and what should be done.

Restorative justice focuses on repairing the harm caused by crime and reducing the likelihood of future harm. It does this by encouraging offenders to take responsibility for their actions and for the harm they have caused, by providing redress for victims, and by promoting reintegration of both within the community. Communities and the government accomplish this through a cooperative effort.

Restorative justice is different from contemporary criminal justice practice in a number of ways. It views criminal acts more comprehensively: rather than limiting crime to lawbreaking, it recognizes that offenders harm victims, communities, and even themselves. It involves more parties: rather than including only the government and the offender in key roles, it invites victims and communities as well. It measures success differently: rather than measuring how much punishment has been inflicted, it measures how much harm has been repaired or prevented. Finally, rather than leaving the problem of crime to the government alone, it recognizes the importance of community involvement and initiative in responding to and reducing crime.

Restorative justice responds to specific crimes by emphasizing recovery of the victim through redress, vindication, and healing, as well as recompense by the offender through reparation, fair treatment, and rehabilitation. It seeks processes through which parties are able to discover the truth about what happened and the harms that resulted, to identify the injustices involved, and to agree on future actions to repair those harms. It considers whether specific crimes suggest the need for new or revised strategies to prevent crime.

Restorative justice seeks to prevent crime by building on the strengths of community and the government. The community can build peace through strong, inclusive, constructive, and just relationships. The government can bring order through fair, effective, and parsimonious use of force. Restorative justice emphasizes the need to repair past harms in order to prepare for the future. It seeks to reconcile offenders with those they have harmed, and it calls on communities to reintegrate victims and offenders.

Restorative processes and practices retain their restorative character as they reflect the values and principles of restorative justice. If these values and principles are lost or violated, the result may not only be less restorative, it may be destructive. Four of these values are particularly important: encounter, amends, reintegration, and inclusion.

References

Brophy, A. L. (2006). *Reparations: Pro and Con*. Oxford University Press.

Cragg, W. (1992). *The practice of punishment: Towards a theory of restorative justice*, (1st ed., p. 62). Routledge.

Gaur, M. (2008). The Child Abuse: A Reality, (1st ed., p. 23). Delhi: Alfa Publication.

Harcarik, C. (2009). *Restorative Justice Is Changing The World*, (1st ed., p. 26). New York: Hartington Press.

Kumari, V. (2010). *Juvenile justice system in India*, (2nd ed., p. 117). Oxford University Press.

McLaughlin, E., & Hughes, G. (Eds.). (2003). *Restorative justice: Critical issues* (1st ed., p. 98). Sage.

Sen, R.K., Dasgupta, A., & Dasgupta, M.K. (2007). *Crime and Corruption in Indian Economy*, (1st ed., p. 53). Delhi: Deep and Deep Publications.

Sawatsky, J. (2009). *Justpeace ethics: A guide to restorative justice and peacebuilding* (p. 26). Cambridge: The Lutterworth Press.

Sharpe, S. (1998). *Restorative justice: a vision for healing and change*, p. 23 Canada: Mediation and Restorative Justice Centre.

Strang, H., & Braithwaite, J. (2001). *Restorative justice and civil society*, (1st ed., p. 53). London Cambridge University Press.

Umbreit, M., Armour, M. P., & Zehr, H. (2011). R*estorative Justice Dialogue. An essential guide for research and practice*, (1st ed., p. 52). Sringer.

Vittal, N. (2000). Corruption: The main problem of Indian Democracy. *Journal of Constitutional and Parliamentary Studies, 34,* 47.

von Hirsch, A., Roberts, J. V., Bottoms, A. E., Roach, K., & Schiff, M. (Eds.). (2003). *Restorative justice and criminal justice: Competing or reconcilable paradigms*. Bloomsbury Publishing

Weitekamp, E. G., & Kerner, H. J. (Eds.). (2012). *Restorative justice: theoretical foundations*, p. 62 United kingdom: Willan Publishing.

Zehr, H. (2002). *The Little Book Of Restorative Justice*, (1st ed., p. 31). Good Books.

Part III
Restorative Justice Practices in India: Restorative Justice and Court

Chapter 7 'Mediation'—An Overview of the Opportunity to Resolve Conflicts

Ramanathan Uma

Opportunity and making use of it appropriately is the key to life and especially so in conflict resolution. Insight into the reality of the event that caused the conflict, skills and abilities to recognize the potential for resolution and the ability to step back and help the disputants to come to an agreement is the core of mediation philosophy. The mediator is a neutral third person, who does not decide, argue, advice or suggest but facilitates a conversation to enable parties to distinguish and accept what would be suitable for them in that context. The attempt to CARE, OBSERVE, CONNECT, IDENTIFY GOALS AND INNOVATIVE APPROACHES assists parties to come to a mutually satisfactory agreement on their own which is effective and workable.

Conflicts are natural and it is essential to note that Newton's law 'Every action has an equal and opposite reaction' is more appropriate with respect to persons in conflict. A disagreement, a different view/perspective, different socio-cultural values and differences can be a few of the causes for persons to be in conflict. Resolution of a conflict therefore would involve unravelling the personal views of the parties and understanding that change is necessary and that we have to adapt to the change. In a way this is the Pythagorean concept of justice- cause & effect.

There is an interconnection in everything in society. The interaction between science, justice and politics is at times in variance as they have different modes of communication. Science talks about what is true and untrue and justice by what is legal and illegal. So the language used to co-ordinate these systems has to transform into a form of communication which can be understood by the different systems, as otherwise, there is a possibility for law and order to be put in a straight jacket in

R. Uma (✉)
Madras High Court and Research Scholar, Madras School of Social Work,
Egmore, Chennai, India
e-mail: umaramanathan1956@gmail.com

R. Thilagaraj and J. Liu (eds.), *Restorative Justice in India*,
DOI 10.1007/978-3-319-47659-9_7

which event the disputants will be constrained to accept a resolution which may not be considered equitable. The present justice dispensation system is within the straight jacket of legislated law and has failed to consider that men make the society and men are ruled by their hearts and their mind.

The mind as apposed to the brain has a way of approaching situations. Differences in the way an event is understood or perceived, capacity to understand, inability to perceive the other way gives rise to annoyance. An annoyance can lead to a disagreement which in turn could turn to a power struggle and thereby a conflict. So factors that escalate the difference to a conflict have to be understood. For that the analysis of the expression of differences, the tone and the language and the attitude with which the conflict is approached, the emotions, the values and the context is essential.

Primarily mediation, therefore, attempts to empower the disputants to understand their part in the conflict, acknowledge responsibility, express appreciation of concessions made, and effectively assist parties to understand what they need. Parties face each other and express their point of view, their concerns and fears. The job of the mediator is to build rapport with the disputants, assist parties to trust each other and learn to LISTEN. The first step is providing the comfort and the ambience for a non-abusive talk. Maslow, a renowned psychologist has drawn a pyramid called the Hierarchy of Needs and says that for every individual the first need is Biological & physiological, then comes Safety, thereafter Belonging and Love, and only then Self-esteem. If these needs are satisfied then comes cognition and only thereafter aesthetics and realisation of self. The resolution of every conflict will have to address these needs for the substantive satisfaction of the parties. Unless these needs are addressed, disputants will be unable to make a decision. It is essential to help disputants to overcome their fears and understand that they have the ability to decide and move forward. Mediation is therefore a way to move from the past into the future. It therefore requires courage and creative thinking.

Courage to face the other side, talk to them and explain the reason for the differences can be ensured only when parties are allowed to understand that the process is totally party centric, voluntary, confidential **{PVC}**. The Mediators need an insight into themselves and into the problem as they have to distance themselves from the disputants and their emotions, steer them to the path that would enable them to come to a decision without coercing and advicing them to accept a solution by just encouraging them to THINK, understand their untold fears and acknowledge what would satisfy them.

In our country, with emotions running high even in political agendas, value has to be placed on the context in which the conflict arose to enable resolution. Every resolution of conflict means change in attitude, perception and evaluation. Basically we are all set in our perceptions and beliefs and so once there is a conflict our automatic thought process is kick started in our brain and then it is controlled by our beliefs, our value systems that gets fed by our emotions which then fuels the way we react. So every incident which causes a conflict has an automatic trajectory: event- automatic thought- belief-emotion-reaction-outcome. The change cannot occur in our thinking pattern unless we overcome **FEAR**.

F.E.A.R

Frustration, **E**go, **A**nimosity and **R**eaction are the support systems for entrenchment of positions of parties in conflict. An understanding of the negative aspects which can be changed to positive with respect to conflict may be enabled by considering factors like:

	Negative [−ve]	Positive [+ve]
C	Confusion/lack of clarity	Clarify/connect
O	Opinion/beliefs	Options/opportunities
N	Negative behaviour	Needs
F	Fear	Feelings validated
L	Lack of data/information	Legitimacy of claim
I	Impressions	Interests
C	Collusion	Consensus
T	Threats	Trade-offs

Primarily concerns of the parties, have to be addressed to enable them to look beyond what they can see. Clarification on issues which are misunderstood or not perceived in the right, and then negotiating by considering the alternatives is enabled by the process of mediation.

Mediation as a process of dispute/conflict resolution is different from any other negotiation per se because parties can withdraw from the process at any stage and any information exchanged during mediation is strictly confidential. The disputants cannot use the information gathered in mediation if the matter is referred back to court, no documents are generated in the process and the mediator cannot be called as a witness. This gives a sense of more space to the disputants to discuss wide issues and possibilities.

Mediation is not possible for every conflict. Generally mediation is possible when:

[A] relationship between the parties
[B] willingness of the parties to collaborate
[C] when opportunities for joint gain will not be available in the litigation process
[D] any other issues which may be considered as a possibility for settlement

While mediation is at present resorted to only in civil cases, criminal actions also can be mediated when the situation reveals possibilities for reconciliation or restoration. The stake holders in the dispute resolution process have to believe in negotiation, formulate areas that are possibilities for discussion, identify issues that will bring out mutual gain, and not the least, not get lost in the frustration with the progression of the litigation system.

The mediator therefore provides the time and space and facilitates the conversation AND effectively controls the process by nudging the disputants to understand the underlying issues and what is apparent to them. The outcome is totally in the hands of the disputants and so autonomy and the fact that they can choose to opt out gives the disputants freedom to explore and come to a conclusion on their own. The **CHANGE** brought about by mediation is a revelation of human behaviour and the skill of the mediator is brining out the latent reasonable approach of every disputant.

C.H.A.N.G.E

Communication, **H**earing, **A**cknowledgment, **N**egotiation, **G**oal and **E**valuation are the factors which help the disputants in mediation to accept reality, understand and come to a conclusion that is satisfying to them. Satisfaction is totally relative and the ultimate decision can vary from person to person, from persons in different socio-cultural backgrounds and so on.

Process

Parties in mediation are welcomed, introduced and seated comfortably. This sets the tone as it puts parties at ease and they feel validated. The parties are told about the procedure at the outset and the ground rules, which is that they should not interfere when the other is talking and that language should be tempered to avoid further discord.

Next each party gives a summary of their case. In this situation the opposite party is hearing the version for the first time maybe in the way it is seen and that itself helps to clarify the conflict in a way. The person who is stating his case, is also hearing it when he talks and that enables him to understand how it could be perceived. The mediator then summarises what is said and rephrases the statements to remove the negatives and to help the parties to focus on what is to be discussed. The other side then gives their version and the same procedure of summarising and rephrasing is followed by the mediator. Thereafter, the parties are asked to set their goals, discuss options and this is done either separately or with both of them together and the mediator can decide when to discuss with them separately. The separate sessions enables parties to give confidential information and to understand reality. The mediator uses open ended or clarifying questions in the joint session to gather more information and closed/cross-examination type of questions in the separate session to enable parties to look at different perspectives. Options are given, which are evaluated by both parties and the mediator's creativeness and ability to assist parties to think laterally and brainstorm enables parties to come to a solution. Even if they do not come to an agreement, the fact that their thinking process has changed enables them to move without rancour and in most cases they end up settling at a later point of time.

An understanding of the **BARRIERS** in decision making helps in assisting the disputants:

1. **SPACE & TIME TO DECIDE**: normally the gut feeling is what assists in making a decision and when lack of time and space denies that opportunity decision is not made.
2. **DECISION MAKERS ARE OTHER PEOPLE**: people look up to elders or those whom they respect to make a decision and unless their input is there, parties will be unable to come to a decision.
3. **INADEQUATE INFORMATION**: even when the odds seem to be evenly balanced decision making becomes a problem unless one more point in favour is made out.
4. **WIN-LOOSE**: the ability to let go of something and gladly make the choice to leave for the sake of an agreement will happen only when parties make a considered decision.
5. **MULTIPLE ISSUES**: prioritizing and handling the easier issues when there are more than one issue, handling one issue at a time and not to insist on overcoming the most difficult issue to discuss by either minimizing [after all this is —] or by forcing a decision to get the best out of the situation.
6. **STRESS DUE TO UNCERTAINITY**: Limited information or inability to understand the natural and logical consequences, time factor and fear of negative consequences can affect the decision process.
7. **ANXIETY AND FEAR ABOUT FAILURE**: the possibility of the worst situation and inability to foresee whether the decision maker would be able to accept what is possible and realise to live with the consequences can call the discussion to a halt.
8. **NEGATIVE PERCEPTIONS ABOUT HOW OUTCOME WILL BE VIEWED**: While considering alternatives, fear of what others would say or how they would be perceived and so understanding the difference between price and value of each decision is essential for a resolution.
9. **COMMENDATION**: Acknowledgment of the decision and why it will work/how it can be made workable, helps in accepting the solution. Pat on the back or a simple recognition of the value will enable bigger decisions, support and acceptance.
10. **SELF ESTEEM**: Recognition of the identity of the person and value, chance to be acknowledged as the winner helps in blocking or making a decision.
11. **SOCIAL/CULTURAL ASPECTS**: Conditioning and perceptions.
12. **REACTING AND NOT RESPONDING**: Taking every word at face value and countering merely to make a point/one upmanship and failing to look at the content of the offers due to lack of trust can hamper decision making.
13. **INCONSISTENT DEMANDS**: When offers are not firm and reasonable, and keep changing, as finality is not guaranteed there is an inability to come to a conclusion.
14. **UNACKNOWLEDGED EMOTIONS**: When the reason behind the demands is not understood, the offers made are not evaluated realistically and this prevents decision making.

Negotiation being the key to arrive at a solution, it is then essential to look at the factors that help to give options, consider probabilities and to evaluate them.

A.L.T.E.R.N.A.T.I.V.E.S

Aspirations-expectations & yearnings
Legitimacy-what is possible
Trade-offs-what can be given up/accepted
Emotions- reason for hate/anger/frustration
Reasoning-information that puts a different perspective
Norms-law or social expectations
Apology-face saving/healing/personal/dignity
Time-appropriate point
Innovations-probabilities and out of the box
Validation-understanding of 'WHY'
Evaluation-possibilities
Spirituality-values/belief systems and acceptance of a higher truth

The attempt to ask the five 'WHY'S is a way of assisting parties to gather more information, consider alternatives and come to a solution on their own volition. The process of problem solving has to be in a concerted manner and it usually entails:

PROBLEM SOLVING

- finding the correct problem
- defining the problem
- analysing the problem
- developing possibilities
- selecting the best option
- implementing/workable
- evaluating

Once this is done and parties accept the solution, the agreement is recorded in simple understandable language of the parties and this agreement once signed and accepted by the court has the force of a decree under Sec. 89 C.P.C in court referred mediation. In private mediation, the agreement to mediate and the agreement must be in accordance with the Arbitration and Conciliation Act and will have the force of an award.

Mediation is possible once disputants have the intention to resolve and the process is used in good faith. Different styles are used by mediators depending on the nature of the disputants and the conflict and so it is essential to learn and use the techniques in a proper manner and not practice mediation without a proper training as that will cause more harm to the disputants and may lead to further conflicts.

An understanding of the "Third Alternative"* as opposed to yours and mine and the ability to reach out will ensure the success of any resolution. What is Just and Proper and what is fair play depends on every individuals understanding. A change in the mind set of disputants, those involved in the resolution and organisation of mediation can alone enable progress and acceptance of mediation as a form for substantial satisfaction of issues. The statement that "you cannot shake hands with a clenched fist" is most appropriate to mediation. The synergy for change and the effective practice of mediation could then be:

*Third Alternative—Stephen R. Covey—synergising to make a change in the thought process.

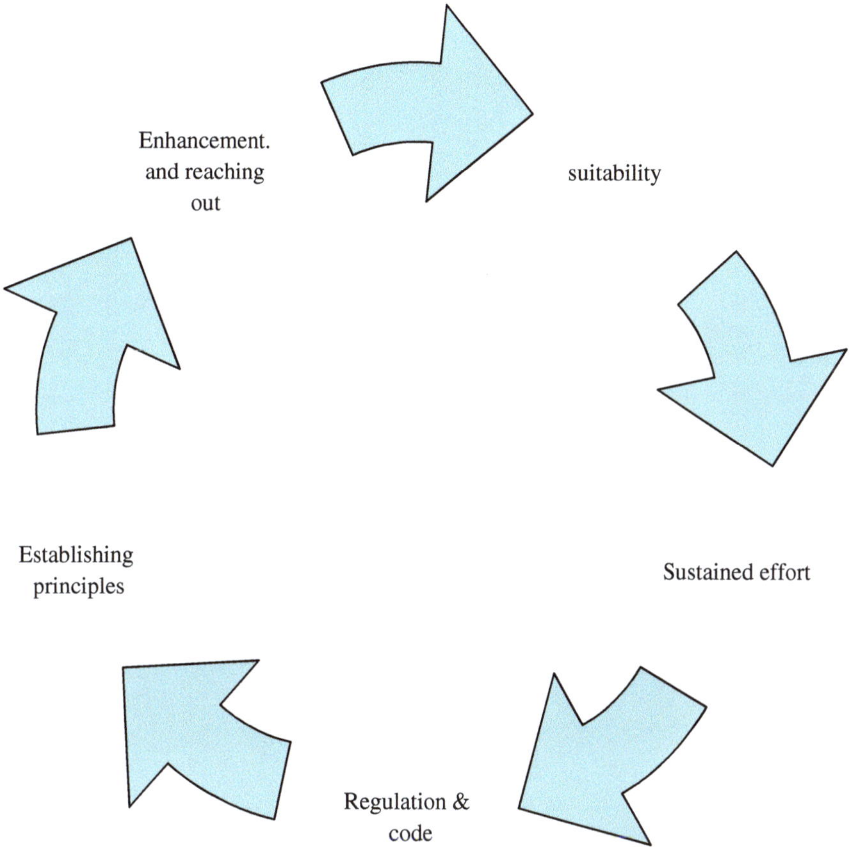

Justice and fair play will have meaning only when the parties in conflict find substantial satisfaction in the resolution and so we have to awake, arise and do the needful for effective practice of mediation.

Chapter 8
Plea Bargaining in India: A Tool to Provide Restorative Justice?

Sarfaraz Ahmad Khan

8.1 Introduction

Restorative justice processes are effective tools for resolving conflicts between victims of crimes and their offenders. It envisages an entirely different outlook toward crime and victimization. Rather than the state being viewed as the primary victim in criminal acts and victims and offenders assuming passive roles, as is the case in the prevailing retributive justice paradigm, restorative justice recognizes crime as an issue which is directed first and foremost against individual people (Umbreit 1998, p. 3). The conventional criminal justice system focuses on three questions: (1) what laws have been broken? (2) who broke the laws? and (3) what do they deserve? From a restorative justice perspective, an entirely different set of questions are asked: (1) who has been hurt? (2) what are their needs? and (3) whose obligation are these? (Zehr 2002, pp. 19–20). The restorative justice process has gradually become the most desirable mode of dispute resolution in most parts of the world. In India also different forms of dispute resolution mechanisms are being followed within the criminal justice administration, which fulfills the basic requirements of restorative justice or which may be instrumental in providing restorative justice such as plea bargaining, compounding of offences, withdrawal from prosecution, Lok Adalats in respect of compoundable offences etc.

As far as plea bargaining in India is concerned, the Law Commission has mooted this concept since long, focusing on pre-trial negotiations between the accused and the prosecution, wherein the accused agrees to plead guilty to the charges leveled against him in exchange for certain concessions which he gets, with the courts

S. A. Khan, Ph.D. Candidate, City University of Hong Kong at Kowloon.

S.A. Khan (✉)
National University of Juridical Sciences, Kolkata, India
e-mail: sarfarazahmedkhan033@gmail.com

R. Thilagaraj and J. Liu (eds.), *Restorative Justice in India*,
DOI 10.1007/978-3-319-47659-9_8

usually adopting a lenient stance, particularly in cases of lesser gravity (LCI 1991, 1996). The Law Commission observed that when an accused feels contrite and wants to make amends or is honest and candid to plead guilty in the hope that the community will enable him to pay the fine for the crime with a degree of compassion, then he deserves to be treated differently from the accused who seeks trial involving considerable time, cost and money and cost of the community (LCI 1991). Such proposals of the Law Commission were corroborated by other bodies in India, particularly Committee on Reforms of Criminal Justice System in India (Malimath 2003). Against this background the plea of "Nolo Contendere" or plea bargaining got legal recognition in India. The advantages of plea bargaining, which can be availed of, is reflected from the following statement of our former Chief Justice of India, "for instance many minor offences against property are still classified as non-bailable, whereas it is evident that classifying them as compoundable offences and relying on methods such as 'plea-bargaining' may be more effective and agreeable to address the injury caused by the same" (Balakrishnan 2012).

This paper argues that the *sui generis* mode of plea bargaining can be considered as a form of restorative justice if implemented properly. It also has the potentiality of bringing about a drastic change in the outlook of our criminal justice system by adhering to restorative justice principle.

8.2 Conceptualizing Restorative Justice

Restorative justice is a philosophy, which gives society a different outlook towards crime and the criminal justice system (Reimund 2004). There are diverse understandings about the nature of restorative justice—parameters which include providing a more humane, participatory, inclusive, need-based, and effective response to state-defined crime to proposing a new way of thinking, not merely focussing on the nature of crime and how to deal with its repercussions, but also devising means of organizing the social life more justly (Johnstone 2004). That is to say, developing means to better organize a social life to meet our individual and collective needs and therefore to decrease the prevalence of harm in our communities and societies (Quinn et al. 2006). One of the first scholars to articulate restorative justice theory was Howard Zehr, who distinguished the response to crime between retributive approach and restorative approach (Ness and Strong 1997, p. 26; Zehr 1990). According to Zehr, "restorative justice is a process to involve, to the extent possible, those who have a stake in a specific offense and to collectively identify and address harms, needs, and obligations, in order to heal and put things as right as possible" (1990, p. 130). The United Nations adopted the basic principle on restorative justice which defined the term as "a process whereby all the parties with a stake in a particular offence come together to resolve collectively how to deal with the aftermath of the offence and its implication for the future" (ECOSOC 2002; Zehr 1990, p. 40). This definition of the ECOSOC is based on the Restorative Justice Consortium proposed in the year 1996 (Quinn et al. 2006, p. 23).

According to Zehr, restorative justice can be contrasted with conventional criminal justice under the following key variables (Zehr 1985, p. 15; Umbreit 2002, pp. 31–32).

Two different views of justice	
Conventional criminal justice	Restorative justice
1. Crime defined as violation of the state	1. Crime defined as violation of one person by another
2. Focus on establishing blame, on guilt; on past (did he/she do it?)	2. Focus on problem-solving, on liabilities and obligations, on future (what should be done?)
3. Adversarial relationship and process normative	3. Dialogue and negotiation normative
4. Imposition of pain to punish and deter/prevent	4. Restitution as a means of restoring both parties' goal of reconciliation/restoration
5. Justice defined by intent and process: right rules	5. Justice defined as right relationships and outcomes
6. Interpersonal, conflictual nature of crime obscured, repressed; conflict seen as individual versus the state	6. Crime recognized as interpersonal conflict; value of conflict is recognized
7. One social injury replaced by another	7. Focus on repair of social injury
8. Community on sideline, represented abstractly by state	8. Community as facilitator in restorative process
9. Encouragement of competitive, individualistic values	9. Encouragement of mutuality
10. Action directed from state to offender-victim ignored and offender passive	10. Victim and offender engaged in the process. Victim rights/needs recognized and offender encouraged to take responsibility
11. Offender accountability defined as taking punishment	11. Offender accountability defined as understanding impact of action and helping decide how to make things right
12. Offense defined in purely legal terms, devoid of moral social, economic and political dimensions	12. Offense understood in whole context-moral, social, economic, political dimensions
13. "Debt" owed to state and society in the abstract	13. Debt/liability to victim recognized
14. Response focused on offender's past behavior	14. Response focused on harmful consequences of offender's behavior
15. Stigma of crime irreparable	15. Stigma of crime reparable through restorative action
16. No encouragement for repentance and forgiveness	16. Possibilities for repentance and forgiveness
17. Dependence upon proxy professionals	17. Direct involvement by participants

In retributive approach, crime is viewed as a violation against the state by the act of law breaking and the guilt associated with it. Justice determines blame and administers pain in contest between the offender and the state by systemic rules.

While restorative justice views crime as a violation of people and relationships, it creates obligations to make things right. It involves the victim, the offender, and the community in search of solutions which promote repair, reconciliation, and reassurance (Umbreit 2002). Taking a restorative approach sees crime as an injury rather than as lawbreaking with the purpose of justice being to heal rather than just punish (Van Ness and Nolan 1998). Accordingly, it is concerned not only with determining appropriate responses to criminal behavior, but also with reparation, that is, actions that attempt to repair the damage caused by the crime, either materially or symbolically. Therefore, restorative justice encourages the victim and the offender to play active roles in resolving conflict through discussion and negotiation. Restorative justice looks at crime and its response is based on the following principles namely (a) crime is first of all a violation of relationships among people, not just an act against the state, (b) all those affected by crime have roles and responsibilities and need to deal collectively with its impact and consequences, and (c) restoration, problem-solving, and the prevention of future harm should be emphasized (LCC 2000).

There are an array of ways and program models in which restorative justice principle are embodied and functional. Few of the most common forms of restorative justice followed in different parts of the world are (1) Victim-Offender Mediation, (2) Family Group Conferencing, and (3) Sentencing Circles, Healing Circles, and Community-Assisted Hearings.

1. ***Victim-Offender Mediation*** was pioneered in Kitchener, Ontario, in 1974. Victim–offender mediation or reconciliation brings the victim and the accused person together with a mediator to discuss the crime and to develop an agreement that resolves the incident. This process allows victims to express their feelings to the accused and to have offenders explain their actions and express remorse. The process is intended to help victims gain a sense of closure while offenders learn to take responsibility for their actions. In many Canadian jurisdictions, this method is commonly used in alternative measures programs. This approach has also been incorporated in hundreds of programs throughout the United States, the United Kingdom, and Western Europe (LCC 2000).
2. ***Family Group Conferencing*** based upon the Maori and Samoan tradition of involving extended families in resolving conflicts, is the primary way of dealing with young offenders in New Zealand. In Canada, mediators or facilitators help accused persons and their families to meet with victims, their supporters, police, and others to discuss and resolve the incident (LCC 2000).
3. ***Sentencing Circles, Healing Circles, and Community-Assisted Hearings*** are based upon Aboriginal practices of having communities, families, elders, and people in conflict discuss and resolve an issue flowing from an offence. Participants sit in a circle and may pass a "talking stick" or "talking feather" from one speaker to another. Traditional Aboriginal ceremonies such as burning sweet grass, passing a tobacco pipe, or entering sweat lodges are often part of circles (LCC 2000).

- In ***Sentencing Circles***, the victim, offender, family, and community members meet with a judge, lawyers, police, and others to recommend to the judge what type of sentence an offender should receive. The victim and the community have the opportunity to express themselves to the offender, and may also take part in developing and implementing a plan relating to the offender's sentence (LCC 2000).
- ***Healing Circles*** are ceremonies intended to bring the conflict to a close, allowing the participants to express their feelings, and indicate that the offender and victim have undergone personal healing (LCC 2000).
- ***Community-Assisted Hearings*** are sometimes also called releasing circles are a type of National Parole Board hearing that is held in an Aboriginal community rather than in a holding institution. These hearings are an opportunity for the justice system, the community, and the offender to be responsible for the successful reintegration of the offender back into the community (LCC 2000).

As there are diverse ways in which restorative justice system functions, the need arises for some basic principle to assess the programs and to ascertain whether the process is a part of restorative justice or not. Zehr and Harry Mika indicated the following criteria to determine whether the program is working towards restorative justice (Van Ness and Nolan 1998, pp. 54–55):

1. Focus on the harms of wrongdoing more than the rules that have been broken;
2. Show equal concern and commitment to victims and offenders, involving both in the process of justice;
3. Works toward the restoration of victims, empowering them and responding to their needs as they see them;
4. Support offenders while encouraging them to understand, accept, and carry out their obligations;
5. Recognize that while obligations may be difficult for offenders, they should not be intended as harms, and they must be achievable;
6. Provide opportunities for dialogue, direct or indirect, between victims and offenders as appropriate;
7. Involve and empower the affected community through the justice process, and increase its capacity to recognize and respond to community-based crimes;
8. Encourage collaboration and reintegration rather than coercion and isolation;
9. Give attention to the unintended consequences of our actions and program; and
10. Show respect to all parties including victims, offenders, and justice colleagues.

Accordingly any program which fulfills the key variables enlisted above can be qualified as restorative justice program.

8.3 Plea Bargaining in India

The concept of plea bargaining as incorporated under the Indian Law is different from other systems followed in the western world. It is in reality, a *sui generis* system of plea bargaining. In the plea bargaining system as incorporated in Chapter XXIA of Code of Criminal Procedure, (CrPC), the number of stakeholders is much higher than in other places. In the course of deliberation, the victims have been empowered to participate effectively in the process and be a party to the mutually satisfactory disposition of plea bargaining process. There are different bodies which suggested for the introduction of plea bargaining in India, which needs little reflection.

The LCI in its 142nd Report stated that it is desirable to infuse life into the reformative provisions embodied in Section 360 CrPC and the Probation of Offenders Act (1958), which according to the Law Commission has remained unutilized. The Law Commission noted that plea-bargaining ensured speedy trial with several benefits such as the end of uncertainty, saving the cost of litigation, relieving the anxiety that a prolonged trial might involve and avoiding legal expenses. The Law Commission observed that plea-bargaining is a viable alternative to be explored to deal with huge arrears of criminal cases. The same might involve pre-trail negotiations, and irrespective of whether it is "charge bargaining" or "sentence bargaining" it results in a reduced sentence and early disposal.

The LCI was of the view that plea-bargaining can be made one of the components of the administration of criminal justice, provided it is properly administered, and could be introduced in cases where the term of imprisonment is less. The Law Commission recommended that when the accused makes a plea of being guilty, the court after hearing the public prosecutor or the de facto complainant can give the accused a suspended sentence while releasing him on probation or the court may order him to pay compensation to the victim and impose a sentence taking into account the plea bargaining or convict him for an offence of lesser gravity.

The Law Commission in its 154th Report again recommended that the concept of plea-bargaining may be made applicable as an experimental measure, to offences which are liable for punishment with imprisonment of less than seven years and or fine, including the offences earmarked as compoundable offences under Section 320 of the CrPC. Plea-bargaining can also be assessed keeping in mind the nature and gravity of offences and the quantum of punishment.

The Commission further suggested that such plea-bargaining can be availed at any stage of the trial after the charge sheet is filed. It recommended that in cases where the accused is entitled to probation under the statute such benefit may be given to the accused. The Commission further recommended that if the offence for which a guilty plea is made provides for a minimum sentence, the Court may impose half of such minimum sentence. The Law Commission also recommended for incorporation of a new chapter in CrPC being Chapter XXIA on Plea Bargaining. Interestingly, the 154th Report of the LCI recommended for both categories of plea-bargaining namely sentence bargaining and charge bargaining.

But, the present legislation has only incorporated sentence bargaining. The LCI recently in another report on Fast Track Magisterial Courts for Dishonoured Cheque Cases advised that the new system of plea-bargaining incorporated in the CrPC shall be available to the under-trial prisoners and the court, the prosecuting agency and the lawyers should make them aware of the benefits of the benevolent provision incorporated in our statute (LCI 2008). It further observed that the challenges before the criminal justice system were to balance the rights of the accused while dispensing speedy and effective justice.

The Malimath Committee observed that plea-bargaining which has been implemented with a great deal of success in the USA had to be considered for India. According to the Committee, the United States experiment shows that plea-bargaining helps to dispose of accumulated cases and expedites delivery of criminal justice (Malimath 2003). The Committee argued that as a provision for compounding of offences is already in existence in the old statute CrPC, there is no reason for plea-bargaining not to be introduced in the criminal justice system.

One of the recommendations of the N. R. Madhava Menon Committee was for the enactment of the Correctional Offences Code (Menon 2007). It suggested that the second group of offences which are more serious than the social welfare offences and which may need police intervention may be brought under legislation to be called Correctional Offences Code (COC). This would include offences punishable up to three years of imprisonment and/or fine. It further suggested that all such cases may be open to settlement through Lok Adalats, plea-bargaining and other alternative methods avoiding trials.

8.4 Plea Bargaining and Its Constitutionality

The Supreme Court of India had examined the concept of plea-bargaining and its constitutionality in the case of *Murlidhar Meghraj Loya* v. *State of Maharastra* (1976) and *Kasambhai* v. *State of Gujarat* (1980), much before the enactment of Criminal Law Amendment Act, 2005, which incorporated the provisions relating to plea-bargaining. In both the cases, the Court did not approve of the procedure of plea-bargaining on the basis of informal inducement. In *Kasambhai's case* (1980) the Court squarely observed that conviction based on plea of guilty entered by the accused as a result of plea-bargaining could not be sustained and that it was opposed to public policy to convict the accused by inducing him to confess to a plea of guilty on allurement being held out to him that if he enters a plea of guilt he will be let off lightly.

The Supreme Court also has time and again blasted the concept of plea-bargaining saying that negotiation in criminal cases is not permissible. A decade back in *State of Uttar Pradesh* v. *Chandrika* (2000), the Apex Court held that it is settled law that the Court cannot dispose of the criminal cases on the basis of plea-bargaining. The Court has to decide it on merits. If the accused confesses his guilt, the appropriate sentence must be implemented. The Court further held in the same case that, mere acceptance or admission of guilt should not be a ground for reduction of sentence. Nor can the accused bargain with the Court on the ground that as he is pleading guilty, the sentence to be reduced. However, all these judgments were passed when there was no legislative mechanism or procedure in place to check its misuse. Similar kind of constitutional issues were raised in the United States regarding the practice of plea bargaining thereby making it essential to ascertain the manner in which the courts in other jurisdictions have reacted to the challenge of the constitutionality of plea-bargaining.

In United States of America, which had taken the lead in plea-bargaining, the judiciary did not address the constitutionality of plea-bargaining until after its establishment as a part of the criminal justice system (Guidorizzi 1998). Initially, the Court questioned the validity of the plea- bargaining process as burdening the defendant's right to a jury trial. In *United States* v. *Jackson* (1968), the Court invalidated a statute that allowed the imposition of the death penalty only after a jury trial. However, the situation changed soon. Just two years later, the Court limited the holding of *Jackson* in *Brady* v. *United States* (1970). In *Brady*, the Court pointed out the positive aspects of plea-bargaining, emphasizing that the practice benefits both sides in the adversary system. Additionally, the Court justified the practice of plea-bargaining by noting that a guilty plea suggests some hope for success in rehabilitation. Justice White, who delivered the opinion of the court, observed, "the issue we deal with is inherent in the criminal law and its administration because guilty pleas are not constitutionally forbidden, because the criminal law characteristically extends to judge or jury a range of choices in setting the sentence, in individual cases, and because both the State and defendant often find it advantageous to preclude the possibility of the maximum penalty authorized by the law" (Brady, para. 752). The Supreme Court also found that the award of lesser punishment pursuant to plea-bargain is not invalid. In *North Carolina* v. *Alford* (1970), the Court abandoned the rehabilitation rationale for plea-bargaining upholding a guilty plea entered to avoid a possible death sentence despite the fact that the defendant had clearly asserted his innocence both before and after the plea. In upholding the guilty plea, the court in *North Carolina* v. *Alford* (1970) emphasized upon the fact that the defendant had made an intelligent and voluntary choice and that there was strong evidence of guilt in the record.

In the following year, the validity of plea-bargaining was also upheld by the U.S. Supreme Court in *Santobello* v. *New York* (1971). Chief Justice Burger, who delivered the opinion of the Court, observed that "disposition of charges after plea discussions is not only an essential part of the process but a highly desirable part for many reasons. It leads to prompt and largely final disposition of most criminal cases; it avoids much of the corrosive impact of enforced idleness during pre-trail confinement for those who are denied release pending trail; it protects the public from those accused persons who are continue criminal conduct even while on pre-trail release; and by shortening the time between charge and disposition, it enhances whatever may be the rehabilitative prospects of the guilty when they are ultimately imprisoned" (para. 260).

Repelling another attack on the constitutionality of plea-bargaining, the U.S. Supreme Court addressed a claim of prosecutorial vindictiveness in *Bordenkircher* v. *Hayes* (1978) in which the prosecutor threatened the accused to re-indict on more serious charges if he did not accept the plea offer. The Court rejected a due process violation claim and found a presumption of equal bargaining power between the prosecutors and the defendants (para. 358). The Court refined this reasoning later in *United States* v. *Goodwin* (1982). In this case, the defendant was indicted on additional charges after plea negotiations had broken down and he requested a jury trial. The Court held that a prosecutor may file additional charges if an initial expectation that a defendant would plead guilty to lesser charges proved unfounded. The Court refused to adopt a presumption of vindictiveness, thereby reaffirming the legitimacy of the plea-bargaining process.

In a series of subsequent decisions, such as *Hutto* v. *Ross* (1976), *Chaffin* v. *Stynchocombe* (1973), *Blackledge* v. *Allison* (1997), *Weatherford* v. *Bursey* (1977) and *Newton* v. *Rumery* (1987), the United States Supreme Court has approved the constitutionality of plea-bargaining. The challenge to constitutionality has gone through similar kind of phase in the United States, from the unconstitutional to constitutional and beyond. In India also, as the legislation with certain safeguards are in place, most importantly provisions which ensure the effective participation of victim in the process of mutually satisfactory disposition, we can now assume that the judiciary will no longer consider plea-bargaining as unconstitutional within the Indian Criminal Justice System (Balakrishnan 2009).

8.5 Laws Relating to Plea Bargaining in India

A new Chapter XXIA on "Plea Bargaining" has been introduced in the CrPC by the Criminal Law (Amendment) Act (2005). The incorporation of plea-bargaining principle has definitely given a new dimension to Indian Criminal Justice System and provided a scope for making restorative justice principle implicit in our administration of justice. Section 20 of the relatively recently enacted the Gram Nyayalayas Act, 2008 also empower the tribunal to accept applications for plea-bargaining. It provides that a person accused of an offence may file an application for plea-bargaining in the Gram Nyayalaya in which such offence is pending trial, and the Gram Nyayalaya shall dispose of the case in accordance with the provisions of Chapter XXIA of the CrPC.

The Criminal Law Amendment Act, 2005, added 12 Sections in Chapter XXI in respect of plea-bargaining. Section 265A CrPC incorporated the principles relating to applicability of the Act in respect of a particular class of offences as well as the stages of the proceeding. The section lays down the jurisdiction, providing that the chapter shall apply to cases where Charge Sheet has been submitted by the police under Section 173 CrPC or court has taken cognizance on complaint and process has been issued under Section 204 CrPC. It further provides that application can only be made in respect of offences other than those punishable with death, life imprisonment, or imprisonment for more than 7 years. The process shall also be inapplicable in respect of socioeconomic offences and offences against women and children below 14 years. Section 265B CrPC provides the procedure for filling application for plea-bargaining. It provides that a brief description of the case shall be stated along with accompanied affidavit where applicant should state that they are making application for plea bargaining voluntarily. Clause (3) obliges the court to issue a notice after receiving the application while clause (4) mandates the court to hear accused in-camera to ascertain voluntariness of application. Once the court is satisfied with the voluntariness of the application, the court can ask the stakeholders for settlement by coming to a mutually satisfactory disposition taking into account, among others, the need of the victim to get compensation. Section 265C CrPC provides guidelines for achieving mutually satisfactory disposition. It mandates for involvement of all stakeholders, for example in a case initiated on police report, the public prosecutor, investigating officer, victim and the accused are to reach at a mutually satisfactory disposition and in a case initiated on complaint, all the aforesaid stakeholders excluding the police and the prosecutor shall decide on a mutually satisfactory disposition. It is important to remember here that in the process of plea-bargaining in other jurisdictions the victim does not play any role while in our system of plea-bargaining the victims' aspiration has to be taken in account to arrive at a mutually satisfactory disposition.

Once the mutually satisfactory disposition is worked out, the court has to prepare a report which shall be signed by all the parties participating in the proceeding and if it is not worked out then the court shall proceed to hear the matter from the pre-application stage as enumerated in Section 265D CrPC. Section 265E CrPC provides the guidelines for disposal of cases where the mutually satisfactory disposition is worked out. Section 265F CrPC obliges the court to pronounce the judgment in open court while 265G CrPC declares that all such judgment shall be binding, and no appeal shall lie against such judgment. However, it further clarifies that such limitation on appeal shall not bar judicial review under the constitutional provisions. Impliedly writ petition may be filed to the High Court if the concerned parties feel that their constitutional rights are violated. Section 265H CrPC vests the court with all power which it exercises in a normal court proceeding while Section 265I CrPC provides that the imprisonment already undergone by the accused shall be set off. Section 265 K CrPC provides protection to the accused by making it clear that the statement of the accused cannot be used for any other purpose other than plea-bargaining under Chapter XXI CrPC. Section 265L CrPC has made the process of plea-bargaining inapplicable to juveniles or children covered under the Juvenile Justice Act.

While on the one hand, CrPC has laid down an elaborate procedure for plea-bargaining, on the other hand it has restricted its applicability in respect of those offences for which punishment of 7 years and above has been provided and also for those offences which are committed against a woman or a child below the age of 14 years. The division bench of the Gujarat High Court in *State of Gujarat* v. *Natwar Harchanji Thakor*m (2005) observed in respect of requirement for reform in administration of criminal justice that the very object of law is to provide easy, cheap, and expeditious justice by resolution of disputes, including the trial of criminal cases and considering the present realistic profile of the pendency and delay in disposal in the administration of law and justice, fundamental reforms are inevitable. Nothing should be static. So it can be said that plea-bargaining is a redressal measure which shall add a new dimension in the realm of judicial reforms.

Plea-bargaining as introduced in India shows significant deviation from the established practices of plea-bargaining adopted the world over. It is important to note of all those shifts which make our plea-bargaining a *sui generis* system and to critically evaluate them. However, this paper does not aim to evaluate critically such deviation, as the focus is on victim participation and restorative justice, nevertheless, it is important to have a glance on such deviations. Some of the deviations from established plea bargaining practices are: (a) Indian plea bargaining does not allow charge bargaining; (b) it has limited applicability to the cases where punishment is up to 7 years; (c) it has also excluded offences against women, children and socioeconomic offences; (d) a large number of stakeholders are made party to the process which may create difficulty in arriving at mutually satisfactory disposition; (e) the legislation is silent about the outcome when one of the stakeholders does not agree to the settlement; and (f) on the occasion of not arriving at mutually satisfactory disposition who will conduct the trial, whether same judge will adjudicate or the case will be referred to another judge has not been clarified.

8.6 Plea Bargaining in India and Restorative Justice

The *sui generis* system of plea-bargaining as incorporated within CrPC in India is an attempt to provide a participatory mode of dispute resolution in criminal cases. It is basically a procedure, incorporated in Chapter XXIA of the CrPC for a mutually satisfactory disposition of criminal cases. The issue which may come up is, whether we can consider such dispute resolution mechanism as a component of restorative justice processes. In plea-bargaining proceedings, the investigating officer, the public prosecutor, the victim of a crime, the complainant and the person accused of an offence join hands to settle voluntarily a pending criminal case to achieve mutual satisfaction. The process is completely voluntary. If the plea bargain succeeds, the criminal case is disposed of in terms of the agreed settlement. If the plea bargain does not succeed, the criminal case proceeds from the stage when the plea bargain application was filed. There are several benefits to plea-bargaining. The process is completely voluntary, the applicant is likely to get a much-reduced punishment, and there will be the quick disposal of the pending criminal case. It satisfies the needs of the victims as victims play an important role, unlike our traditional criminal justice system. If settlement arises the plea bargain will results in an amicable and mutually satisfactory disposition of the pending criminal case. If an admonition or a supervisory order is passed under the Probation of Offenders Act (1958), then Section 12 of the said Act provides that it shall not cast any stigma on the offender. This again helps the accused and saves him from stigma. The application for a plea bargain can be filed: (a) by any adult accused of an offence that is punishable with imprisonment of less than 7 years, (b) the applicant should not have been earlier convicted of a similar offence, (c) the offence shall not be against women, children, or be a socioeconomic offence.

The court which receives the plea bargain application will consider the application and issue notice to the investigating officer of the case, the public prosecutor, the victim of the offence (if any) and the complainant. Whenever necessary, if it is found that the applicant/accused is not represented by a lawyer, he will be provided the services of a free legal aid lawyer. Preferably, before meeting with the judge, all the parties concerned in the plea bargain should try to arrive at a settlement in consultation with the public prosecutor. If it is not possible to reach a settlement in advance, the judge will assist the parties in arriving at an amicable settlement. If a plea bargain is arrived at the settlement the judge will do the following to ensure voluntariness and informed decisions of the parties: (a) the judge will have an in-camera or private discussion with the applicant in the presence of his lawyer to determine whether the plea bargain is voluntary; (b) to ensure whether the plea bargain is acceptable to the applicant; and (c) to assess whether the applicant has understood the meaning and effect of the plea bargain. Judge will also see whether the needs of the victims are taken care of and did the victim give consent to such agreement. If the judge is satisfied that the plea bargain meets all the legal requirements, he will accept it and pass an order disposing of the case in terms of the settlement. All the parties to the plea bargain are required to sign the order recording the settlement. Most importantly, the entire plea bargain proceedings are absolutely confidential. If the plea bargain fails, then no party can use anything said in the plea bargain proceedings in the pending criminal case. Even the trial judge will not ask any question during the trial about the plea bargain proceedings.

According to the ECOSOC definition "restorative justice is a process whereby all the parties with a stake in a particular offence come together to resolve the issue of dealing with the aftermath of the offence and its implication for the future" (ECOSOC 2002). Now if we analyze the process of plea-bargaining in India, the victim plays an important role in the process. The western concept of plea-bargaining distances the victim away from the process. In the USA, the bargaining takes place normally between the prosecutors and the accused. The *sui generis* concept of plea-bargaining in India is a mixture of plea-bargaining and victim-offender mediation as followed in the USA. This mixture of two processes in plea-bargaining without a doubt makes the system compatible with the restorative justice model. The stakeholders come to a "mutually satisfactory disposition" by discussion. This discussion should be victim-centric, acknowledging the harm suffered by the victim, and the ways by which it can be rectified. The needs of the victims have to be taken into account while coming to a "mutually satisfactory disposition". The involvement of such a large number of stakeholders in the process gives a circumstantial guarantee of fulfillment of the needs of all stakeholders as well as the society at large. While one may argue that plea-bargaining as prevalent in the developed world may not take into account the aspiration of the victims and hence is not a restorative justice, but that is not the case of Indian plea-bargaining. Moreover, pleading guilty and negotiating with the victim and others helps the accused to realize the suffering of the victim which in turn helps him to change his behavior in future. All these characteristics are the elements of restorative justice. Accordingly, there is no iota of doubt that the process of plea-bargaining in India is one of the restorative processes and will help in achieving restorative justice.

8.7 Conclusion

The restorative justice movement is having a great impact upon the criminal justice system, policy makers and practitioners throughout the world. The restorative justice movement holds a great deal of promise for the future of the criminal justice system. By drawing upon the several traditional values of the past, from many different cultures, restorative justice system has attempted to build a far more accountable, understandable and healing system of law and justice that can lead to a greater sense of community through the active involvement of victims and citizens in restorative justice initiatives. In restorative justice process, the focus of criminal justice shifts from the accused to the victim. Restorative justice provides a large number of advantages in comparison to the adjudicatory processes, such as speedy disposal, cost effectiveness, maintenance of good relationship and chances of continuity of relationship, less formality, more compliance etc. In different parts of the world, people use restorative justice within the criminal justice system in different ways, such as victim–offender mediation, out of court settlement, etc. Benefits obtained by such processes in other jurisdictions have compelled our legislature to use it within the Indian Criminal Justice System. The result of such incorporation within the criminal justice system is the emergence of "Plea-Bargaining" within the criminal procedure.

The concept of plea-bargaining was, in reality, the expansion of the use of restorative justice within criminal justice administration. It is being used to further justice. Reduction of the backlog of cases was not the sole reason for its extensive use. The process of plea-bargaining can be deemed to be considered as one of the restorative justice processes. As the concept of plea-bargaining is relatively new in India, there is a need to popularize it among the functionaries. The hostile attitude of lawyers is one of the biggest hurdles in effective implementation of plea-bargaining in India. So, the need arises, for effective and proper implementation of *sui generis* concept of plea-bargaining in India. In such circumstances, the benefit of such process can be availed by a large number of people in the country.

References

Balakrishnan, K. G. (2012, October 15). Criminal justice system—Growing responsibility in light of contemporary challenges. Retrieved from http://cbi.gov.in/speech/dpkohli_cji_200904202.pdf
Basic principles on the use of restorative justice programmes in criminal matters, 2002/12, (2002).
Blackledge v. allison, 431 US 63 (1997).
Bordenkircher v. hayes, 434 US 357 (1978).
Brady v. United States, 397 U.S. 742 (1970).
Chaffin v. stynchocombe, 412 US 17 (1973).
Code of criminal procedure, 1973 (Act 2 of 1974).
Criminal Law (Amendment) Act, 2005 (India).
Guidorizzi, D. D. (1998). Should we really ban plea bargaining: The core concerns of plea bargaining critics. *Emory Lj, 47,* 753–1475.
Hutto v. ross, 50L.ed.2d. 876 (1976).
Johnstone, G. (2004). *How, and in what terms should restorative justice be conceived? Critical Issues in Restorative Justice* (pp. 5–15). Cullompton, UK: Willan Publishing.
Kasambhai v. State of Gujarat AIR 1980 SC 854.
Law Commission of Canada (LCC). (2000). *Restorative justice.* Canada: Consultative paper.
Law Commission of India. (2008). Fast track magisterial courts for dishonoured cheque cases. (No. 213).
Malimath, J. V. S. (2003). *Committee on reforms of criminal justice system.* New Delhi: Ministry of Home Affairs, Government of India.
Menon, N. R. M. (2007). *Draft national policy on criminal justice.*
Murlidhar Meghraj Loya v. State of Maharastra, AIR 1976 SC 1929.
Newton v. Rumery, 480 US 386 (1987).
North carolina v. alford, 400 U.S. 25 (1970).
Probation of Offenders Act, 1958.
Quinn, T., Sullivan, D., & Tifft, L. (2006). *Handbook of restorative justice.*
Reimund, M. E. (2004). Is restorative justice on a collision course with the constitution. *Appalachian JL, 3,* 1.
Santobello v. New York, 404 U.S. 257 (1971).
State of Gujarat v. Natwar Harchanji Thakorm, 2005 Cr. L.J. 2957.
State of Uttar Pradesh v. Chandrika, 2000 Cr.L.J. 384.
The Law Commission of India. (1991). Report on *concessional treatment for offenders who on their own initiative choose to plead guilty without any bargaining.* (Commission Report No. 142).
The Law Commission of India. (1996). *The code of criminal procedure, 1973.* (No. 154).
Umbreit, M. (1998). Restorative justice through victim-offender mediation: A multi-site assessment. *Western Criminology Review, 1*(1), 1–29.
Umbreit, M. S. (2002). *The handbook of victim offender mediation: An essential guide to practice and research.* John Wiley & Sons.
United Nation ECOSOC Experts Committee adopts Restorative Justice basic principle in 2002, referred in Id p. 40.
United States v. Jackson, 390 U.S. 570 (1968).
United states v. Goodwin 457 U.S. 368 (1982).
Van Ness, D. W., & Nolan, P. (1998). Legislating for restorative justice. *Regent UL Review, 10,* 53.
Van Ness, D., & Strong, K. (1997). *Restoring justice.* Cincinnati, USA: Anderson Publishing Co.
Weatherford v. bursey, 429 US 545 (1977), 429 545 (USA 1977).
Zehr, H. (1985). *New perspective on crime and justice.* Office of Criminal Justice: MCC U.S.
Zehr, H. (1990). *Changing lenses: A new focus for crime and justice.*
Zehr, H. (2002). *Little book of restorative justice.*
Zehr, H., & Mika, H. (1998). Fundamental concepts of restorative justice. *Contemporary Just Review 1, 47–54–55.*

Part IV
Restorative Justice Practices in India: Restorative Justice and Prisoners

Chapter 9
An Insight into the Importance of Restorative Justice and the Rights of Offenders: An Analysis of Issues of Convergence and Divergence

V. Ramya Krishnan

9.1 Introduction

In the criminal justice system the importance of restorative justice has long been perceived as an approach which promotes an innovative approach with regards to repairing the damage caused by a crime wherein the focus is not solely on the punishment of the offender but also on other issues. Restorative justice has been adopted as an important part of the criminal justice system by a number of countries across the world. Research by Van Ness (2005) reveals that one hundred countries around the world are in favor of adopting a restorative justice system. Restorative justice is a boon as it is often founded at the grass root level and works its way up from the bottom, which is a very healthy alternative to the strong and rigid criminal justice systems found across the world.

This is very important because in today's world there is a perception that the current judicial system is focused on issues of bringing justice to the victim while there is rarely an account of the needs of the offender. The researcher feels that the growth of restorative justice means the adoption of a different approach to criminal justice that not only brings satisfaction to the victim but also takes a hint at rehabilitation of the offender. This type of approach is important in terms of healing the fractures which may have resulted in the community by a simple punishment of offenders in the form of a prison terms without any measures to rehabilitate them.

V. Ramya Krishnan (✉)
KIIT School of Law, Bhubaneshwar, India
e-mail: ramyakrishnan1998@yahoo.co.in

R. Thilagaraj and J. Liu (eds.), *Restorative Justice in India*,
DOI 10.1007/978-3-319-47659-9_9

9.2 Models and Definition of Restorative Justice

Models based on restorative justice are generally taken into consideration on the basis of the process involved or on the basis of the results obtained (Bazemore and Elis 2007; Walgrave 2007; Zernova and Wright 2007). Experts consider that the combined deliberation of the stakeholders is essential to accomplish restoration and to establish restorative justice based upon the process (McCold 2000). "Restorative justice is a process whereby parties with a stake in a specific offence collectively resolve how to deal with the aftermath of the offence and its implications for the future" (Marshall 1999).

Nevertheless, definitions based on the process have been criticized for not taking into account any of the possible results, mainly due to the lack of assurance that the stakeholder's decision on the quantity of amends is requisite or will complete the restoration (Dignan 2005). In contrast, restorative justice based on the results is likely to shift focus and emphasize the completing of restoration, (i.e.,), the particular collection of burdens and benefits that may evolve from the process of restorative decision making (Zernova and Wright 2007). When both these models are taken into consideration, a more complete methodology is supported whereby the "essence of restorative justice… is the adoption of any form [of justice] which reflects restorative values and which aims to achieve restorative processes, outcomes, and objectives" (Morris 2002). Yet this definition fails to give a broad perspective about the meaning of justice or restoration.

It is important to understand what is being restored and by whom is it restored. How can this process be justified and altered? In order to find answers to these questions, it is necessary to take into account the association between the principles involved in restorative justice and its values. Restorative justice is generally considered to be a popular and practical concept but not a hypothetical one (Marshall 2007; Ashworth 2002; Maxwell and Liu 2007). The principles of restorative justice and its associated values offer guidance apart from forming the basis of practice. The three major principles that emphasize and support the initiatives of restorative justice (Zehr and Mika 1998) are as follows:

1. A crime infringes the people involved as well as their relationships with one another. This violation is harmful to every main stakeholder involved which includes the victims, the criminal, and society. Therefore, there must be a way to implement a restorative process to cater to their requirements.
2. Criminal conduct results in both a compulsion and a responsibility for the person who commits the crime. The perpetrator is supposed to be responsible for the criminal act, and hence must try to mend its harmful consequences. Criminals may have to be forced to complete their responsibilities. The main idea behind this is to accomplish some amount of restoration rather than punishment only. Further, the community has an active role in offering aid for both the offender and the victim in facing the consequences of the criminal act.

3. The main intention of this concept is to enable community healing by mending the effects of the criminal act, namely the damages to the relationships between the offenders, the victims and the community that unavoidably arise by criminal acts.

Even though realization of this concept can be witnessed from the abundance of restoration activities across the world (Bazemore at al. 2006; Miers 2001; Van Ness 2005), the comparatively quick implementation and enhancement of such programs are debated. A number of reviewers have criticized and issued warnings in opposition to the extensive adoption of this concept with lack of sufficient substantiation and have questioned the capability of the restoration experts in terms of defending the rights of the stakeholders in the crime (Ashworth 2002; Radzik 2007; Roche 2003; Ward and Langlands 2008; Warner 1994). Further, there exist a few criticisms that the principles and policies of this concept have been motivated by over enthusiasm and oratory rather than by proof and logical reasoning. It has been called the "nirvana story of restorative justice" (Daly 2006).

9.3 The Importance of Human Rights

Numerous substantiations have been projected for the implications of human rights. These vary from a logical and realistic progression that may result in a compromise based on a cluster of privileges and responsibilities, to some specific attributes of humans which include sentience, consistency, fundamental requirements and interests (e.g., Nickel 2007; Orend 2002). In our perspective, the most valid rationalizations are those which originate from requirements/personhood concepts. This is due to the fact that only they seem to expand the aspects related to human rights to all the people living in a community and those living in other countries.

Human rights can be based upon three fundamental attributes (Griffin 2008):

1. Autonomy—the capacity to take major decisions on our own.
2. Possessing a set of resources and abilities, such as education and health
3. Liberty—in which others do not influence the implementation of ideas.

Human rights operate to guard the fundamental attributes for people to function as agents. These agents have the capacity to develop their own way of realizing the attributes (Gewirth 1981, 1996). Every individual has a right to anything that is essential in attaining the idea behind their intentions. In the absence of such assurances, they may not be able to perform efficiently in order to achieve their goals (Gewirth). Human rights are substantiated by their capability to assure that their intrinsic requirements are met. An intrinsic need is defined as "… those items or conditions it is necessary for a person to have if she is to avoid being harmed" (Miller 2007).

Considering the ideologies of the experts, it is clear that any right that is valid for any individual extends to other individuals also. It is also established that the responsibilities and rights of every individual must be respected and must be taken into consideration for any social or political decisions (Ward and Birgden 2007).

9.4 Promotion of a Flexible and Informal Restorative System

Informality and flexibility have been identified as the most important aspects of restorative justice. In order make the current criminal system more clear and beneficial a restorative system offers a viable alternative. As indicated by Radzik (2007) promoting a paradigm of restorative justice will help build up an ethical advantage over the conventional criminal justice system. She identifies that

> In recognizing that wrongdoers have moral obligations, we recognize their status as agents and not 'things', as subjects and not objects. This is crucial to treating them with the respect that all humans deserve (p. 192).

Thus, the principle of human rights and bringing into focus the rights of the offender is promoted in this manner. According to Radzik (2007), when restorative justice is promoted there will definitely be efforts which help uphold the fundamental human rights of the offenders. This will help promote the dignity and respect of the offenders which is the primary aim of restorative justice.

Research by Braithwaite (1999) further supports the views that only when the offender is given an opportunity to do some good in order to atone for the wrong can there be restoration of dignity of both the offender and the victim. The author feels that this is what will lead to rehabilitation and restorative justice. This research also highlights the issue that when measures are taken to promote restorative justice it is possible to promote personal freedom as well as facilitate social recognition for the offenders.

The adoption of restorative justice will thus help to promote freedom of choice and autonomy as well as personal agency. For the proceedings to be truly autonomous as well as freedom oriented the programs should be made voluntary for the offenders, otherwise it will have no effect. This will help the offenders understand their error of their ways and result in measures which promote discussion of criminal actions and their consequences.

One divergence issue which needs to be highlighted is that while these measures may promote the respectful treatment of offenders there is a potential for agency to be undermined unless attention is paid to ways in which offenders may be coerced to participation in the process of restorative justice. There can be competing interests among the victim, the offender and the community. This divergence issue has not been addressed very clearly in the past and there is a need to analyze it more clearly. We need to acknowledge the fact that when considering the interests of different stakeholders it may not be possible to reach a solution which satisfies all parties involved. The rights of the offender are often discarded and rarely treated on a par with the rights of the community or the victim.

We should also highlight that it is important not to ignore the potential of human rights of offenders during the practice of restorative justice, due to the conflicting situations of the different parties are involved. This consideration is very important, especially since some authors like Braithwaite (1999) and Walgrave (2007) are not against coercion. There may be a number of reasons why offenders are forced to participate in the process of restorative justice, including issues of fear, discrimination, and further penalty (Ashworth 2002; Karp et al. 2004). These reasons are easy to understand in cases where a community values restorative justice very highly. Braithwaite (2005), for example, states that "crime should always be confronted with a presumption for mercy that is conditional upon participation in a truth-seeking process that identifies paths to prevention" (p. 283). This means that unless the offender takes part in the program of truth seeking he will be definitely doomed. This comment has not taken into account the different reasons why an offender chooses not to participate in this program which may include lack of trust as a result of a previous experience or issues related to mental health.

The issue of offender competence should be highlighted. As observed by Ward and Birgden (2007):

> In order to be able to form a conception of a worthwhile life and to implement it in the real world, offenders require a minimum level of freedom and well-being goods, plus an environment that is supportive of their aspirations and contains the resources necessary for them to achieve their goals (e.g., training opportunities, supportive networks etc.).

Those who have a history of deprivation and abuse may lack the ability to function in society. In these cases, a rigid restorative justice system may not be a fruitful approach. If a more flexible system were adopted compared to a more formal system, there is a better chance for rehabilitation given that informed consent is obtained from the victims.

9.5 Participation of the Victim in the Process of Justice

Allowing participation of the victim is not a very ideal solution because this will definitely affect the rights of the offender in the form of personal security and social recognition. As indicated by Ashworth (2002), "Impartiality is a key value in justice processes, and yet in restorative justice theory it stands in tension with other values such as participation, involvement, and empowerment" (p. 584). This is valuable because it helps bring about a sense of proportionality involving the enactment of sentences which directly relate to the crime. Ideally, offenders should receive their just deserts; offenders will not be subject to overly harsh or lenient punishments, and because the type of crime committed to a large extent determines what level of punishment is meted out, offenders who commit the same crime will be subject to similar sanctions. This major point of tension between human rights, values and restorative justice occurs because of the wish to respect the autonomy of victims and the good of the community by holding the offender to account, while at the same time overriding the offender's autonomy or freedom and downplaying the importance of equality of treatment.

According to Wright, the lack of proportionality within restorative justice settings should not be viewed as problematic because

> …while courts are aiming at consistency of punishment, where inequalities may indeed cause resentment… conferences aim at reparation, tangible or symbolic, which is rightly determined by the needs and wishes of the victim and the capabilities of the individual offender.

It is observed here is that restoration needs to reflect a system of belief which helps to promote both retribution and restoration. Major emphasis is on holding the offender to account in accordance with the victim's wishes, rather than ensuring that the offender's fundamental rights to equality of treatment in legal proceedings and to social recognition are also met. There is also a suggestion that community balance or social harmony is a superordinate value that trumps the freedom and other core human rights of offenders.

Victim participation therefore needs a practice of restoration which involves promotion of measures which will result in stakeholder views being addressed. Therefore emphasis on the adoption a human rights perspective is needed when working with offenders to ensure that they are treated as fellow human beings rather than as moral strangers.

9.6 Conclusion

The degree of conflict between human rights and the concept of restorative justice needs to be minimized. This chapter has attempted to show that in order to integrate these into the justice system we need to focus on improving measures that will facilitate a more flexible system, wherein the involvement of the victim is optional. The process of restorative justice should ensure that no single aspect is favored whose effect is to dismiss or downplay issues of human rights of the offenders.

References

Ashworth, A. (2002). Responsibilities, rights and restorative justice. *The British Journal of Criminology, 42,* 578–595.

Bazemore, G., & Elis, L. (2007). Evaluation of restorative justice. In G. Johnstone & D. W. Van Ness (Eds.), *Handbook of restorative justice* (pp. 397–425). Cullompton, UK: Willan Publishing.

Bazemore, G., O'Brien, S., & Carey, M. (2006). The synergy and substance of organizational and community change in the response to crime and conflict: The emergence and potential of restorative justice. *Public Organization Review: A Global Journal, 5.*

Braithwaite, J. (1999). Restorative justice: Assessing optimistic and pessimistic accounts. *Crime and Justice, 25,* 1–127.

Braithwaite, J. (2005). For public social science. *British Journal of Sociology,* 56.

Daly, K. (2006). The limits of restorative justice. In D. Sullivan & L. Tifft (Eds.), *Handbook of restorative justice: A global perspective* (pp. 134–145). London: Routledge.

Dignan, J. (2005). *Understanding victims and restorative justice.* Maidenhead, UK: Open University Press.

Gewirth, A. (1981). *Reason and morality*. Chicago, USA: The University of Chicago Press.

Gewirth, A. (1996). *The community of rights*. Chicago, USA: The University of Chicago Press.

Griffin, J. (2008). *On human rights*. Oxford, UK: Oxford University Press.

Karp, D. R,. Sweet, M., Kirshenbaum, A., and Bazemore, G. (2004). Reluctant participants in Restorative Justice? Youthful Offenders and their parents. *Contemporary justice review, 7*(2), 199–216.

Marshall, C. D. (2007). Reflections on the spirit of justice. In G. Maxwell & J. H. Liu (Eds.), *Restorative justice and practices in New Zealand: Towards a restorative society* (pp. 311–319). Wellington: Institute of Policy Studies.

Marshall, T. (1999). *Restorative justice: An overview*. London: Home Office Research Development and Statistics Directorate.

Maxwell, G., & Liu, J. H. (2007). Can a restorative approach heal and restore? In G. Maxwell & J. H. Liu (Eds.), *Restorative justice and practices in New Zealand: Towards a restorative society* (pp. 305–309). Wellington: Institute of Policy Studies.

McCold, P. (2000). Towards a holistic vision of restorative juvenile justice: A reply to the maximalist model. *Contemporary Justice Review, 3,* 357–414.

Miers, D. (2001). *An international review of restorative justice*. London: Home Office Research Development and Statistics Directorate.

Miller, D. (2007). *National responsibility and global justice*. Oxford, UK: Oxford University Press.

Morris, A. (2002). Critiquing the critics: A brief response to critics of restorative justice. *British Journal of Criminology, 42,* 596–615.

Nickel, J. W. (2007). *Making sense of human rights* (2nd ed.). Oxford, UK: Blackwell Publishing.

Orend, B. (2002). *Human rights: Concept and context*. Ontario, Canada: Broadview Press.

Radzik, L. (2007). Offenders, the making of amends and the state. In G. Johnstone & D. W. Van Ness (Eds.), *Handbook of restorative justice* (pp. 192–207). Cullompton, UK: Willan Publishing.

Roche, D. (2003). *Accountability in restorative justice*. Oxford: Oxford University Press.

Van Ness, D. W. (2007) (Ed.). *Handbook of restorative justice* (pp. 91–108). Cullompton, UK: Willan Publishing.

Van Ness, D. W. (Ed.). Handbook of restorative justice (pp. 559–579). Cullompton, UK: Willan Publishing.

Van Ness, D. W. (2005). An overview of restorative justice around the world. Eleventh United Nations Congress on Crime Prevention and Criminal Justice. Retrieved August 21, 2007, from http://www.icclr.law

Walgrave, L. (2007). *Integrating criminal justice and restorative justice*. G. Johnstone and D.

Ward, T., & Birgden, A. (2007). Human rights and correctional clinical practice. *Aggression and Violent Behavior, 12,* 628–643.

Ward, T., & Langlands, R. L. (2008). Restorative justice and the human rights of offenders: Convergences and divergences. *Aggression and Violent Behavior, 13,* 355–372.

Warner, K. (1994). Family group conferences and the rights of the offender. In G. Alder & J. Wundersitz (Eds.), *Family conferencing and juvenile justice: The way forward or misplaced optimism?* (pp. 141–152). Canberra: Australian Institute of Criminology.

Zehr, H., & Mika, H. (1998). Fundamental concepts of restorative justice. *Contemporary Justice Review, 1,* 47–55.

Zernova, M., & Wright, M. (2007). *Alternative visions of restorative justice.*

Daly, K. (2006). The limits of restorative justice. In D. Sullivan & L. Tifft (Eds.), *Handbook of restorative justice: A global perspective* (pp. 134–145). London: Routledge.
Dignan, J. (2005). *Understanding victims and restorative justice*. Maidenhead, UK: Open University Press.
Gewirth, A. (1981). *Reason and morality*. Chicago, USA: The University of Chicago Press.
Gewirth, A. (1996). *The community of rights*. Chicago, USA: The University of Chicago Press.
Griffin, J. (2008). *On human rights*. Oxford: Oxford University Press.
[illegible]

Chapter 10
Justice and Reconciliation in the Aftermath of Mass Atrocities and Collective Violence: The Restorative Justice Lens

Kaushikee

10.1 The Linkage Between Conflict, Violence and Justice

Conflict takes place in relationships over real or perceived incompatible goals or needs. The relationship could be between two or more groups or individuals. In such a situation, conflicts could be expressed either positively or negatively. When expressed constructively, it could direct attention to social injustices, promote change in organizations, structures and systems and lead to creative problem-solving. However, when conflict is expressed destructively, it could lead to violence resulting in loss of life, injury to human beings, destruction of the social fabric, environment and property, and, disruption of social interactions, networks and structures. Thus conflict can fracture relationships and violent conflict, and can do so in a brutal manner, leaving behind traumatized victims with a sense of injustice.

Human beings have an inbuilt desire for justice in the face of harms or injustices done as a result of crime or violent conflict. Justice seeks to *right* the *wrongs* committed. Howard Zehr, a pioneer and exponent of restorative justice, sees justice as a choice—society needs to choose between the three "R's" of justice—revenge, retribution and restoration (Amstutz and Zehr 1998, pp. 37–38). Revenge can lead to an unending cycle of violence, so it is not an option at all. Retribution, in the opinion of Zehr (Amstutz and Zehr 1998) "assumes that justice and healing are separate issues, perhaps even incompatible" (p. 38). Restorative justice, on the other hand, for Zehr (Amstutz and Zehr 1998) is built on the presumption that "justice can and should promote healing, both individual and societal" (p. 38). He sees retributive justice and restorative justice as a continuum, where pure retributive justice and pure restorative justice fall on the two ends (Amstutz and Zehr 1998).

Kaushikee (✉)
Nelson Mandela Centre for Peace and Conflict Resolution,
Jamia Millia Islamia University, New Delhi, India
e-mail: kaushikee28@gmail.com

R. Thilagaraj and J. Liu (eds.), *Restorative Justice in India*,
DOI 10.1007/978-3-319-47659-9_10

However, in practice, justice is neither purely retributive nor can it be purely restorative. But in the absence of some form of justice, victim's can and do take recourse to revenge.

10.1.1 Retributive Justice

Retributive justice makes the following assumptions about crime and justice—crime is essentially lawbreaking; when a law is broken, justice involves establishing guilt; so that "just deserts" ("tit for tat") can be meted out; by inflicting pain; through a conflict or process in which rules and intentions are placed above outcomes (Zehr 1990, p. 81). The most important assumption here is that the state is the real victim. The notion of retributive justice seeks punishment and assumes that inflicting pain on the perpetrator will restore a sense of reciprocity. It looks to punishment to make right, the wrong done to the victim. The punishment generally meted out to offenders is prison term of varying degrees. The prison system while perpetuating a culture of violence, strips the offender of their self-worth and personal autonomy and inflicts on them more physical and emotional violence. Gilligan (2001) is of the view that this increases the chances of their re-offending because crime can be a way of asserting one's identity. When the self-esteem of a human being is violated through insult, humiliation or coercion, it leads to anger and aggressive behaviour (Gilligan 2001).

The retributive system is prosecution-centred. It also results in *secondary victimization* as the victim is re-traumatized because of the adversarial nature of the justice system and the lack of support of the community. This does not let the victim regain a sense of personal power. When a large section of the society sees itself as victims of violent crimes, the process of reconciliation gets more complicated. Moreover, they are not able to contribute effectively to the process of peace-building. Besides, the punitive system does not address the needs of the offender for accountability, closure and healing. Thus, the wounds of both the victim and the offender are not only neglected in the retributive system but these also get compounded further.

10.1.2 Restorative Justice

Restorative justice sees crime as a violation, of the self, a desecration of who we are, of what we believe in or our private space. Crime is devastating because it upsets two fundamental assumptions on which we base our lives: our belief that the world is an orderly, meaningful place and our belief in personal autonomy. In fact, the psychological effects on victims are more serious than the physical loss. It is ironical that the offender gets punishment because of what she/he did to the victim but the latter has very little say in the whole process, is never a part of the resolution and does not even constitute the understanding of the problem. In this context, there is an urgent need to view crime, violence and justice with a different lens and a different paradigm. The notion of restorative justice provides that distinct lens.

Underlying the concept of wrongdoing in restorative justice is the assumption that we are all interconnected. In Hebrew scriptures, this is embedded in the concept of *shalom*. This notion of interconnectedness is represented in other cultures as well —*whakapapa* (Maori); *hozho* (Navajo); *ubuntu* (Africans). All these concepts communicate a similar message: all things are connected to each other in a web of relationships. On the other hand, massive violence represents damaged relationships. Damaged relationships are both a cause and an effect of collective violence. Interrelationships imply mutual obligations and responsibilities. Making amends for wrongdoing is thus an obligation. Accordingly, restorative justice implies a concern for healing of all those involved: victims, perpetrators and communities.

Restorative justice draws on the indigenous roots of the restorative justice processes in the Maori tradition, the Aborigines in Australia and Western Samoa, the Celtic tradition in Ireland, the sentencing circles in Canada and the indigenous African system of justice. The traditional African system of justice, according to Archbishop Desmond Tutu, Chairperson of the South African Truth and Reconciliation Commission (TRC), aimed at

> the healing of breaches, the redressing of imbalances, the restoration of broken relationships. This kind of justice seeks to rehabilitate both the victim and the perpetrator, who should be given the opportunity to be reintegrated into the community he or she has injured by his or her offence (Bloomfield et al. 2003, p. 106)

Restorative justice operates on the following fundamental premises: crime is a violation of people and relationships, justice aims to identify needs and obligations, so that things can be made right; justice encourages dialogue and mutual agreement; gives victims and offenders central role and is judged by the extent to which responsibilities are assumed, needs are met and healing is encouraged. There is place for punishment in restorative justice although its place is not central.

Viewing crime as wrongdoing stresses on the needs of the victims, which the prevalent model of retributive justice totally ignores. Wrongdoing is seen as representing a disharmony in relationships between individuals, families, communities and those between humans and the natural world. Wrongdoing provides an opportunity to rebuild fractured relationships. Restoring the relationship in all the four dimensions—the spiritual, emotional, the physical and the mental—of an individual involved in the justice process are equally important.

The goal of restorative justice is to reintegrate *us* with *them* into a larger whole. Since we normally portray conflict and massive violence in the context of us versus them, the victim and perpetrator both are justified in maintaining their respective positions and protecting the self. The hurt is never attended to and although it heals on the surface but leaves behind a scar and unaddressed emotions and feelings that keep churning. In essence, restorative justice seeks to heal. In order to continue on with life and for the sake of the future, healing is of prime importance. The reintegration of us and them can be done by following the five principles of restorative justice—invite full participation and consensus; heal what has been broken; seek full and direct accountability; reunite what has been divided; and strengthen the community, to prevent further harms. Here *accountability* must be understood broadly—those who benefitted from the injustices—are also guilty in moral terms.

10.2 Post-conflict Peace-building and Reconciliation in the Context of Massive Violence: The Restorative Justice Lens

Can restorative justice provide the lens or framework to facilitate reconciliation, deliver justice and build peace in a society emerging from collective violence? If yes, how? What are the challenges and limitations posed in the process of implementation of restorative justice? Before delving into the intricacies and complexities of these questions, it is pertinent to first look at the terms peace-building and reconciliation.

10.2.1 Peace-building

Peace-building involves addressing the causes of conflict, the grievances of the past and promoting justice, stability and sustainable peace. It comprises of various roles, functions, strategies, interventions, and short- and long-term measures such as ceasefire negotiations, a comprehensive peace agreement, refugee resettlement, establishment of a government, structural reforms, economic regeneration, social reconstruction, rehabilitation and reconciliation.

10.2.2 Reconciliation

Reconciliation has two dimensions: backward-looking and forward-looking. As a backward-looking dimension, it seeks to heal survivors, compensate for past injuries, create an understanding of the divided past and rebuild relationships between individuals and communities. In its forward-looking avatar, reconciliation intends to enable victims and perpetrators to get on with life and cooperate with each other to be able to run the affairs of the society and have a shared future.

Reconciliation is not a linear process where one can follow steps logically. However, there are certain essential ingredients of reconciliation: replace fear with non-violent coexistence (look for alternatives to revenge, establish communication between victims and perpetrators and ensure physical security), build confidence and trust between the victims and perpetrators (help the victims to distinguish degrees of guilt among the perpetrators by individualizing guilt), and develop empathy (acknowledge the pain and suffering, e.g., through truth commissions) (Bloomfield et al. 2003, pp. 19–22). In spite of these ingredients, reconciliation cannot work and will not be sustainable without the codes of democracy and minimum functioning of institutions—judiciary, legislature and the bureaucracy, and a just socioeconomic order. Thus reconciliation must be focused on both psychological as well as social needs.

The elements and mechanisms of reconciliation. Ledearch (1997, p. 29) is of the view that reconciliation is the place where the four elements of truth, mercy, justice and peace meet (see Fig. 10.1). These elements are connected—for without truth there can be no mercy and no justice—and without justice there can be no peace. Disclosure of truth is essential for forgiveness but the latter may not be forthcoming even after the truth has been revealed. Additionally, disclosing the truth and acknowledging it may also not necessarily lead to healing as it does not give the victims a sense of justice. Thus reconciliation cannot take place without justice. Moreover, peace cannot be durable and sustainable without justice.

Truth means acknowledging the wrong and recognizing the pain and suffering. Mercy relates to acceptance and forgiveness and making a new beginning. Justice comprises of making things right, as far as possible, having equality in relationships, social restructuring and restitution. Peace is associated with an interdependent society where there is well-being, security and respect. Reconciliation is "both a *focus* and a *locus*" in the opinion of Lederach (1997, p. 30, emphasis in original). It is focused on relational aspects and as a social process denotes a space where the conflicting parties can meet.

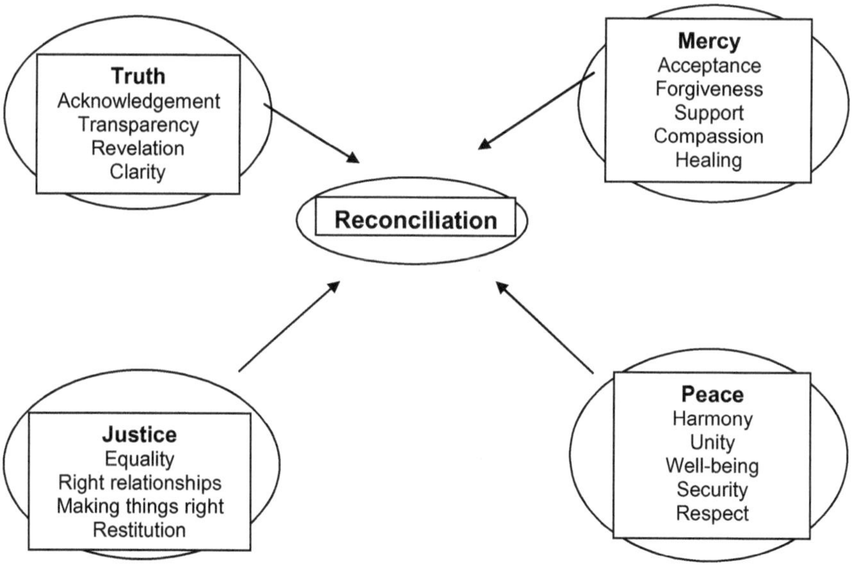

Fig. 10.1 The place called reconciliation. *Source* Lederach (1997, p. 30)

So how do we make the elements of reconciliation functional? According to Bloomfield, Barnes and Huyse, the elements of reconciliation can be translated into four techniques or mechanisms for making them functional (see Fig. 10.2):

- "healing the wounds of the survivors;
- some form of retributive or restorative justice;
- historical accounting via truth-telling; and
- reparation of the material and psychological damage inflicted on the victims" (2003, p. 23).

The mechanism of healing the wounds of the survivors coincides with the element of mercy, historical accounting via truth-telling tallies with the element of truth, and the mechanisms of retributive or restorative justice and reparation

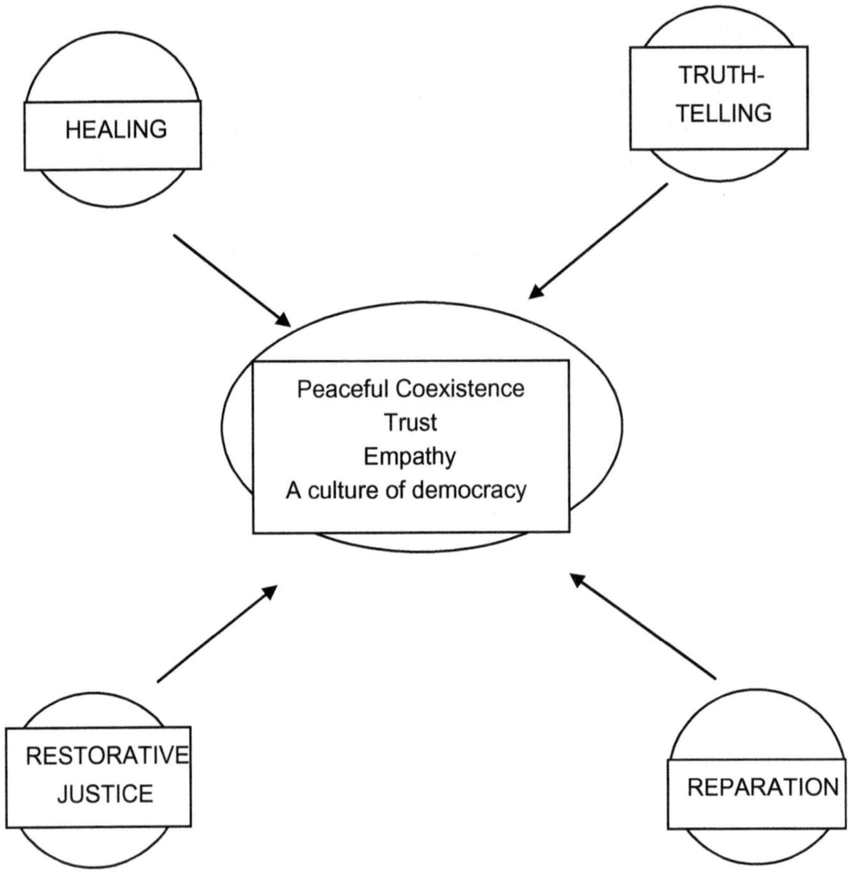

Fig. 10.2 Reconciliation: the instruments. *Source* Bloomfield et al. (2003, p. 24). Adapted from the work of John Paul Lederach

corresponds to the element of justice. When all the four mechanisms are put into practice, they can lead to building of trust and peaceful coexistence or peace.

Just as the four elements are interrelated, the four mechanisms of reconciliation are also closely linked to each other: restitution for the damages can heal the victims; justice and telling his or her own story can lead to the healing of both the victims as well as perpetrators. In this context, the slogan of the South African Truth and Reconciliation Commission (TRC) was very apt—*revealing is healing*. Acknowledgement of the wrongs is thus very critical; silence and justice do not go hand in hand. Tina Rosenberg's thoughts are pertinent in this regard

> If the victims in a society do not feel that their suffering has been acknowledged, then they ….. are not ready to put the past behind them. If they know that the horrible crimes carried out in secret will always remain buried …then they are not ready for reconciliation (As cited in Bloomfield et al. 2003, p. 26).

It can therefore be concluded that victims do not forget or forgive past wrongs easily, especially when there is no closure and no genuine attempt has been made to ensure justice.

10.2.3 Mass Level Atrocities and Collective Violence: Why Restorative Justice Is More Suited for Reconciliation?

When societies and communities become victims of massive atrocities, it is very different from simple wrongdoing or criminal act or an individual committing a grave criminal act. Judge Richard J. Goldstone emphasizes this aspect in the 'Foreword' of the book *Between Vengeance and Forgiveness*

> in a perfect society victims are entitled to full justice, namely trial of the perpetrator and, if found guilty, adequate punishment. That ideal is not possible in the aftermath of massive violence. There are simply too many victims and too many perpetrators. Even the most sophisticated criminal justice system would be completely overwhelmed (Minow 1998, p. x)

The assumption here is that the institutions of criminal justice system are still functional but in many instances of protracted violent conflict, it may be in complete shambles and thus nonfunctional.

Given that the criminal justice system is functional, it being *overwhelmed* by a large number of cases is not the only reason that it is not suited to situations of mass atrocities; there are other problems as well. The political realities in a given circumstance may not be conducive for criminal prosecution. Besides, dealing with perpetrators is not the only task at hand in a post-conflict scenario; peace-building here would involve may other things. Moreover, criminal prosecution of the perpetrators could destabilize the whole peace process, spoil the democratization and reconciliation process and lead to another cycle of violence. This was the reason that the Latin American leaders chose not to go in for criminal trials in the 1980s. Further, in some situations it may not be easy to distinguish between perpetrators and victims. The former may have been victim at some point of time especially in cases where there have been cycles of violence and hatred.

Additionally, if a large number of administrative officers who participated in violent activities are tried, they will be dismissed from their services. This could have severe repercussions on governance, as it will make the bureaucracy almost nonfunctional. Keeping this in mind, administrative officers were not tried in post-communist Central and Eastern Europe. Furthermore, criminal trials individualize guilt which is helpful as then the whole community is not labelled or seen as perpetrators by the victims. However, such trials fail to identify the patterns in atrocities. In addition, if there is lack of evidence then perpetrators cannot be tried. The criminal justice system thus seems incapable of dealing with the eventualities of mass atrocities. So what are the alternatives in such a scenario? Amnesty, truth commissions and/or reparation programmes, and restorative justice based on traditional conflict resolution mechanisms could provide the alternative to retributive justice and facilitate reconciliation.

Amnesty based on the idea of forgiving and forgetting has been used as a mechanism for reconciliation in some cases. The exponents of amnesty laws emphasize that reconciliation can only be achieved if the successor regimes desist from prosecuting the officers of the preceding establishment. Collective amnesia has even succeeded, e.g., in post-Franco Spain (Jeong 2006). However, Judge Richard J. Goldstone rejects the mechanism of forgetting the past as an option and points out the negative effects of doing so

> Some countries simply forget the past and attempt to induce a national amnesia in its people. Of course that is bound to fail—the victims do not—indeed cannot forget. And their unanswered calls for retribution develop into hate and invariably that hate is directed collectively at the group from which the perpetrators came. In the former Yugoslavia and Rwanda the hate induced in that way provided the tool which evil leaders used to induce those under their power to commit genocide, crimes against humanity, and other gross violations of human rights (Minow 1998, p. x)

Tina Rosenberg too, does not favour the mechanism of amnesty as it does not lead to genuine reconciliation. She says, "The kind of reconciliation that lets bygones be bygones is not true reconciliation. It is reconciliation at gunpoint and should not be confused with real thing" (As cited in Bloomfield et al. 2003, pp. 26–27). Thus amnesty based on amnesia is not a tenable proposition. However, a variant of the amnesty clause, the concept of limited amnesty, was applied in the case of Sierra Leone where serious crimes like rape and murder were not reprieved but small and petty offences were pardoned. In East Timor, grave crimes such as murder, torture and rape were put under the jurisdiction of legal procedures set up by the United Nations Transitional Administration in East Timor (UNTAET). In Chile, Argentina and El Salvador, too, excessive human rights violations were denied amnesty.

Another option is to go for historical accounting so that the past can be dealt with by recording it. Dealing with the past is a painful process but an essential one if a society is to move towards durable peace. Contested histories must be dealt with and addressed as a part of this process. However, it is not essential that all the parties agree on one history; it could include an acknowledgement and perhaps an apology for the harms done in the past. This acknowledgement facilitates trauma healing and reconciliation. According to Ho-Won Jeong, "public truth telling has become the preferred path since the Latin American experience of the late 1980s and early 1990s" (2006, p. 163). Indeed, truth-telling was the basis of reconciliation in both Guatemala and South Africa. The Guatemalan truth-telling process was "characterized by the participation of civil society in reconstructing memory. In particular, its grassroots politics of memory served as a means to further justice with an extensive report prepared by Catholic churches" (Jeong 2006, p. 164).

Public testimony was the feature of the South African Truth and Reconciliation Commission (TRC) formed to facilitate the memory of the past racial killings. Reconstructing memory through truth-telling rather than forgetting helps communities and individuals to heal and reconcile. Truth commissions can be complemented with reparation or restitution mechanisms which makes it more meaningful and relevant. However, compensation for damages can be used as a stand-alone means as well, though this format may not be that effective as the other needs of the victims, for instance, the desire to know the truth is not fulfilled.

Restorative justice in practice: The TRC of South Africa and the Gacaca Tribunals of Rwanda. Amnesty, truth-telling, reparation and restorative justice principles, a combination of one or more of these mechanisms have been applied in some countries which had been witness to massive violence in the past. Here two cases, the TRC of South Africa and the Gacaca tribunals of Rwanda, are briefly being discussed. In both these cases, restorative justice principles and mechanisms were used for restoring the damaged relations in the society.

The TRC of South Africa. The TRC was set up in South Africa in 1994 to deal with the large number of human rights violations that were committed during the apartheid rule. The leaders of post-apartheid South Africa realized that criminal trial was not an alternative as the conflict had been a long-drawn one, which had resulted in a large number of victims and perpetrators. Moreover, the court system was not in a position to handle such large number of cases. Hence the TRC focused on the holistic healing of victims and perpetrators and not on retributive justice.

Restorative principles and values were adapted for setting up the TRC. It comprised of three interconnected committees: Human Rights Violations Committee, Reparation and Rehabilitation Committee and the Amnesty Committee. The Human Rights Violations Committee was responsible for collecting statements from victims and witnesses and recording the degree of violations. The Reparations and Rehabilitation Committee (RRC) was meant to design and recommend reparation programmes. The Amnesty Committee was given the task of processing and deciding individual amnesty cases. This was seen as a very controversial power and thus challenged constitutionally.

As per the amnesty clause, if an individual fully confessed to the crime committed by him/her in the past and disclosed all the facts or the truth pertaining to it and also proved that the crime was politically motivated, the Amnesty Committee could decide whether s/he could be granted amnesty and be exempted from criminal prosecution. The perpetrator also had to show that "there was proportionality between the crime committed and the political objective pursued" (Bloomfield et al. 2003, p. 141). Crimes, however, committed as a result of some hatred or animosity or for some personal gain were not eligible for amnesty. Moreover, apology or remorse was not a precondition for amnesty. Individuals responsible for serious crimes had to appear in a public hearing, wherein they had to answer questions posed by the TRC, the victims and the lawyers representing the victims and their families. Those perpetrators whose amnesty application was rejected or those who chose not to come before the TRC had to undergo trials. It is generally perceived that perpetrators benefitted from the amnesty clause. However, in reality only 849 out of 7112 applications were granted amnesty ("Amnesty hearings and decisions"). Thus the TRC applied the principle of limited amnesty—not blanket or general amnesty—and took into account individual circumstances.

Truth was a central component of the TRC. However, the purpose of finding out the truth was not to prosecute people but to use it for healing and make it the basis for amnesty—*truth-for-amnesty*. In the TRC, the concept of truth was broken down into four notions: factual or forensic truth; personal and narrative truth; social truth; and healing and restorative truth. Factual truth consisted of corroborated evidence. The narrative truth comprised of stories, of both the victim and the perpetrator. Social truth was defined by Judge Albie Sachs as "the truth of experience that is established through interaction, discussion and debate" (Boraine and Levy 1995, p. 105). The TRC of South Africa Report, Volume One, 1998 defines healing truth as "the kind of truth that places facts and what they mean within the context of human relationships—both amongst citizens and between the state and its citizens. This kind of truth was central to the Commission" (paragraph 43, p. 114).

Apart from amnesty, reparation was the other point of debate in South Africa. The process of giving reparations was a slow one. The TRC submitted its final two-volume report in March 2003. After this, the government agreed to make the final reparation payouts to about 22,000 South Africans who were declared apartheid victims by the TRC (Final TRC Reparations Payouts 2003). Most victims were given compensation except for those that could not be traced. Earlier, the government had paid urgent interim reparation grant of R50-million to 16,500 of the 18,000 victims identified by the TRC (Final TRC Reparations Payouts 2003).

The TRC focused on individual human rights violations but sidetracked responsibility of the broader apartheid structures and people who benefitted from those structures. Only the government contributed to the reparation scheme while businesses and corporations and individuals who profited from the discriminatory policies of the apartheid regime did not compensate the victims in any way. They did not own responsibility or show any remorse for their acts. As a result, some victims and local groups filed for reparation claims against multinational corporations in the courts of the United States of America. The government did not support the victims in these lawsuits. Besides, the government rejected the TRC's recommendation of imposing a once-off wealth tax on businesses and companies that benefitted from the apartheid system by contending that they had a role to play in the economic revival and growth of the country. Instead, it created a reparation trust fund wherein businesses, civil society and the government could contribute money. This fund was to be used for compensation to apartheid victims as well as for community development. The government, however, agreed to the TRC recommendation to declare a national day of prayer and traditional sacrifice to pay tribute to the people who either suffered or lost their lives during the apartheid regime, with the intention of healing memory and honouring those who were executed. Most of all, the government has failed to dismantle and address the structural and economic inequalities in the post-apartheid era. Economic wealth is still largely confined in the hands of white South Africans. Thus it needs to be recognized that "true social transformation—and healing of victims—will only come about if the issues of economic justice and the myriad problems that post-apartheid South Africa faces are addressed" (Gobodo-Madikizela 2002, p. 28).

In South Africa, striking balance between individual claims and rights and reconciliation had proved to be a challenge. Individual claims and rights were sidetracked for the sake of reconciliation at the national level. Further, trauma and counselling resources were inadequate and thus survivors and victims' families underwent a process of secondary victimization as a result of the processes initiated by the TRC. Since neither remorse nor apology was a precondition for amnesty, several victims did not feel healed.

So although many questions have been raised about the efficacy and the gaps in the TRC, it cannot be denied that several survivors experienced some "closure" and healing as a result of it. The same would have not happened if the South Africans had opted for a retributive system of justice. This has been pointed out by Gobodo-Madikizela, a psychologist who served on the TRC

> South Africans faced the challenge of how to embrace the past without being swallowed by the tide of vengeful thinking. The TRC was a strategy that not only broke the cycles of politically motivated violence but also taught us important lessons about how the human spirit can prevail even as victims remember the cruelty visited on them in the past. If memory is kept alive to kindle and cultivate old hatreds and resentments, memory is likely to culminate in hateful vengeance and in a repetition of cycles of violence. But if memory is kept alive to transcend hateful emotions, to free oneself or one's society from the burden of hatred, then remembering, just to acknowledge what happened can be healing (2002, p. 28)

The Gacaca Tribunals of Rwanda. The 1994 genocide in Rwanda left the country devastated. There was a huge loss of life and the social fabric of the country was torn apart. The Rwandan criminal justice system was in a miserable state right after the genocide. As a result, the International Criminal Tribunal for Rwanda was authorized by the UN Security Council. The first judgement was made by this international tribunal.

In 1996, the Rwandan National Assembly adopted a genocide law. The genocide law created categories of crime—ranging from crimes against humanity to property offences—and prescribed punishments for the same. Trials started towards the end of 1996 and by mid-2001, only 3500 people had been judged (Bloomfield et al. 2003, p. 116). Besides, the trials were seriously flawed. First, the quality of justice delivered was poor as a result of corruption, biases and pressures. Second, the number of people undergoing the trial was huge. After the genocide, around 115,000 people were arrested by the Tutsi government but there were less than 50 lawyers to defend the accused (Jeong 2006, p. 170). Moreover, the government wanted to decrease the number of cases brought to the formal judicial system and speed up the judicial process in order to promote a peaceful resolution and reconciliation. Thus it transformed and modernized the traditional conflict resolution mechanism called Gacaca into a tool for judging the massacre accused.

Judges, who were persons of integrity were elected and trained. The entire community including the victims was present during the public hearing and acted as a general assembly. The community had to establish the truth and help the victims and perpetrators to heal so as to promote reconciliation. One creative aspect of the Gacaca was the confession procedure. Penalties were reduced for prisoners who confessed and asked for forgiveness. Sentences could be changed into community service if the accused asked for forgiveness publicly. On the other hand, survivors of genocide were entitled to receive reparations from a public fund for all sorts of damages suffered by them: loss of property, physical loss or loss of family members and relatives.

In spite of the Gacaca tribunal being an ingenious mechanism, it had several limitations. There was no demarcation between the prosecutor and the judge in the tribunals and there were no lawyers, which was against the principles of internationally agreed human rights and criminal law. Moreover, traditionally the Gacaca was used in cases of civil nature such as land use, cattle and inheritance rights. It could also settle minor criminal offences, though not through criminal sanctions but through some civil settlement like compensation. Also, in the traditional system, the objective was not to determine guilt or to apply the legal norms but to restore order and harmony in the society. Thus the outcomes of the traditional Gacaca could be in conflict with the state laws. But after the genocide, the Gacaca tribunal was expected to apply the state laws. Moreover, the tribunal followed a top-down approach of reconciliation while the traditional Gacaca was essentially a community-based reconciliation mechanism, which had been created for dealing with ordinary conflicts and not genocide like situations.

In the Gacaca tribunals, women's participation was very limited. Traditionally also women did not take part in the Gacaca unless they were party to the conflict. There were no provisions for trauma counselling and psychosocial support systems in the tribunal, leaving the trauma of the victims' and survivor's unaddressed. Additionally, social dynamics could harm the process of reconciliation as powerful people could have a say in and influence the tribunal proceedings. Further, the traditional mechanism was based on common values and reciprocal norms but the genocide devastated the value structure, destroyed the existing communities and altered the composition of the local population.

In spite of all its misgivings and limitations, most Rwandans still preferred the Gacaca system of justice as it is an indigenous mechanism which also has the potential to contribute to reconciliation. Moreover, there were no practical alternatives available to them.

10.2.4 Mass-level Atrocities and Collective Violence in India: Can Restorative Justice Fulfil the Need for Justice and Bring About Reconciliation?

India has been witnessed to a chain of violent conflicts since its independence. In some violent cases, one community was targeted by another as in the anti-Sikh riots of 1984, the Gujarat riots of 2002, the Kandhamal riots in 2008 to name a few. Second, left wing extremists, Kashmiri separatists and several identity-based insurgents in the northeast have also perpetrated violence. Third, the state itself has been an aggressor and indulged in violence through its various agencies, functionaries and legal mechanisms, e.g., through laws such as the Armed Forces Special Powers Act (AFSPA), encounter killings. The victims of these violent atrocities, whether at the hand of state agencies or that of insurgent groups or that of other communities, have not forgotten their pain and trauma as there have been no genuine attempts to ensure justice.

India can no longer ignore the various conflicts that continue to brew in different parts of the country. If the pain and trauma of the present generation of victims is not attended to, it could lead to major outbursts in the near past, leading to several smaller fragments of the nation. India thus needs to reconcile. The process of reconciliation should take place at different levels: between the state and citizens, between states and non-state actors, and between communities. This is easier said than done as there is trust deficit—communities do not trust each other, the state does not trust its citizens, and pockets of communities and citizens do not trust the state. In such a scenario, the first step is trust building.

The process of reconciliation needs to start from the top. The process has to be initiated by the government as was done by the Nelson Mandela led South African government that set up the TRC. The civil society and widely respected individuals of the country need to be active participants in this process and give shape to it by having dialogue with all the stakeholders and listening to them with an open mind and heart. This will help in building trust among the people and give credence to the process of reconciliation that is to follow.

Restorative justice can provide the platform for reconciliation to take place. However, we need not go in for the western definition of restorative justice. Restorative justice is a flexible concept, which can be redefined in our context as per our ethical and cultural values and norms. In any case the concept of restorative justice is not new to India. Mander (2011) says in this regard: "Ideas of reconciliation and forgiveness—as well as justice—are intrinsic in varied but related ways to virtually every major strand of diverse religious and secular convictions that have impinged through the centuries on the consciousness of Indian people." Restorative justice was thus a part of our culture but was lost somewhere in between. In contemporary times, however, it needs to be contextualized as per our needs and must be based on certain human rights principles and norms.

From the standpoint of restorative justice, the first key aspect is that the perpetrators acknowledge or accept the wrongs committed, whether it is the state or a community or a non-state actor. Even those groups, individuals and communities who benefitted from the injustice or did not raise their voice against it are guilty in some ways and they need to acknowledge this. Next, some sort of a public apology or remorse, a sincere and genuine one, for the wrongs committed, could provide the healing touch to victims. Here again the government should lead the process and offer sincere apologies for its omissions and commissions. Besides, where ever practically possible, the victims should be given some compensation for their losses. In 2008, the government of New Zealand agreed to pay out hundreds of millions of dollars to settle century old grievances of the Maori community. However, loss of human life must be dealt with sensitively as far as compensating for them is concerned.

The next key element is justice for the victims. This would entail a process that facilitates bringing the culprits to book. However, weak laws and an ineffective criminal justice system means that the culprits will be let off either very lightly or without any punishment. Therefore, laws need to be strengthened and implemented seriously and the criminal justice system needs to be reformed. Additionally, it may not be possible to punish each and every perpetrator, therefore some sort of a limited amnesty, as was done by the TRC in South Africa, could be provided to people who indulged in minor acts, but only if they come forward and tell the truth. For this, the government could form some sort of a Truth Commission. Grave crimes, however, should not go unpunished and can be dealt with through either a fast track criminal justice process or through a time-bound commission of enquiry which has powers of prosecution.

Besides the above measures, efforts must be made to strengthen inter-community relationships so as to prevent violent conflict from recurring. Restoring the damaged relationships between communities is a time-taking process and so efforts must be pooled towards building at least a minimum level of understanding in the short and middle term; this way the affairs of the state and the government could be carried on. Structural and systemic changes would be necessary as well, e.g., draconian laws like the AFSPA would have to be repealed; the government and its agencies would have to be held accountable for its acts, etc. It is also essential to create some sort of a common understanding of the violent past; for this, a group consisting of the representatives of the former belligerents and academic and non-academic experts should be formed. They need not agree on each and every aspect of the past incidents but will have to decide on how the violent incident has to be communicated to future generations and put the same in black and white.

To sum up, the onus for starting the process of reconciliation is on the Indian state and its government. Taking cue from there, other levels might also take recourse to the process of reconciliation.

10.3 In Conclusion

Restorative justice is trying to bring in a major paradigm shift in terms of the meaning of crime and justice and how society should relate to victims and perpetrators. However, in choosing to go for restorative justice approaches, leaders, societies, and communities should be aware of some of the knotty issues around it. First, the process of restorative justice counts a lot on the goodness of the individual and the community and this can be problematic. Second, restorative justice desires a lead role for the community in its processes but then the community itself is not a cohesive unit—it has its own problems of hierarchical social arrangements based on class, caste, gender, etc. Next, without addressing the systemic and structural roots of crime and violence which lead to unemployment, economic inequality, poverty, etc., restorative justice cannot have a holistic view. But addressing systemic issues is a long-drawn work. Also, fundamental human rights should be the norm for negotiating reparation in restorative justice processes but the problem is that these are defined differently in different cultural settings. Further, there is a need to be alert for while restorative justice will try to make things better, there might be unintended consequences, which could make things worse. Striking the right balance and treading this path cautiously is critical. Though restorative justice is preferable to retributive justice when working towards sustainable peace and reconciliation, however, this does not mean that there is no place for punishment; those who commit violent acts must be brought under the rule of law. On a retributive-restorative justice continuum, efforts should be made to move as far as possible towards the restorative end.

Restorative justice in situations of massive violence should not be seen just as an ideal based on high moral grounds, for in the words of Archbishop Desmond Tutu (2004), "Confession, forgiveness and reconciliation in the lives of nations are not just airy-fairy religious and spiritual things, nebulous and unrealistic. They are the stuff of practical politics." Restorative justice has emerged as a field of study that can be beneficial for communities recovering from genocide, war, violence and trauma. It can facilitate individual healing, of both the victims and the perpetrators and sustain the process of reconciliation. Restorative justice is not primarily about forgiveness or reconciliation but it does provide a context where this might happen.

References

Amnesty hearings & decisions. Retrieved from http://www.justice.gov.za/trc/amntrans/index.htm

Amstutz, L. S., & Zehr, H. (1998). *Victim offender conferencing in Pennsylvania's juvenile justice system*. Harrisburg, PA: Commonwealth of Pennsylvania.

Bloomfield, D., Barnes, T., & Huyse, L. (Eds.). (2003). *Reconciliation after violent conflict: A handbook*. Stockholm, Sweden: International IDEA.

Final TRC Reparations Payouts. (2003, November 18). Retrieved from http://www.southafrica.info/public_services/citizens/your_rights/reparations_171103.htm

Gilligan, J. (2001). *Preventing violence*. New York: Thames and Hudson.

Gobodo-Madikizela, P. (2002). Remorse, forgiveness, and rehumanization: Stories from South Africa. *Journal of Humanistic Psychology, 42*(1), 7–32.

Jeong, H. (2006). *Peacebuilding in post conflict societies: Strategy & Process*. New Delhi: Viva Books Private Ltd.

Lederach, J. P. (1997). *Building peace: Sustainable reconciliation in divided societies*. Washington, DC, USA: United States Institute of Peace Press.

Mander, H. (2011, July 2). Barefoot—Some paths to forgiveness. *The Hindu*. Retrieved from http://www.thehindu.com/opinion/columns/Harsh_Mander/barefoot-some-paths-to-forgiveness/article2150128.ece

Minow, M. (1998). *Between vengeance and forgiveness: Facing History after genocide and mass violence*. Boston, Massachusetts: Beacon Press.

Sachs, A. (1995). The task for civil society. In A. Boraine & J. Levy (Eds.), *The healing of a nation?* (pp. 103–109). Cape Town: Justice in Transition.

Tutu, D. (2004, September 1). Truth and reconciliation. *Greater Good*. Retrieved from http://greatergood.berkeley.edu/article/item/truth_and_reconciliation

Zehr, H. (1990). *Changing lenses: A new focus for crime and justice*. Scottdale, Pennsylvania & Waterloo, Ontario: Herald Press.

Part V
Restorative Justice Practices in India: Restorative Justice and Juveniles

Chapter 11
Scope and Applicability of Restorative Justice for Juveniles in Conflict with the Law

A. Vijayalakshmi

11.1 Introduction

Restorative justice is a tool to recognize the rightful place of the child in society. It is a paradigm shift from a need-based approach to a rights-based approach which seems aims to mainstream the development of children. When we speak about the rights, liabilities, etc. of children, we think about a child-centric approach to rights and laws as basic to social reintegration. Whether a law or a right, what we have to concentrate on is what is the objective, scope and applicability of either one to children. Before the enactment of child-centric laws or acts meant exclusively for juveniles, we depend on existing constitutional remedies like Articles 15(3) and 39 (e). What is the justice that the law or act is going to provide for the welfare of the juveniles who are in need of it? Under what law is the child who committed crimes going to be tried? Criminal law or any other supplementary laws? If tried for the offence committed, what would be the sanction? Here a reformative theory of punishment arises. International conventions, covenants and declarations speak about the rehabilitation process of children who commit crimes and punitive sanctions relevant to them. What is this reformative, rehabilitative, restorative justice towards a child who commits or is alleged to have committed a crime?

When we think about the application of restorative justice to juveniles in conflict with the law, the issue lies with both society and the government, not between the parties. It lies on the community and the statutory agencies. In India, more than 40% of the population are children who should be considered out national asset. Various UN conventions and declarations work to implement the agenda and rights of children. This chapter discusses the legislative view on juvenile justice nationally

A. Vijayalakshmi (✉)
School of Excellence in Law, The Tamil Nadu
Dr. Ambedkar Law University, Chennai, India
e-mail: vijayalakshmi_ml@yahoo.co.in

R. Thilagaraj and J. Liu (eds.), *Restorative Justice in India*,
DOI 10.1007/978-3-319-47659-9_11

and internationally, the need to invoke restorative justice for juveniles, and how to apply and attain these goals.

11.2 Legislative View on Juvenile Justice: International Perspective

The first step regarding child welfare law came into force after the outcome of abuses of children in factories in England. In the years, 1852 and 1892 two articles with the titles "The rights of Children" and "Children's Right" acted as wake-up calls internationally for the want of children-centred law. The declaration of the General Assembly of United Nations, The Convention on Child Rights,[1] has encouraged the international community to recognize the needs of children. Other declarations and conventions are the Universal Declaration of Human Rights, which emphasizes that motherhood and childhood are entitled to special care and assistance. Act 10(1) and (3) of ICESCR[2] upheld special protections and assistance for youth without discrimination. The contribution of ICCPR with regards to child welfare was remarkable, as it stressed the elimination of discrimination, the right to have a name and the right to acquire nationality.[3] The root for the existing Juvenile Justice Act in India is the contribution of the Convention on the Rights of the Child, 1989, in which attention was drawn to a set of four civil, political, social, economic and cultural as the right to survival, the right to protection, the right to development, the right to participation. By these numerous declarations the international organizations now and then speak and work for the development of children.[4] The four main guidelines which specifically speak about the juveniles in conflict with the law are the Beijing Rule, 1985; the Riyadh guideline 1990; Juvenile Delinquency law rules 1990; the Tokyo Rules 1990.

11.3 The Indian Scenario: Pre-independence Era[5]

Differential treatment for children can be traced as far back as the Code of Hammurabi in 1790 B.C.E., the responsibility for their supervision and maintenance being vested on the family. During the colonial regime in India the first center for destitute children, called the "Ragged School", was established in 1843 by Lord Cornwallis. The period between 1850 and 1919, marked by social and

[1]1898.

[2]International covenant on Economic, Social and Cultural Rights.

[3]Art 24 of International Convention on Civil and Political Rights.

[4]Law Relating to women and Children, Mamta Rao, 2nd edition, pp. 413–433.

[5]www.mightylaws.in/740/juvenile-justice-system-india.

industrial upheavals, called for the enactment of the Apprentice Act (1850), the IPC (1860), the CrPC (1861), and the Reformatory Act (1876 and 1897), announcing a paradigm shift in the penal philosophy in India from punitive to reformative.

As the country moved towards independence, recommendation to establish a special children's act came from the Indian Jail Committee (1919–1920). Individual provincial governments chose to enact separate legislation for juveniles in their respective jurisdictions. The provinces of Madras, Bengal and Bombay passed their own Children Acts in 1920, 1922 and 1924, respectively.

11.4 The Indian Scenario: Post-independence Era

Constitutional protection: Article 15(3), gives special procedure for the enactment of free education, Articles 23 and 24 protect fundamental rights. Based on the International Convention on Prevention of Crime and Treatment of Offenders in India, our government passed a central act in 1960, the Central Children Act, followed by a Child Right convention 1989. The government then passed the National Charter 2003 and the National Plan for Action in 2005. The Central Children Act 1960 was replaced by the Juvenile Justice Act 1986. With the effect of Beijing Rule and to upheld the protocols the then Act was again amended. We now follow the Juvenile Justice (Care and Protection of Children) Act, 2000. There are vast differences between the 1986 act and the 2000 act. In the first, children are under one category, no separate authority, no individual homes, no separate process for rehabilitation and reformation, etc. But the later Act rectified every thing and gave a crystal clear view regarding who is juvenile, the two different category of children as Juvenile in conflict with law,[6] and Child in need of care and protection,[7] authorities are different for these category as Juvenile Justice Board and Child welfare committee, separate homes like Observation Home[8] and Special. Home[9] and children's home[10] and Shelter Home,[11] respectively. As we are pointing on only regarding Juvenile in Conflict with law, it is fair to discus briefly about the general causative factor for committing crime. In our country one can find that urchins are destroying public properties like street bulbs, buses, school property, and so on. Then theft is also prevalent. Different types of cases are found. To give an example there are youngsters who are employed in households as servants or cooks. Generally these boys if they get opportunities depart secretly with valuables. There are also pilfering cases. In fact the most vulnerable part is railways, juveniles

[6]Sec 2(l).

[7]Sec 2(d).

[8]Sec 8.

[9]Sec 9.

[10]Sec 34.

[11]Sec 37.

are doing pilfering of whose property generally. A large number of neglected or destitute children take shelter in railway stations. It is the valuables of railway station very often tempt a common sight that neglected child. Neglected children, who are allowed to hawk in the streets, learn smoking and get addicted to cinema and bad literature and like. So in order to get money for this, they try to steal, cheat, and thereby involving themselves in many other wrongful activities.

Another reason is that they are more often very easily tempted by asocial elements and are being used for circumventing law. These children who are in need of basic needs want money even for their bread. They get money by involving themselves in minimum of labour. In this way, the anti-social, corrupt their morals and they in the long run develop delinquent propensities. Syed Hussiain who has discussed about the nature and extent of juvenile rebellion has also mentioned vandalism, theft, pilfering and street hawking as the nature as well as the source of juvenile delinquency in India.[12] This fact is well reflected by the crime rate in India and the number of juveniles involved in the same.[13] JJ Act 2000 lays special emphasis on the rehabilitation and social integration of the children. The Act has provided for institutional and non-institutional measures for care and protection of children. The act also envisages a system of partnerships with local communities and local governments to implement the legislation. JJ Act further provides for the establishment of children's homes, for the care, treatment and protection of neglected and abandoned children. Institutional care still appears to be the largest service for the care of the destitute and orphan children. The JJ act also speaks for the setting up of Observation homes, Juvenile homes, Special homes, Aftercare homes and recognizing fit persons/institutions for the temporary reception of both children in need of care and protection and that of children in conflict with law.

The role of Probation officers in bring out the change in the attitude of juveniles seems to be the back bone of the Act and its object. Without their help the purpose of the Act would not be fulfilled. It is time to pick children who easily get into the world of criminals and become a recidivist. To achieve this goal the best way to attain the target is Concept of Restoration, reformation and rehabilitation. This can be achieved only with the support of civil society and non-institutional agencies. Greater care and caution has to be taken to apply this principle towards Juvenile in Conflict with law as it includes social responsibility and awareness.

11.5 Need for Invoking Restorative Justice

Though we are having various laws which relates to the welfare and development of children and for their reformation, the problem exists with the correctional bodies due to various reason like lack of in taking the children, providing proper method of

[12]www.legalservisesindia.com.

[13]ibid.

rehabilitation. Thus the problem arises in the execution of law.[14] Another complication in India is the special status accorded to the state of Jammu and Kashmir. Meant as a temporary provision in 1950, Article 370 of the Indian Constitution allows the State of Jammu and Kashmir unprecedented legal independence with relation to all other regions of India. Thus, acts such as the Juvenile Justice (Care and Protection) Act (2000) do not extend to the Jammu and Kashmir judiciary. Owing to the turbulent history of the region, the legal system in Jammu and Kashmir is not as developed as the rest of the Indian judiciary, and has minimal provisions for the rights to children.[15] The ultimate goal of the Act is to rehabilitation, and social reintegration of juvenile in conflict with law and the paves way for the natural justice of speedy disposal by way of disposing the case against the juvenile with in 4–6 months.[16] The amended Act of 2006 gives additional remedy towards this aspect that the records has to be destroyed within 7 years from the date of order. The Act also favours the juveniles by the that no where in the record there should not be the mentioning of matter which relates to the accommodation of the juvenile in the particular home during so and so period. Even then the curse of reforming, rehabilitating the juveniles in conflict with law is lacking or staying behind is due the process of reformation.

In that regard, here it arises the need for applying restorative justice principle for these children. Prescribing different treatment for juvenile offenders is an offshoot of the new penology, which came to be applied with the realization that courts, procedures and prisons meant for adult offenders could hardly be expected to serve the interests of juvenile offenders. Erstwhile system exposed delinquents to contamination due to incarceration with other criminals. The nation's future citizens deserve compassion and best care. A child is born innocent, and responsibility should be attributed to such environmental factors that have stirred his criminal tendencies, whose removal might mould him into a person of stature and excellence.

Even our Judiciary now and then passing various directing order through the litigations like, "Sanjay Suri V. Delhi Adminstration",[17] by which the apex court gave direction for separate home for juveniles. The crucial question regarding determining juvenility is based in what? Whether the date of commission of offence or the date of arrest? There are various cases which dealt with these issues. The predominant cases which stand as the land mark cases are,[18]

#Krishna Bhagwan V. State of Bihar,[19] —date of commission of offence,
#Bhola Bhagat V. State of Bihar,[20] —Do,

[14]"The Status of Children in India", www.Crin.org/docs/resource/treatiescrc.35/India.

[15]Art 370 of Constitution of India, http://indiacode.nic.in/coiweb/coifiles.

[16]Sec 14 of Juvenile Justice Act, 2000.

[17]AIR 1988 SC 414.

[18]Criminology And Penology, Prof N.V. Paranjape, 12th edition, pp. 501, 502.

[19]AIR 1989 Pat. 217.

[20]AIR 1998 SC 236.

#Umesh Chandra V. State of Rajasthan,[21] —Do,
#Arnit Das V. State of Bihar,[22] —Do,

Where these cases are sticked on the principle, that the determining age of the juvenile in conflict with law, is at the time of commission of offence only. Speedy disposal of cases which are pending before the court comes to the knowledge of the court and it passes the order in case like "Sanat Sinha V. State of Bihar.[23] By way of this directions the Apex court and other High Court has fulfilled their responsibility with regard to the implementation of the law."

Restorative Justice is a problem-solving approach to crime which involves the parties themselves, and the community generally, in an active relationship with statutory agencies. It is not any particular practice, but a set of principles which may orientate the general practice of any agency or group in relation to crime. Restorative Justice may be seen as criminal justice embedded in its social context, with the stress on its relationship to the other components, rather than a closed system in isolation.

Restorative Justice is centrally concerned with restoration: restoration of the victim, restoration of the offender to a law—abiding life, restoration of the damage caused by crime to the community. Restoration is not solely backward-looking; it is equally, if not more, concerned with the construction of a better society in the present and future.

11.6 Concept and Enforcement

Regarding the conceptual issue and its implication in India, it is a blunder question as our Juvenile system is in terms of terror, not healing, not cure, so that it convert the culture of homes into jails literally. Undoubtedly juvenile detention concept is need of new focus and rationale. The real purpose of detaining the juvenile is to reform them and to bring about a constructive change in the minds of them and help them to confront with the society when they released from the home. But the present situation which prevails in the non-institutional homes is not up to that level.

The Juvenile judge is charged with the solemn determination whether to deprive juveniles of liberty or whether they can be released in their parents' custody or to a third party and, if so, what conditions should apply to the release. In making such a decision the judge should follow due process, that is, hearing procedures and in all probability the legal presumption should favour release. If the decision is to detain, the judge must make a record to support that decision. The legality of preventive

[21]1982 (1) 335 (SC).

[22]AIR 2004 (5)617.

[23]1991 (2) Crimes, 241.

detention in the juvenile court needs to be tested. If the power is upheld, the procedural safeguards should be as precise as they are for adults. We should abandon the notion that secure detention is good for the child.

"Justice and the Child" is a distinct jurisprudential-criminological branch of socio-legal specialty which is still in its infant status in India and many other countries, the Children Act is a preliminary exercise, the Borstal School is an experiment in reformation and even Section 360 Cr. P.C. tends in the same direction. Correction informed by compassion, not incarceration leading to degeneration, is the primary aim of this field of criminal justice. Juvenile justice has constitutional roots in Articles 15(3) and 39(e) and the pervasive humanism which bespeaks the super parental concern of the State for its child-citizens including the most vulnerable, juvenile delinquents.[24] Despite of multiple process of reformative theory with regards to the restoration of juveniles as a part of provision under the Act of 2000[25] the authorities those who are involved in the correctional process for handling the juvenile in conflict with law, are not taking the issue as much of importance and they are discharging their duties like that of 9 to 5 job. If the authorities like the commissioner, Directors, Superintendents, Wardens, Residential Wardens, Technical Staffs who are directly connected with this institutions, discharge their functions with some concern over the children, definitely we can expect the change what we are looking for. The residential staffs inside the home have to be close with the inmates by way of gaining their faith, so that they could move freely with them, share their needs with them and it is also easy for the implement of the correctional procedure with them. Apart from the role of authorities regarding rehab and reform and restore them, the next category who is having the responsibility over the juvenile justice programme is Society, Judiciary and the Educational institution and last but not the lease the MEDIA. Nowadays children are spending one-third of the time with technologies like Television, Internet, iPad, Tablet, etc. If we compare the mass communication, the impact and influence of magazines and books is less when the impression of visual communication is high. Today the visual media has become the demonstration tool for all crimes. They put sketch and diagram on the commission of any nature of offence right from pickpocketing to gruesome murder. They are not realizing their role and responsibility over the younger generation, more particularly juvenile, who can become a prey to this. As the Act 2000, simply lay down the provision regarding publication of identification of juvenile against whom any proceedings is initiated and prescribe the punishment also, which seems to be very minimal.[26] When all these agencies joined together in one hand and for the welfare of the juvenile in conflict with law, the goal is not too far.

The enforcement of this restorative justice can be attain by way of three process like,

[24]www.legalservicesindia.com.

[25]Sec 39 of the Act, 2000.

[26]Sec 21 of Act, 2000.

ENFORCEMENT PROCESS

(i)JUDICIAL PROCESS	NON-JUDICIAL PROCESS	COMMUNITY PROCESS
under this method judiciary and the functionaries like Judges, Advocates has to Apply the judicial Process for their Restoration	under this method, the correctional institute, experts in child psychology has to take part. Non-judicial process like protection and well being has to be attain by family counseling	under this method active participation of agencies like educational institution, media NGO's and probation officers has to work together to create awareness without Legal intervention.

11.7 Recommendation

It is the time to make some amendment in the existing law, Juvenile Justice (care and Protection of Children) Act, 2000, due to the recent shocking incident of 15-year-school-boy stabbed his teacher because of the adverse remarks made by her regarding his poor performance in studies. We are creating some notion in the minds of the children that only the numerical values, i.e. marks gives them pride and future. For what we are preparing our children, like horses running in races and we are like jockeys shouting "Come on, Come on". Where is the moral values, where is the moral education class, where is the leisure class like physical training?

We erased all these golden ideologies which gave the children refreshment and breathing time. By making all these things, we ourselves create opportunity for them to commit the delinquent activities and blaming them later. The need for amendment of the Act is not only to the children covered under the Act but also to the entire juvenile community for their betterment of future.

1. Inclusion of all categories of children (child in conflict with law and need of care and protection), like school children, child labours, etc. without limitation.
2. The concern government has to recruit the members those who are working in the homes (institutions) by way of finding out whether they are really work for them and bring out the change in their attitude. Because if they work their with this notion we would not come out the news like inmates escaped from the observation home, children home, etc. to avoid this it has to be concentrated more.
3. Need for making the provision regarding publication of identification of juveniles those who are facing trail by media has to be more stringent by the way of imposing sentence for rigorous punishment and fine, that fine amount can be either utilized for the correctional process or grant to that juvenile as matter of compensation.
4. The most important thing is, the law itself has to pave way by way of inserting provision for prescribing condition and circumstance for which selection of juvenile for awarding this restorative principle.
5. Minimum punishment to be prescribed for escaping inmates and recidivist juveniles. Because nowadays the juveniles are misusing the Act, as there is no punishment for any nature of crime committed by them, they are repeating the same offence after coming out of the house and indulge in further offence and come to institution just like taking rest.
6. Minimum prescription of punishment for the authorities who either misuse the procedure or non-usages of process or recommending for departmental action. These are some of the recommendations for attaining the real purpose of applicability of restorative justice for the juvenile in conflict with law. Again, it lies in three wings called, judiciary, community and correctional institutions.

11.8 Conclusion

Despite the elucidation of comprehensive beneficial schemes for children, implementation is defective. Appropriate training is absent; there is tussle in granting bail to the delinquents, serious accountability concerns, and overall apathy. There are unprecedented incidents of police brutality and abuse in the Observation Homes, along with incompetence and delay on the part of probation officers.

Attempts have been made to ensure enforcement by drafting Model Rules 2007 as an addendum to the Act and by creating an Integrated Child Protection Scheme.

A ray of hope glimmers in the form of the Protection of Children from Sexual Offences Bill 2011, which not only aspires to curb the sexual atrocities against our children, but also to rein the media by prohibiting comments on child, either accused or victim of an offence, which may lower character or infringe privacy. It is high time now that the social workers take up the role of a friend, adviser, reformer and healer simultaneously, and NGOs come forward to seek charge of juveniles pending or on completion of inquiry. Juvenile justice, sometimes called child justice, is often perceived as the natural playground for restorative justice. Justice concerns the proper ordering of things and persons within a society. In this respect, restorative justice refers to the implementation of a theory of justice that focuses on crime and wrongdoing as perpetrated against the individual or community rather than the state. The wide and deep implementation of restorative justice principles, in particular when dealing with young people, has been recognized as the "green" way to go. This is so, because the principles of restorative justice do not, either actually or symbolically, reduce incidents otherwise recognized as offences/crimes and, which give rise to societal reaction and censure, to a bundle of predefined and pre-structured rights relations. A broader focus, which includes as the case may be the perspective of individuals, encompasses the social environment from which a conflict emerged. In this process, in which young people are recognized as persons in formation, and where the emphasis is on reparation, also with regard to victims, the full potential for personal development is maintained.

Restorative justice is a different way of thinking about crime and our response to crime. It focuses on repairing the harm caused by crime and reducing future harm through crime prevention. It also requires offenders to take responsibility for their actions and for the harm they have caused. However, it seeks redress for victims, recompense by offenders and reintegration of both within the community through a co-operative effort by communities and the government.

Part VI
Restorative Justice Practices in India: Restorative Justice and Woman

Chapter 12 Applicability and Reception of Restorative Justice for Rape Victims

D. Umamaheswari

12.1 Introduction

One area often questioned is the use of restorative processes in cases of victims of physical and sexual abuse. For the victims of physical and sexual abuse it can be just to argue that criminalization of domestic violence was important in changing societal views towards violence in relationships and that the use of restorative practices can give a platform to return domestic violence to a private sphere and the resultant continued victimization. Mere an aggressive response to crimes does not benefit the victims. The victim does not get any substantial gain to mitigate his victimization and the victims of crime are often marginalized in the criminal justice process. Survivors legal needs are most poorly met due to justice delivery system problems that can be summarized as attrition, re-traumatisation, and disparate treatment across gender, class, and ethnic lines.[1] With the growing interest in restorative justice by governments and communities, several questions about appropriateness arise.

Realization of mistake, admittance of guilt and forgiveness are some of the essential requirements of restorative justice. Physical and sexual abuse such as rape results in injury to the mental and physical health and also the results in social and legal consequences. For the latter, restorative justice-based programmes might augment community response.[2] This paper address these issues by way of a collaboration between victim services, prosecutors, legal scholars and public health

[1]Restorative justice—History, www.experiencefestival.com (Accessed on 31 March 2012).
[2]John R. Gehm "Victim-Offender Mediation Programs: An Exploration of Practice and Theoretical Frameworks", *Western Criminology Review* 1, wcr.sonoma.edu (Accessed on 23 February 2012).

D. Umamaheswari (✉)
Labour Law and Administrative Law, The Tamil Nadu
Dr. Ambedkar Law University, Chennai, India
e-mail: uma.akirtim@gmail.com; dr.umamaheswari@tndalu.ac.in

R. Thilagaraj and J. Liu (eds.), *Restorative Justice in India*,
DOI 10.1007/978-3-319-47659-9_12

professionals implementing and evaluating the concept of '*restore*', a victim-driven, community-based restorative justice programme for the person victimized by physical and sexual abuse. '*Restore*' here is meant as to, prepares survivors, offenders, and both parties' families and friends to identify the harm and develop a redress plan.[3] The article highlights the need of the community collaboration in building and sustaining the restorative justice programme, processes and its goals, thus tries to identify the need and use of some appropriate functional restorative justice programmes encompassing survivor's needs and existing community responses for the victims of physical and sexual abuses.

12.2 Restorative Justice

In common parlance, Restorative Justice is a way of seeing crime as more than an act of breaking the law but as a source which causes harm to people, relationships and the community at large. Any discussion on restorative justice remains incomplete without reference to Alternative Dispute Resolution (ADR). The ADR, as technique, helps the restorative justice to achieve its objectives. These programmes operate both voluntary and mandatory basis.[4]

Restorative justice is not a 'new wave' movement on the fringe of legal practice. John Braithwaite observes "restorative justice has been the dominant model of criminal justice throughout most of human history for all the worlds' people."[5] The notion of restorative justice, in some form or the other, appears to have been with human societies since long.[6] Zehr, in 1997 defined it as, Restorative justice seeks to heal and put right the wrongs. It is a form of criminal justice based on reparation, that is, actions which attempt to repair the damage caused by the crime, either materially at least in part or symbolically.[7] Marshall in 1995 defines restorative justice as: "...a way of dealing with victims and offenders by focusing on the settlement of conflicts arising from crime and resolving the underlying problems which cause it. It is also, more widely, a way of dealing with crime generally in a rational problem solving way. Central to restorative justice is recognition of the

[3]Dr. N.V. Paranjape, Studies in Jurisprudence and Legal Theory, 5th Edition, Central Law Agency, Allahabad, 1998, p. 172–73.

[4]Melissa Lewis and Les McCrimmon, The Role of ADR Processes in the Criminal Justice System: A View from Australia, www.doj.gov.za (Accessed on 5th June 2012).

[5]Braithwaite, J, Crime, Shame and Reintegration., 1989, Cambridge: Cambridge University Press. p. 32.

[6]Albert Eglash first coined the term "restorative justice" in his 1977 article "Beyond Restitution: Creative Restitution".

[7]Howard Zehr, Changing Lenses: A New Focus for Crime and Justice, Scottdale, Ontario: Herald Press, 1990. p. 181.

community, rather than criminal justice agencies, as the prime site of crime control…".[8]

In countries like North America, Europe, Australia and New Zealand, the concept of restorative justice are linked to diverse practices, such as conferencing, sentencing circles and victim–offender mediation schemes. These practices focus on repairing the harm caused by crime, by holding moderated meetings of crime victims, offenders, and others affected by crime. They are used at different sites in the justice system: as a diversion from court, as a pre-sentencing option, and following the release of a person from prison. Restorative justice practices are also applied in the handling of family welfare and child protection matters, and in workplace disputes.[9] The conferencing idea was subsequently borrowed and adapted by jurisdictions in United States, Canada, the United Kingdom, Ireland, Singapore and South Africa.[10] Conferences can differ from victim–offender mediation schemes in that they bring more community people into the discussion, acknowledge a wider range of victimized people and emphasize participation by the family members of offenders. The operational procedure in the restorative programmes tends to vary. Essentially, these programmes require the victims, offenders and the community act together in repairing the damage of crime as per the procedure of law under the authority of the state.[11] Restorative justice is a theory of justice that emphasizes repairing the harm caused or revealed by criminal behaviour. It can be accomplished through cooperative processes that include identifying and taking steps to repair harm, involving all stakeholders, and transforming the traditional relationship between communities and their governments in responding to crime.[12]

Restorative justice thus emphasizes the importance of role of crime victims and community members through more active involvement in the justice process, holding offenders directly accountable to the people and communities they have violated, restoring the emotional and material losses of victims and providing a range of opportunities for dialogue, negotiation, and problem solving, whenever possible, which can lead to a greater sense of community safety, social harmony and peace for all involved.

---

[8]Tony Marshall, Restorative Justice: An Overview, Research Development and Statistics Directorate, 1999. p. 5.

[9]Ministry of Justice. (2004). Restorative justice in New Zealand: Best practice. www.justice.govt.nz, (Accessed on May 13, 2012).

[10]Marty Price, Crime and Punishment: Can Mediation Produce Restorative Justice for Victims and Offenders? VORP, www.vorp.com (Accessed on 14th April 2012).

[11]Mark S. Umbreit, "Restorative Justice Through Victim Offender Mediation: A Multi-Site Assessment", llwcr sopoma.edu, (Accessed on 1st February 2012).

[12]Kevin I. Minor and J.T. Morrison "A Theoretical Study and Critique of Restorative Justice." in Restorative Justice: International Perspectives, edited by Burt Galaway and Joe Hudson. Monsey, NY; Amsterdam, The Netherlands: Criminal Justice Press and Kugler Publications, 1996. p. 117.

12.3 Restorative Justice in India

The criminal justice system, as a means of formal social control, is still steeped in the retributive model, and centres on the State. In India Restorative justice finds little place in criminal jurisprudence. The Constitution of India guarantees equality of sexes. Article 14 says that the government shall not deny to any person equality before law or the equal protection of the laws. Article 15 declares that government shall not discriminate against any citizen on the ground of sex. Article 15(3) makes a special provision enabling the State to make affirmative discriminations in favour of women. Moreover, the government can pass special laws in favour of women. Article 16 guarantees that no citizen shall be discriminated against in matters of public employment on the grounds of sex. Article 42 directs the State to make provision for ensuring just and humane conditions of work and maternity relief. Above all, the Constitution imposes a fundamental duty on every citizen through Articles 15(A) (e) to renounce the practices derogatory to the dignity of women.

Section 376 Indian Penal Code (IPC) states that, the crime of rape, when committed by a private actor, is punishable by a minimum of seven to ten years and a maximum of life imprisonment.[13] According to India's constitution, sexual harassment infringes the fundamental right of a woman to gender equality under Article 14 of the Constitution of India and her right to life and live with dignity under Article 21 of the Constitution. United Nation Population Fund in its Report (2009–2010) has stated that, around two-third of married Indian women are victims of domestic violence and as many as 70% of married women in India between the age of 15 and 49 are victims of beating, rape or forced sex. In India, more than 55% of the women suffer from domestic violence, especially in the states of Bihar, U.P., M.P. and other northern states.[14] Although victim assistance is a rarity in India, its bases exists under the Indian Constitution, which provides that the state is mandated to secure the right to public assistance in cases of disablement and in other cases of undeserved want. Much of the progress made in the sphere of victimology is yet to pervade the penal mechanism in India. The victim is still largely restricted to the role of a witness.

12.3.1 Compounding of Offences

The provisions of the Criminal Procedure Code, 1973 (CrPC) for instance, the compounding of offences under Section 320 of the Code has been provided in an

[13]Law Commission Of India Reports (101–169), www.lawcommissionofindia.nic.in (Accessed on 11th May 2012).

[14]Section 354, IPC deals with "assault or criminal force to a woman with the intent to outrage her modesty" and Section 509, IPC deals with "word, gesture or act intended to insult the modesty of a woman".

effort to incorporate restorative justice into the prevailing system.[15] The victim and offenders can reach to settlement of the matter in accordance with the Section 320 (Compoundable offences) of the Criminal Procedure Code, 1973. Compounding the offences has connotations to what is popularly being voiced as "restorative justice". There are some offences which affect individuals and do not affect the society. This type of offences can be compounded without the permission of the court under the *sub-section (1) of 320* of the Criminal Procedure Code, 1973. The offences under this category are: *hurting religious feeling of a person, hurt, confinement, mischief, criminal trespass, adultery, defamation,* etc. The offences under sub-section of 2 of this law contains those offences which are of grave nature and likely to affect people at large. These cannot be compounded without the permission of the court. The offences under this class include: *grievous hurt, wrongful confinement, misappropriation of property, breach of trust involving heavy amount, fraud, counterfeiting, indecent behaviour towards women,* etc. The offences reached to successful compounding always result in acquittal. Under this provision, the victim may opt to compound the case, thus providing an opportunity for the victim to go for compromise or to mediate with the accused.

The compounding of offences need not necessarily result in mediation at all, and the victim may be left of a remedy due to the fact that, the victim and the offender may not be placed on an equal footing, due to coercion and fear. This would render the entire exercise a mere means to dispose the cases in the name of restorative justice. Further, the implementation of this provision is dependent entirely on the order of the court to that effect.[16] This provision merely seeks to appease the victim by providing monetary relief, while continuing to exclude the victim from playing any significant role. Therefore, some sort of restitution is provided to the victims, this provision pays attention, although in a pecuniary manner, to the victim, and is still a step towards a restorative paradigm. The compounding of offences was an attempt towards the incorporation of restorative justice into the present system. Thus, it is the empowerment of affected stakeholders on both sides that is the crucial feature of restorative justice, the absence of which causes both conventional and retributive justice systems not to succeed.[17]

The study highlights the facts that, the existing system of compounding of cases could have become a viable mechanism of restorative justice but there are impediments in the way such as: it becomes the matter of interest to many that the conflict between the victim and offender should not subside; the victim and offender do not take much interest in this process because of not being able to foresee the implications of this process; presently there is no active backing and support to this

---

[15]Upendra Baxi, Introductory Critique in "The (Malimath) Committee on Reforms of Criminal Justice System: Premises, Politics and Implications for Human Rights", (2003) p. 38.

[16]In *Hari Singh v. Sukhvir Singh,* (1998) 4 SCC 551 at 558} the Supreme Court had to exhort the criminal courts to use this provision since this power was intended to do something to reassure the victim that he or she is not forgotten in the criminal justice system.

[17]DR Singh, "Victimological Studies in India", paper Submitted for the 11th International Symposium on Victimology, South Africa (2000) p. 4–6.

type of initiatives and thus the compromise, which is effected, by middlemen and others is generally not in the interest of the victim. At times the victims are forcibly compelled to undergo the compromise; for not getting properly institutionalized within the system of criminal justice, this practice has not been able to produce the desired results. In some areas this has become a profitable business for many who by inducing fear to the parties try to settle the matter and charge heavy money from the interested party.[18] These scenarios have been equally dismal in many countries of the world and systematically implemented the restorative model of justice had offered highly imperative results. In India, the reformative approach is now very much intertwined with the rehabilitative aspect, as held in State of Gujarat v. High Court of Gujarat, case.[19]

12.3.2 *Cash Compensation*

As regards compensation, some highly inadequate and restricting provisions are available in the Sections 357 and 358 of the Criminal Procedure Code, 1973. The procedure to get the prescribed compensation is too cumbersome to practically help the victim. Compensation, obviously, can be paid only after the charge is established in court, which is a tall order in itself. Strangely, the scheme is sought to be justified by the need to help the victim financially so that she can fight it out in court. How this contradiction gets resolved, remains to be seen. Article 38 (1) of the Constitution of India provides for Criminal Injuries Compensation Boards in every state. The Supreme Court has ruled in favour of setting up the boards. The National Women's Commission, the Working Women's Commission, and several legal associations have spoken about probable benefits.[20] Till date, the board exists only on official papers. Therefore, the redressal of individuated grievances does not feature to the same extent as it does in restorative justice. However, in so far as some sort of restitution is provided to the victims, this provision pays attention, although in a pecuniary manner, to the victim, and is still a step towards a restorative paradigm.

Courts have ordered for compensation to be paid under provisions contained in the statutes. Several state governments too have found it convenient to pay sums depending upon the extent of the public outrage and media exposure. The experience with Prevention of Atrocities Act 1989 (for the SC and ST), tribal and dalit victims of rape victims was required to produce a certificate of their (tribal or dalit) status for receiving a compensation of Rs. 25,000. Thus, getting the certificate in

[18]Report of the Committee on Reforms of Criminal Justice System, Vol. 1, Government of India, Ministry of Home Affairs, p. 79–80 (2003).

[19]AIR 1998 SC 3164 at 3172.

[20]V. Unnikrishnan, "Supreme Court on Sentencing Rapists—Recent Trends", 25 ACD. L. REV. 109, 128 (2001).

itself became a profit-making proposition for brokers. It does not require great imagination to understand how these laws end up as bait for attracting more abuse for women.[21] On the one hand, rape cases are held in camera, on the other hand this display of 'help' discourages victims to report rape. The attitude is, since the money has already been paid, why fuss over prosecution? As far as monetary compensation is concerned, it finds justification in offering help to the victim by the state to fight her case legally, which is often long-drawn. If the state takes responsibility, then that cannot be altogether a bad thing. Otherwise it becomes like the flesh-trade.

12.3.3 Marry the Rapist

The former CJ of Supreme Court of India K.G. Balakrishnan is reported to have said that society and the state must respect the decision of a rape victim if she chooses to marry the rapist.[22] Imagine the trauma of a woman having to spend her life with a man who has raped her? It is like inflicting a lifelong sentence of mental and physical cruelty on her, while the man goes scot free. And then, what would prevent the rapist from marrying the victim to escape punishment and then deserting her? This kind of a mindset furthers the warped view society holds that marriage is the be all and end all for a woman. And that it is better to marry a man who has raped you than not marry at all!

The judges worry about marital prospects of victims and many rapists thus get lighter sentences when they agree to marry their victims. Another absurd idea often encouraged by the judiciary is that of compromise. Whenever witnesses turn hostile, victims are advised to accept a compromise, which the court witnesses, but is unable and unwilling to act upon. The court thus 'restores' her chastity in the public eye.[23] To meet extremely rare contingencies and very exceptional situations, discretion was conferred on the court to award subminimum sentence. The consequential effect of the proviso appended to the section 376 was that it nullified the effect of the provision prescribing minimum sentence for rapists. We find umpteen instances wherein some reason is carved out by the judiciary as a "special and adequate reason" for awarding a sub-minimum sentence.[24] Fortunately, the courts are prohibited from compounding a rape case. Being a non-compoundable offence,

---

[21]Dr. N.S. Soman and Dr. K. N. Chandrasekharan Pillai, Rarest of Rare Case—A Myth, 25 ACD. L, REV. 157, 184 (2001).

[22]www.tribuneindia.com (Accessed on 2nd February 2011).

[23]The Indian Penal Code, 1860 (hereinafter "I.P.C."), provides that whoever commits rape shall be punished with imprisonment of either description for a term which shall not be less than 7 years but which may be for life or for a term which may extend to 10 years and shall also be liable to fine 3. For the special category of cases covered under Section 376 (2), the sentence cannot be less than 10 years but which may be for life and shall also be liable to fine. Enhanced sentences for gang rape were introduced by way of an amendment in 1983.

[24]*Baldev Singh & Ors. v. State of Punjab*, A.I.R. 2011 S.C. 1231.

compromise in rape cases has been confined to the bargains between community elders, victims' kin, local authorities and the police. It is sad the way we treat this kind of abuse of women with total disregard for the feelings of a woman. We need to shame the perpetrators; we need to talk more and more in the open about these issues because, as we know, a rapist gets caught usually after a number of successful or unsuccessful attempts. What makes the perpetrators so daring is the silence of the women.

12.3.4 Judicial Review

The study highlights the fact that, criminal justice system in India is modelled largely on the lines of retributive justice. This system indulges in an exercise of quantifying crime in terms of monetary and physical punishment.[25] Thus, the focus primarily is on the offender, disregarding the need for victim participation. Some of the mile stone cases in this regard are discussed herewith. In Tukaram v. State of Maharashtra[26] case which is also known as Mathura Rape Case where, Mathura, one 18-year-old Harijan girl was called to the police station on an abduction report filed by her brother at the police station—Desaui Ganj in Maharashtra on 26 March, 1972. When they were about to leave the police station, Mathura was kept back at the police station in the late hours of the night by one of the constables, named Ganpat, who was on duty. She was taken to a toilet and raped by Ganpat. Then another constable, named Tukaram, molested and tried to rape her, but being too heavily drunk did not succeed. It was alleged that the two constables, while on duty, had bolted the doors of the police station from inside and plunged the place into darkness. But the court held that the victim's failure to appeal to companions and her conduct is meekly following the constable and allowing him to have his way to the extent of satisfying his lust amounts to consent for the sexual intercourse and thus, the act not amounting to rape. The judgment of Supreme Court was widely criticized both inside and outside the Parliament as an extraordinary decision sacrificing human rights and a slander on women under the law and the Constitution.

Later in the year 1991, Supreme Court in the case of State of Maharashtra versus Madhukar N. Mardikar,[27] held that "the un-chastity of a woman does not make her open to any and every person to violate her person as and when he wishes. She is entitled to protect her person if there is an attempt to violate her person against her wish. She is equally entitled to the protection of law. Therefore merely because she is of easy virtue, her evidence cannot be thrown overboard." Whereas, in State of

[25]Mark S. Umbreit, "Restorative Justice Through Victim Offender Mediation: A Multi-Site Assessment", llwcr sopoma.edu (Accessed on 1st February 2012).

[26]AIR 1979 SC 185.

[27](1991) 1 SCC 57.

Punjab versus Gurmit Singh,[28] the Supreme Court has advised the lower judiciary, that even if the victim girl is shown to be habituated to sex, the Court should not describe her to be of loose character.

In view of the above changes, the Supreme Court in Delhi Domestic Working Women's Forum versus UOI[29] has laid down the following guidelines for the trial of rape cases:

1. The complaints of sexual assault cases should be provided with legal representation. Such a person should be well acquainted. The advocate's role should not merely be of explaining to the victim the nature of the proceedings, to prepare for the case and assist her, but to provide her with guidance as to how she might obtain help of a different nature from other agencies—for example, psychiatric consultation or medical assistance.
2. Legal assistance should be provided at the police station, since the victim may be in a distressed state. Guidance and support of a lawyer at this stage would be of great help.
3. The police should be under a duty to inform the victim of her right to a counsel before being interrogated.
4. A list of lawyers willing to act in these cases should be kept at the police station.
5. Advocates shall be appointed by the Court on an application by the police at the earliest, but in order that the victim is not questioned without one, the advocate shall be authorized to act at the police station before leave of the Court is sought or obtained.
6. In all rape trials, anonymity of the victim must be maintained.
7. It is necessary to setup Criminal Injuries Compensation Board with regard to the Directive Principles contained under Article. 38(1) of the Constitution of India, as some victims also undergoes substantial losses.
8. Compensation for the victims shall be awarded by the Court on the conviction of the offender and by the Criminal Injuries Compensation Board—whether or not a conviction has taken place. The board will take into account pain, suffering, shock as well as loss of earnings due to pregnancy and child birth if this accrued as a result of rape.

In India, the case of Vishaka versus State of Rajasthan[30] in 1997 established sexual harassment as illegal. In this case, the litigation resulted from a brutal gang rape of a publicly employed social worker in a village in Rajasthan during the course of her employment. The petitioners bringing the action were various social activists and non-governmental organizations. The primary basis of bringing such an action to the Supreme Court in India was to find suitable methods for the realization of the true concept of 'gender equality' in the workplace for women. In turn, the prevention of sexual harassment of women would be addressed by

---

[28](1996) 2 SCC 384.

[29](1995) 1 SCC 14.

[30]AIR 1997 SC 1997.

applying the judicial process. Under Article 32 of the Indian Constitution, an action was filed in order to establish the enforcement of the fundamental rights relating to the women in the workplace. In particular, it sought to establish the enforcement of Articles 14, 15, 19(1) (g) and 21 of the Constitution of India and Articles 11 and 24 of the Convention on the Elimination of All Forms of Discrimination against Women[31] (CEDAW). In disposing of the writ petition with directions, it was held that, the fundamental right to carry on any occupation, trade or profession depends on the availability of a 'safe' working environment. The right to life means life with dignity. The primary responsibility for ensuring such safety and dignity through suitable legislation, and the creation of a mechanism for its enforcement, belongs to the legislature and the executive. When, however, instances of sexual harassment resulting in violations of Arts 14, 19 and 21 are brought under Art 32, effective redress requires that some guidelines for the protection of these rights should be laid down to fill the legislative vacuum.[32]

In Mohd. Umar v. State[33] case the allegation against the appellant was that he had abducted the prosecutrix aged about 12 years daughter of Ameeruddin on 7 October, 2004 and had taken her to village Saifini, district Rampur, U.P. and had repeated sexual intercourse with her. It is alleged that the prosecutrix was enticed, kidnapped and abducted from the lawful custody of her parents. It is alleged that the prosecutrix knew the appellant, who use to work in a meat shop near her house. It is alleged that the prosecutrix had stayed with the appellant from 7 October, 2004 till the night intervening 27–28 October, 2004. The appellate court upheld and confirmed the judgment of the learned trial court convicting the appellant under Sections 363, 366 and 377 IPC. On the question of sentence also the court did not see any reason to interfere, keeping in view the age of the prosecutrix and the conduct of the appellant. The appellant at the time of offence himself was 40 years of age and was father of eight children. The eldest daughter of the appellant was 15–16 years of age. Appeal was accordingly dismissed.

The news about the post-crime trauma suffered by a teenaged rape victim and her family members and the state's apathy to their plight has shocked a Delhi court, prompting it to order Rs. one lakh as interim compensation to her.[34] In the Ruchika Girhotra molestation case, the protector, an IG, Haryana Police, S.P. Rathore became the tormentor. After 19 years, 40 adjournments, and more than 400 hearings, the court finally pronounced him guilty under Section 354 and gave him six months imprisonment. It is reminiscent of Bhanwri Devi's case, a Sathin volunteer

---

[31]Article 11 ([State] takes all appropriate measures to eliminate discrimination against women in the field of employment) and Article 24 ([State shall] undertake to adopt all necessary measures at the national level aimed at achieving the full realization).

[32]The judgement of the above mentioned case [*Vishaka Vs. State of Rajasthan* (AIR 1997 SC 1997)], is still referred by our H'ble courts to give judgement for recent cases. *State of Karnataka* v. *Krishnappa (2000) 4 S.C.C. 75,* and *Kamal Kishore v. State of Himachal Pradesh, (2000) 4 S.C. C. 502.*

[33]MANU/DE/2974/2010.

[34]www.articles.timesofindia.indiatimes.com (Accessed on 2nd February 2012).

in Rajasthan, when she tried to stop a child marriage in 1992, she was gang raped by five men, including Ramkaran Gujjar, whose daughter's marriage she had tried to stop. The male doctor at the primary health centre refused to conduct medical examination and at a Jaipur hospital the doctor certified only her age. Subjected to sustained humiliation, she was asked by the policemen to leave her lehenga as an evidence of rape. Bhanwri's case inspired Visakha case, which brought about legislation against sexual exploitation of women at work place but Bhanwri could not get justice in a caste-ridden system.[35] There was a time when, after the Bhawnri Devi case, women's groups demanded compensation, because Bhawnri was raped in the course of carrying out her duties as a government functionary, therefore she was entitled to compensation. She was eventually given compensation but she did not use it, it created more problems for her. The community started saying rape was an excuse for taking money.[36]

Apathy of Supreme Court Bench comprising of Justices Markandeya Katju and Gyan Sudha Mishra in an unusual order have let off three gang-rapists with a fine of Rs. 50,000 each after the rapists reached a 'compromising-formula' with the victim. The Bench has reduced the ten-year sentence to three and half years, and has agreed to let the rapists Baldev Singh, Gurmail Singh and Hardeep Singh get away with fine of Rs. 50,000 each. NDTV news report quoting the Counsel for the rapists Rajat Sharma said, "His clients had reached a compromise with the victim and it was decided, to drop the case. Both the convicts and the victim want to bring an end to the case as they were all now married and leading their respective lives". The plea of the rapists was that it was more than 15 years ago, when the incident had occurred.[37] Thus there are directions of Supreme Court with regard to compensation to victims. In some cases the court's order for the award of interim compensation as the offence of rape is can undoubtedly held as against the victim's basic human rights and violation of her fundamental right to life and liberty. In Bhupinder Sharma v. State of Himachal Pradesh,[38] the Supreme Court reiterated that in order to exercise the discretion of reducing the sentence provided in I.P.C. for rape, the Court has to record "adequate and special reasons" in the judgment. Sub-minimum sentence cannot be awarded on the ground of fanciful reasons. The colonial law based on the moral history of the woman was in application while looking at a rape victim, which meant that a woman's sexual history would have a say on the writing of the verdict. The reason recorded by the sentencing court has not only to be adequate but also special. Even after the much talked about Mathura case, which led to the amendment of Evidence Act in 1983, which allowed the woman's word to be trusted for her non-consent, there has been no monitoring of judgements.[39] The

---

[35]www.tribuneindia.com (Accessed on 18 September 2011).

[36]*Bhanwari Devi v. Union of India and others*, AIR 2004 Rajasthan 60.

[37]*Baldev Singh & Ors. v. State of Punjab*, A.I.R. 2011 S.C. 1231.

[38]A.I.R. 2003 S.C. 4684. And also *State of M.P. v. Bala @ Balaram*, A.I.R. 2005 S.C. 3567.

[39]The legislative intent to curb the offence of rape with iron hand can be inferred from the Criminal Law (Amendment) Act, 1983 which provided enhanced sentences for gang rape.

Supreme Court observed that what is adequate and special would depend upon several factors and no strait-jacket formula can be imposed. When the discretion becomes wide and unfettered the result would be wide disparity and variation in sentences.

The widespread dissatisfaction by battered women and rape victims with the current system of mandatory law enforcement opens the door for consideration of alternative forms of dealing with its effectiveness and relevance to women who have been victimized by physical and sexual abuse.[40] Hence the study on the sentencing practices followed in India has revealed that subjectivity of the judge plays a crucial role in the decision making process.[41] This is not at all desirable for a criminal justice system and a solution to this problem needs to be found at the earliest.

12.4 Applicability of Restorative Justice

While talking about the concept of restorative justice in these circumstances and to introduce the concept of restorative justice in cases of rape and sexual violence it is to be remembered that Restorative Justice Model, while holding offenders accountable, also encourages them to engage in a dialogue which attempts to repair the harm done not only to the victim, but to a community or society at large. Understanding the concept of restorative justice provides the possibilities of changing the behaviour of offenders and empowering victims.[42] Thus, there is need of the approach which is compatible with the principles of republican criminology which suggest that, the justice system can be reformed to give voice to victims and to continue the struggle against physical and sexual abuse. Bringing the victim and the offenders along with their family and friend face to face under the concept of stake holders of the crime can make a way to look at the victim of such crime and the offender as a human.[43]

Restorative Justice is not primarily about forgiveness and it does not require forgiveness. But its different way of understanding and responding to matters of crime and justice often creates a context in which forgiveness may occur—if and when people choose it. None of the people involved are saints. They are ordinary

[40]A Google search for kanoon.com and rape cases will throw up several judgements, which are deeply patriarchal and explain why conviction rates are so abysmally low.

[41]Dr. N.S. Soman & Dr. K.N. Chandrasekharan Pillai, Rarest of Rare Case—A Myth, 25 ACD. L, REV. 157, 184 (2001).

[42]Mary Koss and Mary Achilles, "Restorative Justice Responses to Sexual Assault" 2006-Restorative justice, 6–5 March-Ilan University Bar- Restorative justice Conference. www.1202.0rg.il (Accessed on 24 March 2012).

[43]John R. Gehm "Victim-Offender Mediation Programs: An Exploration of Practice and Theoretical Frameworks", *Western Criminology Review* 1(1). wcr.sonoma.edu (Accessed on 9th June 2012).

people who chose extraordinary ways to deal with one of the worst tragedies anyone could imagine. In each case a Restorative Justice programme can help them see and adopt alternatives to the life-devouring responses of hate and revenge. The Economic and Social Council of the United Nations has developed a blueprint of the Basic Principles of the Use of Restorative Justice Programmes in Criminal matters.[44] It provides: The parties should have the right to legal advice before and after the restorative process and, where necessary, to translation and/or interpretation. Minors should, in addition, have the right to parental assistance; Before agreeing to participate in restorative processes, the parties should be fully informed of their rights, the nature of the process and the possible consequences of their decision; Neither the victim nor the offender should be induced by unfair means to participate in restorative processes or outcomes. Facilitators should be recruited from all sections of society and should generally possess good understanding of local cultures and communities.[45] These can be effectively used by us as the basis for making the appropriate restorative justice programmes for the rape or other physical and sexual violence cases.

Feminists resist the idea of responding to rape or other physical and sexual violence through restorative justice. The criticisms is that, this move would trivialize rape and provide only a 'cheap justice' and that, the restorative justice cannot address or appropriately account for the gendered power imbalances between the victim and offender, as a result, it may cause further harm to the victim and fail to protect her and others from future violence.[46] But there are good reasons for turning to alternative or additional legal responses to rape. By further exploring restorative justice as either an alternative or addition to the criminal justice system, it could at least in some cases provide justice for physical and sexual abuses and rape victims; or at the least it might shed light on ways in which to improve the criminal justice response to it.

12.5 Conclusion and Suggestion

The above study highlights the fact that criminal justice system in India can be said as a hangover of the colonial times and thus hardly bears any semblance to instances of restorative justice or forgiveness of the ancient times or the modern ones outside the formal system. The crime is against the State and State interests drive the process of doing justice. Victims of crime are left on the sidelines of

[44]The Economic and Social Council of the United Nations has developed a blueprint of the Basic Principles of the Use of Restorative Justice Programmes in Criminal matters (2000).

[45]Curtis-Fawley, S. & Daly, K. (2005). Gendered violence and restorative justice: The views of victim advocates. Violence Against Women, *11*, p. 603–638.

[46]Daly, K. & Stubbs, J, "Feminist theory, feminist and anti-racist politics, and restorative justice." In G. Johnstone & D. Van Ness (Eds.), Handbook of restorative justice. Cullompton Devon, (2005) UK: Willan Publishing.

justice, with little or no input and thus feel twice victimized; first, by the offender and second, by the disregard of their interests by the criminal justice system. In this context, the need for a dilution of the existing offender driven approach to construct a system more sensitive to needs of victims, is addressed. The study provided an insight indication of the use of restorative justice as a process and examines its effectiveness and relevance to the victims of physical and sexual abuse. These methods can operate on a parallel plane with those of court processes and may act as an alternative to the justice system in settling disputes about offences.

Restorative justice initiatives that function as alternatives to influence the disposal of cases within the criminal justice system tend to be part of formal programmes. Thus, these integrated programmes have systems and processes linked with those of the criminal justice system. Their aims often include the general aims of the criminal justice system in addition to those specifically related to restorative justice.[47] Restorative justice strategies has several major advantages as these strategies are solution-based rather than problem-based processes, gives voice to marginalized people, and focus on healing and reconciliation.[48] From the above study it is thus concluded that, there is a need for identifying common ground in advocacy and restorative justice goals and calls for a holistic approach to the needs of rape survivors and for physical and sexual abuses victims that includes advocating for expanded justice alternatives. Conventional and restorative justice is often viewed as mutually exclusive whereas they are complementary.

To combat the failings of the retributive system, crime is to be recognized as being directed first and foremost against an individual and then the State. A positive approach is indeed needed to implement restorative alternatives to expand survivor choice and offender accountability. Along with the Basic Principles of the Use of Restorative Justice Programmes in Criminal matters the Judicial provided by the Economic and Social Council of the United Nations as discussed above, it is further suggested that, the issues discharges based on agreements arising out of restorative justice process should have the same status as judicial decisions or judgments and should preclude prosecution in respect of the same facts. Failure to implement an agreement made in the course of a restorative process should be referred back to the restorative programme may not be used as justification for a more severe sentence in subsequent criminal justice proceedings and the decision as to how to proceed should be taken without delay. Where no agreement can be made between the parties, the case should be referred back to the criminal justice authorities and may not be used as justification for a more severe sentence in subsequent criminal justice proceedings. Facilitators should be responsible for providing a safe and appropriate environment for the restorative process. They should be sensitive to any vulnerability of the parties. Thus the facilitators should receive initial training before taking

[47]Feeley, Malcolm and Jonathan Simon 'The new penology; notes on the emerging strategy of corrections and its implications', Criminology (1992): p. 449–74.

[48]Restorative Justice Online: Victim Offender Panels, www.restorativejustice.org (Accessed on 5th May 2012).

up facilitation duties and should also receive in-service training with the aim of providing skills in conflict resolution, taking into account the particular needs of victims and offenders, at providing basic knowledge of the criminal justice system and at providing a thorough knowledge of the operation of the restorative programme in which they will do their work. Facilitators should be recruited from all sections of society and should generally possess good understanding of local cultures and communities, with sound judgment and interpersonal skills necessary to conducting restorative processes. Along with all these things there should be regular consultation between criminal justice authorities and administrators of restorative justice programmes to develop a common understanding of restorative processes and outcomes, to increase the extent to which restorative programmes. It is further suggested that research activities in this area is to be encouraged and promoted in India to explore new forms and ways in which restorative approaches might be incorporated into criminal justice practices in concrete form over time.

Index

R. Thilagaraj and J. Liu (eds.), *Restorative Justice in India*,
DOI 10.1007/978-3-319-47659-9

MIX
Papier aus verantwortungsvollen Quellen
Paper from responsible sources
FSC® C105338

If you have any concerns about our products,
you can contact us on
ProductSafety@springernature.com

In case Publisher is established outside the EU,
the EU authorized representative is:
Springer Nature Customer Service Center GmbH
Europaplatz 3, 69115 Heidelberg, Germany

Printed by Libri Plureos GmbH
in Hamburg, Germany